T H E

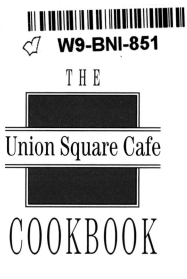

Union Square Cafe

COOKBOOK

THE

Union Square Cafe

COOKBOOK

*160 Favorite Recipes
from New York's
Acclaimed Restaurant*

DANNY MEYER
and
MICHAEL ROMANO

Photography by
RICHARD BOWDITCH

Paintings by
RICHARD POLSKY

ecco

An Imprint of HarperCollinsPublishers

HarperCollins books may be purchased for educational, business, or sales promotional use. For information please write: Special Markets Department, HarperCollins Publishers, 10 East 53rd Street, New York, NY 10022.

A hardcover edition of this book was published in 1994 by HarperCollins Publishers.

FIRST ECCO PAPERBACK EDITION PUBLISHED 2013.

Designed by Joel Avirom
Design Assistant: Jason Snyder

Library of Congress Cataloging-in-Publication Data

Meyer, Danny.
   The Union Square Cafe cookbook / Danny Meyer and Michael Romano.—1st ed.
      p.   cm.
   Includes index.
   ISBN 978-0-06-017013-4
   1. Union Square Cafe. 2. Cookery. I. Romano, Michael.
II. Title.
TX715.M6217   1994
641.5—dc20   94-1110

ISBN 978-0-06-223239-7 (pbk.)

13 14 15 16 17 ❖/RRD 10 9 8 7 6 5 4 3 2 1

To our parents, with love

CONTENTS

Acknowledgments ix

Preface xi

Introduction xv

Appetizers 1

Salads 69

Soups 89

Sandwiches, Eggs
    & Lunch Salads 109

Main Courses 131

Vegetables, Side Dishes
    & Condiments 215

Desserts 267

Pantry Staples 309

Mail-Order Sources for
    Special Products 321

Metric Conversion Charts 322

Index 323

$\mathcal{W}$riting *The Union Square Cafe Cookbook* while running Union Square Cafe has been an extraordinary experience, challenging and gratifying beyond our wildest dreams. We are indebted to so many wonderful people for giving us the inspiration and support we needed throughout the entire process:

To our families, whose guidance, encouragement, patience, and generous support has allowed us to thrive in the career we love.

To Audrey and Hallie Meyer, who nurtured us with honest feedback and good humor through countless all-night writing sessions.

To our ever-loyal family of Union Square Cafe guests, whose faith in us, constructive criticism, and heartfelt accolades keep us going every day.

To the special family of Union Square Cafe staff members, present and past, whose genuine care for making other people happy has always been the secret of our success.

To Susan and Bob Lescher, whose years of gentle goading and fervent belief in the wisdom of this project convinced us that yes, perhaps the world *could* use another restaurant cookbook.

To our editor, Susan Friedland, whose confidence in our recipes, on-target advice, twenty-twenty vision, and unfailing energy has turned our labor of love into a book we're proud of.

To Katherine Alford and Bianca Henry for lovingly testing every recipe in this book, and then some.

To Molly O'Neill, our cookbook "rabbi," for generously allowing us to feel that this book could and would get written, and for shedding a lot of light on how to make that happen.

To Paul Bolles-Beaven, Ellen Campbell, Larry Goldenberg, and Joshua Moulton, whose hard work and tireless contributions during the writing of the book convinced our guests that Union Square Cafe was just fine without Danny and Michael, thank you.

To Ali Barker, Michel Floranc, Larry Hayden, Nancy Hiller, and Jamie Leeds, many of whose enlightened culinary contributions to Union Square Cafe grace this cookbook.

To our friends and mentors, Andrée Abramoff, Thomas Ahrens, Jim Berrien, Pat Cetta, Robert Chadderdon, Susy Davidson, Roger Fessaguet, Joyce Goldstein, Michel Guérard, Deborah Madison, Richard Melman, Didier Oudill, Phil Panzarino, Gilbert Radix, Tom Ryder, Richard Sax, Lindsey Shere, Bill Shore, Alex von Bidder, and Alice Waters, whose ideas, writings, wisdom, and encouragement have influenced us to be the best we can be.

To Yogi Amrit Desai, whose love has opened the door to a life of peace and joy.

To the extraordinary people who grow Union Square Cafe's food and wine, without whom we'd have little opportunity to serve good meals.

And in loving memory of Morton Meyer, who enjoyed red wine, colorful people, lively language, and dreaming a good dream.

*T*wenty-five minutes before the mahogany door to Union Square Cafe swung open for the very first dinner on October 21, 1985, I broke into sobbing tears, brimming with bittersweet emotion. On one hand, the restaurant's debut marked the realization of a lifelong dream—ever since it was clear I didn't have what it took to be a major league baseball player or play-by-play announcer. I had worked toward and focused on this very moment for the previous three years, and perhaps for my first twenty-seven years as well. Nothing should have made me happier and prouder than this day. But something was troubling me. I had absolutely no business opening a 125-seat restaurant in the middle of New York City, and for the first time, at just that moment, I knew it.

I had grown up loving to cook, remembering practically every meal I had ever eaten, adoring festive family get-togethers, longing to try new restaurants and to return to old favorites, savoring the anticipation of every next meal, equating each one with great adventure. Friends and family found it odd when I would mix and match every ingredient and flavor on my dinner plate, trying to come up with something new, something better. A bite of lima beans always tasted better with a forkful of buttered egg noodles than it did on its own. And the noodles improved when I chewed them together with my mother's broiled chicken thighs with herbs. It was a gastronomic epiphany for me when, as a six-year-old, I discovered the taste combination of buttered spinach noodles sprinkled with Kraft Parmesan.

By the time I was seven, my palate began to find exciting stimulation. My father—who always included me in his cooking exploits—was in the business of custom-designing driving tours through the French countryside, and our Saint Louis home was like an ongoing foreign-exchange program, hosting daughters and sons of the *Relais & Chateau* patrons with whom he did business. Many meals at home had a French touch, and no dinner began without a bottle of Beaujolais-Villages. In 1965 I took my first family voyage to France, and I was forced by my parents to keep a diary. One day's entry highlighted my fascination with the "wonderful quiche Lorraine" I had tasted in a private home in Nancy. In another, I remarked about loving "fraises des bois and crem fresh [*sic*]" in Saint Paul-de-Vence. This is not my first book on food!

Back at home, it had become my household responsibility to feed my family's pet dog, a neurotic and epileptic French poodle named Ratatouille. Third-grade friends looked at me with disbelief when I tried to explain the meaning of his name. I enjoyed slipping "Rata" my leftover tastes of things like steak tartare, spicy tacos, Usinger's Milwaukee braunschweiger and Wilno kosher salami, because it was important to me that he could enjoy my favorite foods in addition to his foul-smelling Alpo. Once I even tried feeding him peanut butter. He ate it, but it took him at least ten minutes to quit smacking his tongue and get it down the hatch. In retrospect, Ratatouille was my first regular customer. It made me happy to please him with good food. I may not have known it then, but that's about all it takes to be a successful restaurateur.

Success was a long way off, however, for Union Square Cafe. On the first night of business we served just twenty-eight diners. Never mind that sixteen were well-wishing guinea pigs who had been invited with our compliments, another two had come primarily to teach us how to use our computerized cash registers, and of the ten intrepid diners who actually qualified as true restaurant pioneers, two ended up walking out of the restaurant hungry and angry because the food they ordered never arrived.

It was on that night that I realized what an orchestrational miracle it would one day be if we could ever figure out how to deliver the right food at the right temperature to the right person at the right table at the right time. I reasoned with myself that others before me had solved this mystery, but I knew that we were a long way off.

Union Square Cafe opened with an abundance of good intentions, yet with a sad dearth of hard restaurant experience—from the top down. My idea of a successful restaurant had been one where I took the orders, cooked the food, and then did the dishes. That quickly changed.

I was a complete novice, having had only eight months' training as an assistant manager at a downtown Manhattan restaurant, which is where I met Michael Romano. I had spent another handful of months chopping shallots, opening oysters, and observing as a kitchen *stagière* in Italy and Bordeaux.

Our first chef, a twenty-six-year-old named Ali Barker, had certainly cooked in some good restaurants in his short career, but had no previous chef's experience, and in fact had never even attained the rank of *sous-chef*. The general manager, Gordon Dudash, had once been a decent bartender, but had never managed people; the head bartender, Paul Bolles-Beaven, came from a distinguished family of clerics yet had never mixed a cocktail; and the bookkeeper, who was undeniably honest, had never so much as balanced his own checkbook. And yes, the first waiter I hired thought it proper to use a corkscrew to open a bottle of champagne. For other reasons of ineptitude, he was also the first person I ever had to fire.

Union Square Cafe has come a long way since those early days. The restaurant has always attracted an ambitious and caring family of staff members bent on making good things even better. We've been fortunate to have a loyal following of friends who always let us know when we need to improve and are equally quick to praise us when we do.

Danny Meyer (left) *and Michael Romano*

When Union Square Cafe needed to find a chef in 1988, I immediately thought of Michael Romano. We had worked together for a short while in 1984 at the now-defunct Pesca. Michael had just returned from several years of cooking in Michelin-starred restaurants in France and Switzerland and I remember being terribly impressed with his knowledge, patience, crisp presence, and talent. While Union Square Cafe's cooking was rustic and straightforward from day one, in Michael's hands comfort food has become excellent food.

My collaboration with Michael has included several trips abroad, dining in too many restaurants, tasting in more than our share of dark, dank wine cellars, innumerable seasonal menu changes, and thousands of lunches and dinners served. But this cookbook—an anthology of Union Square Cafe's cooking—is the highlight of our years together and makes me especially proud.

Union Square Cafe's Essential Ingredients

☐ The Role of Hospitality

Service has become a restaurant buzzword of our time, and while most people agree on how bad things are when service is miserable, the public hasn't arrived at a consensus about great service. The point is, there are thousands of kinds of "good service," and every industry defines it slightly differently. A bank can provide it by giving you your own private account representative, even though you're not worth a million dollars. A shoe store clerk can do it by urgently trying to please, even after he's just gone to fetch the fifth pair of shoes for you to try on. Your butcher can give good service by voluntarily trimming that extra ounce of fat you'd just as soon not pay for. When Union Square Cafe won the first-ever James Beard Award for Service Excellence in 1992, we were proud, but a bit humbled and mystified. It was crystal clear to all of us that many other restaurants provided better service than we did—as the term had classically been defined. We don't wear tuxedos, we don't fillet fish or sauce pasta at tableside, and though we do decant our nicest bottles of red wine, we don't have a *sommelier* with a silver-plated tastevin hanging around his neck, and we don't force our guests to sniff the cork.

We were similarly bewildered one year when Union Square Cafe had attained the New York Zagat Survey's third highest rating for overall popularity, even though our food, service, and decor ratings had not even made the top ten. Slowly but surely it started to dawn on us that there had to be an intangible factor that no one was talking about, rating, or perhaps even aware of: hospitality.

When we select from hundreds of applicants to work on Union Square Cafe's staff, the single most important personality trait we look for is a genuine love of making other people feel good. We know we can always teach a caring person how we want our tables to be set. But we can't teach an otherwise expert waiter how to care about making our guests feel happy. We're also acutely aware that while warm service can overcome practically any honest mistake made by a cook, there's no amount of delicious food that will conquer an inhospitable reception from a dining room staff.

No matter what the industry, we think the true measure of service is the level of honest hospitality and value being offered. How well people feel treated will always be the determining factor in whether they'll come back for more, and that goes for home entertaining as well. Though it's omitted from our recipes, the tender loving care we put into our food and service is our secret ingredient.

☐ The Role of Wine at Union Square Cafe

To identify Union Square Cafe as a "wine restaurant" is a bit like calling Yankee Stadium a "mustard ballpark." Just as any self-respecting ballpark better offer decent mustard, ketchup, onions, and pickle relish to accompany the thousands of hot dogs it sells, a restaurant that serves a menu of good food owes it to its guests to carry a variety of tasty wines— red, white, and rosé—to satisfy the many tastes of its diners. Wine, just like mustard or ketchup, is a wonderful condiment to make good food taste even better. The fun is in experimenting to find out which wines you like best to accompany your favorite foods.

The joy of wine—no matter what color, cost, or variety—begins with the pleasant anticipation of what lies ahead, even before you've opened the bottle. It continues when you and someone you like a lot pull the cork to reveal the mystery. If the wine is good, you'll remember it and seek it out again. It will undoubtedly taste somewhat different next time, since the atmosphere in which you last drank it can never be precisely repeated, and because the wine will age and change slightly anyway.

There is no such thing as a universally perfect marriage of wine and food. That would presume that everyone was born with the same set of taste buds and flavor preferences. On the other hand, there are plenty of sensational combinations, and as we love to do for our guests in the restaurant, we'll share some of our favorite wine ideas for the recipes in this book. Even without our advice, you can spot a great wine and food match on your own, simply by doing the following: Next time you have dinner and feel like having some wine, open a familiar bottle and take a sip. Ask yourself what it is you like about the flavor and think of a couple of descriptive words that explain what kind of wine you like (for example, "oaky," "appley," "light-bodied," "refreshing"). Next, taste the wine alongside each different piece of food on your plate. Try a sip separately with a little piece of meat or fish, then with a forkful of the pasta, then with the vegetable, the sauce, and so on. The wine will taste different with each sip, but one of the combinations will stand out as your favorite. You'll know you've hit a great match when the wine tastes even better with the food than it did on its own, and when it brings out even more intense flavors in the food. Remember what combination you liked best, and ask yourself whether the match succeeded because of the food itself (chicken), what it was spiced with (black pepper), what it was

sauced with (herb jus), or how it was cooked (grilled and smoky). While these may seem like a lot of mental steps when you're just trying to enjoy your dinner, in no time you'll be doing this personal wine and food analysis without even being aware of it, just as you *know* Dijon is your mustard of choice with *saucisson à l'ail*.

Union Square Cafe's wine list has seven times won the *Wine Spectator*'s Award of Excellence. Our list—rich in ready-to-drink values— is lovingly chosen with great care and with a keen eye to our menu. In fact, before we choose a wine for our list, three criteria must always be met: It must be delicious and make you excited to take a second sip; as a condiment or seasoning, it must improve the flavor of at least two dishes from our menu; and our guests must feel the wine represents outstanding value. That all may sound simple, but how often have you gone to a restaurant and not liked the flavor of the wine you ordered, found it impossible to find a wine that seems to go well with the restaurant's food, or feared that you'd have to use all three of your credit cards just to cover the exorbitant cost of the one wine you really wanted to drink.

We try to select wines from small estate bottlers, preferably ones whose vineyards we've visited, in whose cellars we've tasted, and whose families we've met. We know the people who bake our bread, make our goat cheese, grow our lettuces, and pick our strawberries. Why wouldn't we want to know the growers who produce our wines as well? It's particularly rewarding to buy wines made by the same people who grow the grapes, and to be able to get to know each winemaker's personality—generous, elegant, humble, fastidious—since those same traits almost always end up as flavor characteristics in the glass. When recommending a bottle to interested Union Square Cafe diners, it's a pleasure to share stories of the people who put the wine into the bottle, and it always adds a nice dimension to their enjoyment of the wine.

Since Union Square Cafe's food is always well seasoned, we tend to seek out wines that taste equally generous, with full flavors and long finishes. A profound wine is usually produced when a winemaker is courageous enough to cut back his vines, sacrificing a large grape production and potentially valuable crop in favor of a smaller harvest with fewer, better nourished, and more intensely flavored grapes. No matter how good a winemaker is, it's the quality of the grapes that will most determine the quality of the wine.

It has become distressingly difficult to find great wines on the market where either the producer or distributor had the restraint not to raise his prices beyond a reasonable level. By the time a restaurant diner asks for the wine list, a wine has often been marked up three or four times. If either the producer, importer, distributor, or restaurateur is greedy, the biggest victim is the wine itself, since it can only be judged against its unfairly high price. It's sad to note how many wines we've tasted through the years, no matter how delicious, that we never got to share with our guests, only because someone price-gouged along the way. Unfortunately, wine simply doesn't taste as good when you're getting ripped off.

Sometimes our guests ask why we don't have many recognizable names on our wine list. We explain that many of the vineyards whose wines we serve have no marketing budget, and that whatever profits they do make usually end up back in the vineyard, not on a billboard. Of course that puts the onus on us to educate and train our staff properly so our guests won't be intimidated by a list of unfamiliar names. We conduct regular wine classes with our staff, always sharing stories about the winemakers and always tasting the wines with food from our menu. What good would a mustard tasting be without trying it with some decent sausage to put things in perspective?

☐ Using Union Square Cafe's Cookbook

There are two approaches to deciding on a menu. One is to meticulously plan out what you feel like eating, what you want to serve, what you have time to prepare—and then to search for all the ingredients needed for the recipes. The other method is to go to the market with no specific plans in mind, see what looks, feels, and smells best, and only then decide what to cook. That's how we plan our daily off-the-menu specials, and it's also how we love to cook if we're entertaining guests at home.

The Union Square Greenmarket gives our restaurant a culinary advantage. When we walk to work, it forces us to stop, look, and smell. When yellow daffodils and forsythia branches are blooming, you know it's spring. If the air is perfumed with the scent of basil, it must be summer. In fall, the farm stands overflow with crisp red apples, orange pumpkins, and gourds. And in winter, the pungent aroma of pine tree sap fills the air and fills the void left behind by yesterday's bountiful harvest. We know we're extremely fortunate to be next door to such a wonderful resource for food and culinary inspiration and we benefit from it almost daily. Countless times we've been at a loss for that night's dinner special, only to be inspired by a morning stroll through the greenmarket.

Though we have chosen to organize our cookbook according to menu courses, we urge you to be the judge of which dishes to cook when. Our suggestion is to use the book as if it were a marketplace, skimming through the different chapters to collect ideas, as you would peruse the stalls of your favorite farmer's market. When you see a recipe that makes you salivate, chances are good that its primary ingredients are in tune with the season, because whether you know it or not, you are, too. For example, if you're eager to cook the braised lamb shank, the outside air probably has a chill to it. Our bodies know when it's time to eat heartily and when to eat lightly, and if you listen to those instincts, your menu choices will probably be right on target. You'll have no trouble deciding about when to cook most of our main courses—for example, the Fillet Mignon of Tuna will taste delicious any time of year. So will roast chicken, grilled lamb chops, or sautéed salmon. But what you serve *with* each dish will give it the seasonal flair needed to be truly successful.

We have purposely included more side dish and vegetable recipes than anything else in this cookbook, and our hope is that you will mix and match these accompaniments creatively with our main courses according to what time of year it is and what's in season. Or, by varying the vegetable accompaniment, you can make any main course taste new and exciting each time. That's how we do it at Union Square Cafe, and we hope you will, too.

In adapting our restaurant recipes for this book, we've made a few procedural changes that should make things a lot simpler for you at home. One standard restaurant convention we've kept, however, is the frequent use of *mise-en-place*. Forgetting its fancy French name, *mise-en-place* (literally "put-in-place") makes cooking a lot easier by having your ingredients prepared and ready to go *before* you start cooking, rather than chopping, trimming, and slicing as you go. You'll notice that in most of our recipes the ingredient lists themselves have built-in instructions that will make recipe preparation a lot more efficient.

Here are a few tips about the ingredients we use most frequently in the cookbook:

Olive oil is by far the preferred cooking fat at Union Square Cafe. When a recipe simply calls for olive oil, use a good quality pure olive oil. Light, pure olive oil is best for sautéing or deep-frying, or for making mayonnaise. When dressing a salad or drizzling oil over cooked vegetables, fish, or meat, a fine extra-virgin olive oil, with its concentrated aroma and fruity flavor, is best.

Butter always refers to unsalted, sweet butter in our recipes. It pays to seek out the finest butter you can find, and salted butter is often of an inferior quality. Salted butter may also alter the seasoning of the recipes.

Kosher salt is used almost exclusively at the restaurant. It is purer than table salt, which generally contains additives to keep it pouring. It is coarser than table salt, so a little goes a longer way. Sea salt—available both coarse and ground—is also an excellent seasoning, with a milder, sweeter flavor than table salt.

Black pepper is always called for as "freshly ground." It pays to use a pepper mill, since the aromatic flavor and potency of black pepper dissipates quickly after it is ground.

Spices such as cumin, coriander, nutmeg, and allspice are widely available preground, but are at their pungent best when freshly ground just before using. It's well worth having an electric spice mill on hand to grind spices.

Zest of any citrus fruit refers to the outer peel, completely free of the bitter white pith found just under the skin. If you don't have a zester—the tool for removing citrus skin—a European-style vegetable peeler does the job quite well. Always wash fruit well before removing the zest.

We prefer fresh herbs to dried. If the fresh herb called for isn't available, substitute one that is: Use fresh parsley, for example, instead of marjoram, or tarragon instead of chervil.

Anchovy fillets refer to oil packed. If yours are salt packed, be sure to rinse them well before using.

APPETIZERS

RICHARD POLSKY

Roman-Style Marinated Olives

Steamed Asparagus with Sauternes Vinaigrette

Bar Nuts

Artichoke and Potato Ragout

Bruschetta Rossa

Bruschetta Bianca

Fried Calamari with Spicy Anchovy Mayonnaise

Corn Pudding with Red Peppers and Okra

Braised Escarole and White Beans with Tomatoes, Mushrooms, and Pecorino

Matzo Polenta with Sautéed Mushrooms

Baked Ricotta and Spinach Tart

Warm Seafood and White Bean Salad

Roast Stuffed Eggplant with Spicy Tomato Sauce

Hot Garlic Potato Chips

Cotechino with Wine-Soaked Crostini

Ratatouille-Stuffed Zucchini Blossoms

Pappardelle of Zucchini

Bombolotti al Modo Mio

Linguine with Spinach, Garlic, and Olive Oil

Malloreddus alla Campidanese

Orecchiette with Broccoli Rabe and Tomatoes

Bucatini all'Amatriciana

Penne with Asparagus and Red Peppers

Penne with Gorgonzola, Beets, and Toasted Walnuts

Penne with Eggplant and Roasted Pepper

Porcini Gnocchi with Prosciutto and Parmigiano Cream

Risotto with Chicken Livers, Moscato d'Asti, and Mushrooms

Pumpkin Risotto

Risotto d'Oro

Shrimp Risotto with Cucumber and Jalapeño

Risotto with Snails, Pancetta, and Red Wine

*M*ore than any other course on the menu, our palate-whetting appetizers are inspired by the Mediterranean diet. Most of the first-course dishes feature olive oil, pasta, rice, and vegetables, with less emphasis on butter, meat, and fish.

In the Italian tradition we've always proposed our pasta and rice dishes as a first course, rather than as the centerpiece of a meal. Still, many of our guests request appetizer dishes served in larger meal-size portions, and you should feel equally free to double any recipe from this section so that it becomes your main course.

Since pasta and rice are vehicles for flavor, we let the seasons determine which sauces and ingredients we'll cook when. For example, we like Pumpkin Risotto in the cold months, even though canned pumpkin is available year-round. Likewise, even though you can find zucchini 365 days a year in your local supermarket, Pappardelle of Zucchini is at its best when made in the height of summer squash season.

For years, cookbooks have advised their readers to boil pasta only until it resists the tooth, or al dente, and we agree. In several of our recipes, we'll even stop the cooking process short of al dente, and finish cooking the pasta right in its sauce. The pasta will absorb the flavors of the sauce, and in turn, the sauce will be enriched by the released starch of the pasta.

Here are a couple more tricks we use at Union Square Cafe to improve our pasta dishes: Just before you drain your cooked noodles,

save a cup of the flavorful cooking water. A few tablespoons of it added to a tomato or olive oil-based sauce provide extra flavor, lightness, and smoothness to the ultimate dish. It's also useful for thinning out an overly reduced cream sauce. If a recipe calls for grated Parmigiano-Reggiano or Pecorino Romano cheese, sprinkle some of the cheese directly onto your piping hot pasta just after it has been drained. Shake the colander to distribute the cheese evenly. The cheese will melt directly onto the pasta, adding flavor to each bite. It will also give added texture to each individual noodle, allowing more of the sauce to adhere.

Interestingly, the most popular appetizer on our menu since the day Union Square Cafe opened is neither a pasta nor particularly Italian in its preparation: It's our addictive Fried Calamari with Spicy Anchovy Mayonnaise—the secret of which is revealed in this chapter.

ROMAN-STYLE MARINATED OLIVES

*G*uests at Union Square Cafe are always greeted with three things: a warm welcome, a basket of local artisanal sourdough bread, and a ramekin of these marinated black olives. At home, they can be served as an hors d'oeuvre; they're great for guests to snack on while you're putting the final touches on dinner. The recipe works best with brine-packed, firm-fleshed gaeta, niçoise, or picholine olives. If the olives you select are oil-packed, omit the first step of the recipe.

SERVES 8 TO 12

> *1 pound brine-packed gaeta, niçoise, or picholine olives*
> *1 cup extra-virgin olive oil*
> *2 to 3 garlic cloves, peeled and flattened with the side of*
> *   a knife*
> *1 tablespoon dried red pepper flakes*
> *1 tablespoon fennel seeds, lightly toasted*
> *Zest of 1 orange, julienned*

1.   Drain the olives, place them in a bowl, and rinse under cold running water until the water in the bowl is clear. Drain the olives well. Shake in a sieve to remove excess water.

2.   In a large, clean, dry jar, combine the olives and the remaining ingredients. Cover tightly and shake to combine well. Marinate at room temperature for 3 to 5 hours, then store the olives in the refrigerator. They will keep for up to 1 month.

Steamed Asparagus with Sauternes Vinaigrette

Sauternes has enough natural sweetness to be one of the few wines that go well with asparagus. This wonderful vinaigrette also works quite well as a dip for chilled artichoke leaves. If you can't find Sauternes—a Bordeaux dessert wine made from botrytised sauvignon blanc and sémillon grapes—it's perfectly acceptable to substitute Barsac or one of the good California dessert wines made from "rotted" overripe sauvignon blanc and sémillon.

SERVES 4

> 2 cups Sauternes
> 2 teaspoons Dijon mustard
> 1 teaspoon lemon juice
> $1/4$ teaspoon kosher salt
> Freshly ground black pepper
> $3/4$ cup grapeseed oil
> 2 pounds asparagus, washed, tough ends snapped off,
>   stalks peeled
> 1 egg, hard-boiled and sieved
> 1 tablespoon chopped parsley
> $1/4$ cup peeled and chopped pistachio nuts

Serve a chilled glass of the same wine you use for the vinaigrette on the side.

1. Place the Sauternes in a saucepan and reduce over high heat to $1/3$ cup. Allow to cool.

2. Pour the Sauternes reduction into a jar with the mustard, lemon juice, salt, and pepper. Add the grapeseed oil, cover tightly with a lid, and shake vigorously to form a creamy vinaigrette.

3. Steam the asparagus until tender. Immediately plunge the cooked asparagus into ice water to stop the cooking. Drain and reserve until ready to serve.

4. Combine the sieved hard-boiled egg with the chopped parsley to make "mimosa."

5. To serve, place the asparagus on a platter and dress evenly with two-thirds of the vinaigrette. Sprinkle with the mimosa and chopped pistachios. Serve and pass the remaining vinaigrette.

NOTE: For a more substantial salad, try the asparagus served with some leaves of Bibb lettuce, or sprinkle with a handful of coarsely chopped mizuna or frisée in addition to the pistachios and mimosa.

BAR NUTS

These nuts won The New York Press award for "best bar nuts in New York." Every afternoon at about 4:45, a piping hot batch emerges from our ovens and is sent out to the bar, where the sweet rosemary fragrance wafts throughout the restaurant. Though we don't have a television set at our bar, these nuts would probably be a hit in your living room accompanied by a football game and some ice-cold beer.

YIELDS 5 CUPS

> *1/4 pound each peeled peanuts, cashews, brazil nuts,*
> *hazelnuts, walnuts, pecans, and whole unpeeled*
> *almonds, or 1 1/4 pounds unsalted, assorted nuts*
> *2 tablespoons coarsely chopped fresh rosemary*
> *1/2 teaspoon cayenne*
> *2 teaspoons dark brown sugar*
> *2 teaspoons kosher salt*
> *1 tablespoon butter, melted*

1. Preheat the oven to 350 degrees F.

2. Toss the nuts in a large bowl to combine and spread them out on a cookie sheet. Toast in the oven until they become light golden brown, about 10 minutes.

3. In the large bowl, combine the rosemary, cayenne, brown sugar, salt, and melted butter.

4. Thoroughly toss the warm toasted nuts with the spiced butter and serve warm.

ARTICHOKE AND POTATO RAGOUT

One intoxicating whiff of the heady fragrance of this ragout will transport you directly to Provence. A great appetizer for an outdoor summer dinner party, serve the ragout with hunks of warmed rosemary focaccia. You could follow the artichoke ragout with a main course of juicy grilled lamb.

SERVES 4

1 lemon
12 baby artichokes, or 4 large artichokes
10 ounces Yukon Gold potatoes, peeled
1 tablespoon thinly sliced garlic
$1/2$ teaspoon coriander seed, crushed
$1/2$ teaspoon black peppercorns, crushed
$1/3$ cup dry white vermouth or white wine
$1/3$ cup extra-virgin olive oil
$1/2$ teaspoon kosher salt
$1/2$ cup pitted black niçoise or gaeta olives
$3/4$ cup Oven-Dried Tomatoes, drained (page 318)
2 tablespoons coarsely chopped fresh mint leaves
2 tablespoons coarsely chopped basil
1 tablespoon coarsely chopped parsley

Cassis rosé, Tavel, and Châteauneuf-du-Pape blanc are heady enough to complement the herbs and still stand up to the wine-unfriendly artichokes.

1. Squeeze the juice of the lemon into a bowl of cold water large enough to hold the artichokes. If using baby artichokes, cut off only the very tips of the stems. Peel the outer layer of the remaining stems with a paring knife or vegetable peeler. Slice off the tops of the artichokes, about $1/4$ inch down, and peel away 2 to 3 layers of the tough outer leaves until the tender yellow inner leaves are exposed. Cut each artichoke in half through the choke. With the tip of a paring knife, pry out the small choke.

2.   If using larger artichokes, snap off the outer, dark green leaves until you get to the innermost light yellow ones. With a paring knife, trim away the ends of the leaves still attached to the artichoke bottom and cut the top of the artichoke, about $1/2$ inch down. Cut the artichokes into 6 or more pieces and remove the choke. In both cases, as you finish trimming each artichoke, place it in the acidulated water to prevent discoloring.

3.   Quarter the potatoes lengthwise and slice each quarter into $1/4$-inch pieces.

4.   In a 3-quart saucepan, combine the artichokes, potatoes, garlic, coriander, peppercorns, vermouth, $1 1/2$ cups water, olive oil, and salt. Bring to a boil, lower the flame, and simmer, covered, for 10 to 12 minutes.

5.   Add the remaining ingredients to the ragout and continue simmering, uncovered, an additional 5 minutes to concentrate the broth. Serve immediately or at room temperature.

BRUSCHETTA ROSSA

*B*ruschetta illustrates the Italian genius of letting great ingredients sing for themselves. At its basic best, bruschetta simply combines good bread, just pressed extra-virgin olive oil, sweet garlic, and coarse salt. In August, at the height of tomato season, it's hard to resist topping the bruschetta with juicy, ripe tomatoes marinated with garlic, basil, and olive oil. Bruschetta Rossa makes a perfect late-summer appetizer or pass-around hors d'oeuvre. Follow with Grilled Veal Lombatina and some steamed corn on the cob.

SERVES 6

6 large vine-ripened tomatoes
1 1/2 teaspoons salt
1/2 teaspoon freshly ground black pepper
1/2 cup (firmly packed) basil leaves, washed and dried
1/2 cup extra-virgin olive oil
8 garlic cloves, peeled and split lengthwise
6 1-inch slices of sourdough or whole wheat
    peasant bread

A refreshing combination with bruschetta are crisply acidic whites like Ribolla Gialla, Sauvignon Blanc, and Soave Classico.

1.   To peel the tomatoes, bring 3 quarts of water to a boil in a large pot. Prepare a bowl of ice water large enough to hold the tomatoes. Plunge the tomatoes into the boiling water for 30 seconds. Remove with a slotted spoon and immediately immerse them in the ice water until cool. Using the tip of a paring knife, core and peel the tomatoes.

2.   Cut the tomatoes in half crosswise and squeeze them gently to remove their seeds and excess juice. (The juice can be strained, frozen, and used later for a sauce, soup, or vinaigrette.) With the palm of your hand, flatten the tomato halves on the cutting board and chop them into 1-inch pieces. Place the chopped tomatoes in a large bowl and season with the salt and pepper.

3.   Thinly slice all but 6 of the basil leaves and toss with the tomatoes. Add the olive oil and all but 4 of the garlic halves. Stir well to combine and marinate for 1 to 2 hours at room temperature.

4.   To serve, grill or toast the bread until golden brown. While the toast is still warm, rub each piece on both sides with the reserved garlic halves. The garlic will melt into the bread and give it an intense flavor.

5.   Use a slotted spoon to heap a generous serving of the tomatoes onto each garlic-rubbed toast, leaving the garlic cloves in the marinade (see note). Garnish with the reserved basil leaves, and serve immediately to prevent the bread from getting soggy.

NOTE: The garlic cloves can be reused for more bruschetta, or finely chopped and combined with the remaining marinating juice to make a delicious sauce for steaming-hot spaghetti or linguine. Sprinkle the pasta with freshly grated Pecorino Romano cheese.

BRUSCHETTA BIANCA

*T*his is a terrific appetizer we created one winter day when tomatoes were woefully pallid and yet the craving still struck for bruschetta. White truffle oil and good balsamic vinegar transform what would normally be a rustic bread dish into an elegantly zesty hors d'oeuvre. While there are plenty of good balsamic vinegars available these days, don't hesitate to invest in a tiny bottle of aged *balsamico tradizionale,* an exquisite product whose every detail of production and barrel aging is carefully monitored by a special consortium. Beyond being useful for this recipe, a drop or two of authentic *balsamico tradizionale* drizzled over a finished omelet, a chunk of Parmigiano-Reggiano, or a bowl of fresh strawberries will transform those dishes into something remarkable. Likewise, Italian white truffle oil—while not inexpensive—is a luxurious way to bring the heady fragrance of white truffles to your table year round at a far lower cost than buying fresh white truffles.

SERVES 4 TO 6

> 6 1-inch slices sourdough or whole wheat peasant bread
> 1 large garlic clove, cut in half lengthwise
> $^{1}/_{2}$ teaspoon coarse sea salt
> $^{1}/_{2}$ teaspoon balsamic vinegar
> $^{1}/_{4}$ cup white truffle oil (see page 321 for mail-order
>   source)
> 3 ounces Parmigiano-Reggiano cheese, shaved with a
>   vegetable peeler into thin shards ($^{3}/_{4}$ cup)
> $^{1}/_{4}$ teaspoon freshly ground black pepper

1. Grill or toast the bread until golden brown. While the toast is still warm, rub each piece on both sides with the garlic halves. The garlic will melt into the bread and give it an intense flavor. Season with the sea salt.

This is a special-occasion appetizer that calls for a festive glass of Champagne, Prosecco, or any good sparkling wine.

2. Drizzle each piece of toast with equal amounts of the balsamic vinegar and half the truffle oil.

3. Place the shaved Parmigiano on the toasts and drizzle the remaining truffle oil over the cheese. Sprinkle each bruschetta with pepper and serve.

Fried Calamari with Spicy Anchovy Mayonnaise

*T*he unusual idea of using graham cracker crumbs to flavor calamari came to Danny accidentally while enjoying a quick bite one afternoon at a San Francisco bar. He was with the cafe's first chef, Ali Barker, and while munching on some tender calamari tentacles, asked why they tasted so good. Barker answered: "I think it's cardamom. You know, the spice that tastes like graham crackers." The bar's chef revealed he used "nothing but flour, salt, and pepper." Even though the two had mis-guessed the ingredients, the idea still sounded intriguing, and they experimented with a mixture of graham cracker crumbs and flour. The results were fantastic. The sugar in the crumbs caramelizes while the calamari are frying, allowing them to reach a perfect golden brown long before they've become overcooked and rubbery. Lastly, the sweet contrast with the spicy, salty dip is addictive.

If you clean the calamari yourself, separate the tentacles from the body. Remove the ink sac and cartilage from inside the head, and under cold running water, peel the dark skin from the body. Rinse well.

SERVES 4

ANCHOVY MAYONNAISE

    1 egg, at room temperature
    4 to 5 anchovy fillets
    2 tablespoons lemon juice
    1 tablespoon finely chopped parsley
    1/2 teaspoon cayenne
    3/4 cup light olive oil or vegetable oil

For an incredible match, try a glass of chilled fino sherry with the calamari. They're also delicious with kabinett and spätlese German Rieslings, as well as Vouvray.

CALAMARI

1 pound fresh, clean calamari
4 cups light olive or vegetable oil
1 cup all-purpose flour
1 cup graham cracker crumbs
1 teaspoon kosher salt

1. In a food processor, combine the egg, anchovies, lemon juice, parsley, and cayenne. Blend until smooth. With the motor running, slowly add the oil to make a mayonnaise. Transfer the sauce to a bowl and refrigerate, covered tightly, for up to 2 days, until ready to serve.

2. Cut the calamari into ¼-inch rings. If the tentacles are large, halve or quarter them lengthwise. Refrigerate until ready to use.

3. Pour the oil into a heavy-bottomed, straight-sided 3-quart saucepan, about 8 inches in diameter. To prevent the oil from bubbling over when frying the calamari, the pan should be no more than one third full. Heat the oil to 360 degrees F on a deep-fat thermometer. (To check the temperature without a thermometer, drop a small piece of bread the size of a crouton into the oil. It should float to the surface immediately and brown lightly in about 45 seconds.)

4. Combine the flour and graham cracker crumbs in a bowl. Divide the calamari into two or three batches for easier frying. Toss each batch in the flour mixture to coat evenly. Shake the calamari in a mesh strainer to shed excess coating. Using tongs or a slotted spoon, gently lower each batch of calamari into the hot oil and fry until golden brown, about 2 minutes. Remove with a slotted spoon and drain on paper towels. Sprinkle with salt. The cooked calamari can be kept warm in a low oven while you continue. Check your oil temperature (360 degrees) and repeat with the remaining calamari. Serve hot with the chilled anchovy mayonnaise.

CORN PUDDING WITH RED PEPPERS AND OKRA

*H*ere's a twist on an American classic, using roast red peppers, cumin, and cilantro for added color and spice. We love the crunch and flavor the okra provides, but feel free to omit if you desire.

As an alternative to the cream sauce, you can substitute Tomato Coulis.

SERVES 4 TO 6

PUDDING

   3 cups fresh corn kernels (cut from 6 to 8 ears)
   1¹/₂ cups half-and-half
   2 large eggs
   Pinch of sugar
   Pinch of ground allspice
   ¹/₈ teaspoon cayenne
   1¹/₂ teaspoons kosher salt
   ¹/₄ teaspoon freshly ground black pepper
   ¹/₂ cup roasted, peeled, and diced red bell pepper
   1 tablespoon chopped parsley
   1 tablespoon chopped cilantro

SAUCE

   2 tablespoons butter
   1 cup thinly sliced okra rounds
   1 tablespoon minced shallots
   2 teaspoons minced garlic
   ¹/₄ teaspoon ground cumin
   1 cup heavy cream
   1 medium tomato, peeled, seeded, and diced (see
      Bruschetta Rossa, page 12)
   1¹/₂ teaspoons fresh lime juice

Choose a fruity Chardonnay, Sauvignon Blanc, or Loire Valley Chenin Blanc for the rich-tasting, sweet-spicy pudding.

1.   Preheat the oven to 325 degrees F. Butter a 5-cup soufflé mold and refrigerate.

2.   In a blender, combine 1 cup of the corn, the half-and-half, eggs, sugar, allspice, half the cayenne, 1 teaspoon salt, and half the pepper. Purée until smooth.

3.   In a large bowl, combine the puréed corn with the remaining corn kernels, diced red pepper, parsley, and cilantro. Check the seasoning and adjust to your taste.

4.   Fill the refrigerated mold three-quarters full with the corn mixture. Place the mold in a roasting pan and pour in hot water to reach halfway up the outside of the mold. Bake for $1^{1}/_{2}$ hours, until set but still slightly soft on top. Remove from the oven and let rest 10 to 15 minutes before serving.

5.   To make the sauce, melt the butter over medium heat in a saucepan. Add the okra and sauté for 2 to 3 minutes, until just softened. Remove from the pan with a slotted spoon and set aside in a warm place.

6.   Stir the shallots, garlic, and cumin into the pan and cook without browning for 1 minute over medium heat. Add the cream, bring to a boil, and cook until the sauce is reduced in volume and lightly coats the back of a spoon.

7.   Add the diced tomato, lime juice, and remaining cayenne. Season with the remaining salt and pepper. Return the sauce to a boil and then remove from the heat.

8.   Spoon equal amounts of pudding onto warm dinner plates and serve the sauce around the pudding. Sprinkle cooked okra rounds over each plate and serve.

BRAISED ESCAROLE AND WHITE BEANS WITH TOMATOES, MUSHROOMS, AND PECORINO

*H*ere's a rustic all-vegetable recipe that serves well as an appetizer, and also satisfies as a main course. It's a hearty dish that is particularly warming in chilly months. Our favorite accompaniment is a thick slice of sourdough or peasant bread, toasted and drizzled with extra-virgin olive oil, covered with grated Parmigiano-Reggiano, and melted under the broiler. Leftovers can be enjoyed as room-temperature hors d'oeuvres, spooned onto a piece of toast or a cracker.
SERVES 4 TO 6

TOMATO SAUCE

$1^1/2$ pounds (3 to 4 medium) fresh ripe tomatoes, chopped

1 35-ounce can Italian plum tomatoes

2 tablespoons olive oil

$^1/2$ cup diced onion

1 teaspoon minced garlic

1 teaspoon minced fresh rosemary

1 tablespoon chopped basil

$^1/2$ teaspoon salt

$^1/2$ teaspoon freshly ground black pepper

ESCAROLE AND BEANS

$^1/4$ pound shiitake mushrooms

$^1/4$ pound white mushrooms

2 tablespoons olive oil

1 teaspoon minced garlic

$1^1/4$ pounds escarole, washed, dried, and cut into 2- to 3-inch pieces

Enjoy a glass of Cahors, Côtes-du-Rhône, or a northern Italian Cabernet Sauvignon with the escarole and beans.

1¹/₂ cups cooked cannellini beans (see Fagioli alla
   Toscana, steps 1 and 2, page 253)
³/₄ cup grated Pecorino Romano
1 teaspoon kosher salt
¹/₄ teaspoon freshly ground black pepper

1.   Combine the fresh and canned tomatoes in a 3-quart saucepan and cook over medium heat until juicy, about 15 minutes. Pass the tomatoes through a food mill to remove the seeds and skins.

2.   Heat the olive oil over medium heat in the saucepan and sauté the onion and garlic for 2 to 3 minutes. Add the tomato purée and the herbs. Cook, stirring occasionally, until the sauce thickens, about 30 minutes. Season with salt and pepper and set aside.

3.   Wipe the mushrooms clean. Remove the shiitake stems, and slice both kinds of mushrooms into ¹/₄-inch slices.

4.   Heat the olive oil over high heat in a 3-quart saucepan and add the mushrooms. Sauté until lightly browned and add the minced garlic. Cook 1 minute, stirring to prevent burning. Add the escarole and continue to cook over high heat until the greens have completely wilted. Stir in the tomato sauce and the cannellini beans, bring to a simmer, and cook 5 to 8 minutes to blend the flavors. Add the cheese, salt, and pepper and serve.

MATZO POLENTA WITH SAUTÉED MUSHROOMS

*T*his is a tasty twist on polenta, substituting matzo meal for yellow cornmeal. Matzo "polenta" was one of the first collaborations we made when Meyer met Romano. It's delicious topped with garlicky sautéed mushrooms or as a sauce-soaking side dish for roast meats and poultry. Just as turkey has successfully flown the coop from its typecast Thanksgiving role, perhaps matzo will one day enjoy an exodus from Passover.

Some purists may raise an eyebrow at the recipe's use of chicken bouillon cubes. We've found that the judicious use of a quality stock base can intensify the flavors of some preparations.

SERVES 4 TO 6

MATZO POLENTA

1 1/4 cups chicken stock

1 cup milk

2 chicken bouillon cubes

1/4 teaspoon each minced fresh rosemary, sage, and thyme

3/4 cup matzo meal, plus extra for coating the cakes

1 large egg

1 egg yolk

Kosher salt

Freshly ground black pepper

1/3 cup olive oil

MUSHROOMS

2 tablespoons olive oil

1/2 pound assorted mushrooms, cleaned and very thinly sliced (use any combination of white, shiitake, cremini, or wild mushrooms)

1/2 teaspoon minced garlic

2 anchovy fillets, very finely minced (optional)

1/4 cup white wine

With primary flavors of mushrooms, garlic, and herbs, look for a white wine like Vouvray, Pinot Bianco, or Sauvignon Blanc to complement the matzo polenta. While sometimes difficult to obtain, it would be worth the effort to seek out a quality Swiss white like Fendant or Dézaley for this dish.

1 tablespoon lemon juice
¹/₄ teaspoon salt
¹/₈ teaspoon freshly ground black pepper
1 tablespoon chopped parsley

1.　Lightly oil an 8-inch cake pan or straight-sided tart pan.

2.　In a 2-quart saucepan, bring to a boil the chicken stock, milk, bouillon cubes, and herbs. Reduce the heat and simmer until the bouillon cubes are completely dissolved, about 3 minutes.

3.　Slowly pour the matzo meal into the liquid with one hand while whisking constantly with the other. (Be sure to use a firm whisk.) Continue whisking until smooth and creamy. The mixture will become quite thick. Reduce the heat to low and cook for 5 minutes, stirring occasionally to prevent sticking.

4.　Beat the egg and egg yolk together in a bowl; whisk into the matzo polenta. Raise the heat slightly and return the mixture to a boil. Whisk constantly for 1 minute, season with salt and pepper to taste, and remove from the heat.

5.　Pour the cooked matzo polenta into the oiled pan. With a spatula, spread the mixture evenly and smoothly. Cover, refrigerate, and chill thoroughly, at least 30 minutes and up to 24 hours.

6.　Preheat the oven to 250 degrees F. Cut the polenta into pie-shaped wedges. In a large sauté pan, heat the ¹/₃ cup olive oil over a moderate flame. Dredge the matzo wedges in the extra matzo meal and sauté on both sides until golden brown. Transfer to an ovenproof platter and hold, uncovered, in the oven while you cook the mushrooms.

7.　Wipe the sauté pan clean and heat the 2 tablespoons olive oil over high heat until it just begins to smoke. Add the mushrooms and sauté to brown and soften them, 3 to 5 minutes. Add the garlic, anchovy, white wine, and lemon juice and toss together to blend the flavors. Season with salt and pepper and cook 1 to 2 minutes. Spoon the mushrooms and their juice over the matzo polenta cakes and serve, sprinkled with chopped parsley.

BAKED RICOTTA AND SPINACH TART

*U*nspired by a treasured Romano family recipe, this savory deep-dish tart is wonderful as an appetizer or as a meal in itself accompanied by a crisp salad. Served on the side, hot Tomato Coulis further enlivens the tart.

SERVES 6 TO 8

30 ounces whole-milk ricotta cheese (4 cups)
2 cups all-purpose flour
1 teaspoon kosher salt
12 tablespoons (1 1/2 sticks) butter, cut into 1/2-inch pieces
  and chilled
5 tablespoons ice water
2 tablespoons olive oil
1 pound spinach, stemmed and cleaned
1/8 teaspoon freshly ground black pepper
1/2 cup peeled and diced onion
1 1/2 teaspoons minced fresh marjoram
1/4 pound prosciutto, diced (1 cup)
3 large eggs
1/8 teaspoon freshly grated nutmeg

This rustic tart calls for a country Italian red like Chianti Classico, Valpolicella, or Salice Salentino.

1.   Place the ricotta in a strainer lined with cheesecloth and allow to drain over a bowl, covered and refrigerated, for 2 hours.

2.   To prepare the tart dough, combine the flour and 1/2 teaspoon of the salt in a bowl. Add the chilled butter and, using your fingertips or two knives, blend until the mixture resembles coarse meal. Work in the ice water until the dough holds together. Form the dough into a smooth, flat disk, wrap in plastic, and refrigerate for at least 1 hour.

3. Lightly flour a clean work surface and roll the dough into a 16-inch disk. Place the rolled-out dough into a 10 x $2^1/_2$-inch-deep cake pan or springform mold. Pressing with your fingertips, flute the top edges of the dough. Place in the freezer and chill thoroughly, about 30 minutes.

4. In a medium skillet, heat 1 tablespoon of the olive oil over high heat and sauté the spinach, stirring constantly until wilted, about 2 minutes. Season with $^1/_4$ teaspoon salt and half the pepper. Place the cooked spinach in a colander and drain. Chop fine and reserve.

5. In the same skillet, add the remaining tablespoon olive oil and cook the onion 3 to 5 minutes over medium heat until translucent. Add the marjoram and prosciutto. Stir and cook an additional 2 minutes. Set aside.

6. Preheat the oven to 425 degrees F.

7. In a large bowl, beat the eggs and add the drained ricotta, spinach, onion, and prosciutto. Season with the nutmeg and remaining salt and pepper. Set aside.

8. Line the tart shell with aluminum foil and fill with dried beans or pastry weights. Bake for 12 to 15 minutes, until the dough is set. Remove the foil and beans and cook an additional 10 minutes, or until the dough is light brown.

9. Lower the oven temperature to 375 degrees. Spread the ricotta and spinach mixture evenly in the tart, place on the middle rack of the oven, and bake for 1 hour and 10 minutes, until the filling is set and the top golden brown. Let rest for 15 to 20 minutes, slice into wedges, and serve.

WARM SEAFOOD AND WHITE BEAN SALAD

*H*ere's our warm twist on the classic Italian *insalata di frutti di mare,* enlivened with simmered white beans, curly greens, and fines herbes. You could follow the seafood-bean salad with Seared Filet Mignon or Grilled Veal Lombatina; or double the portion and make the salad a meal on its own. In either case, make sure to have a crusty loaf of bread on hand to sop up the savory juice.

SERVES 4

4 cups frisée, cored, cleaned, dried, and torn into pieces

$^1/_4$ cup extra-virgin olive oil, plus 1 tablespoon
    for drizzling

2 teaspoons minced garlic

12 small mussels, beards removed and scrubbed

$^1/_2$ pound calamari, cleaned and sliced into
    $^1/_4$-inch rings

8 medium shrimp ($^1/_4$ pound), shelled, deveined,
    and butterflied

$1^1/_2$ cups cooked cannellini or Great Northern beans
    (liquid reserved) (see Fagioli alla Toscana, steps 1
    and 2, p. 253)

1 tablespoon each minced tarragon, chives, parsley,
    and chervil

1 teaspoon kosher salt

$^1/_4$ teaspoon freshly ground black pepper

2 teaspoons fresh lemon juice

To complement the seafood salad, choose an herbaceous bottle of Sancerre, or a lively Tocai Friulano or Ribolla Gialla from Italy's Friuli-Venezia-Giulia region.

1. Arrange the frisée on a serving platter or in a large salad bowl. Set aside.

2.   Heat the $1/4$ cup olive oil and the garlic in a 10-inch skillet over moderate heat for 1 minute. Do not brown the garlic. Add the mussels and cook until they open, 3 to 4 minutes.

3.   Add the sliced calamari and shrimp. Cook over high heat, stirring, until the seafood is firm but not tough, about 2 minutes. Add the cooked beans and $1/4$ cup bean cooking liquid. Bring to a boil, stir in the herbs, and season with salt, pepper, and lemon juice.

4.   Spoon the warm seafood and beans atop the frisée. Drizzle with 1 tablespoon extra-virgin olive oil and serve immediately.

NOTE: If you clean the calamari yourself, separate the tentacles from the body. Remove the ink sac and cartilage from inside the head, and under cold running water, peel the dark skin from the body. Rinse well.

To trim the mussels, grasp the beard between your thumb and the blade of a paring knife. Snip the beard as you pull it away from the shell.

To butterfly the shrimp, place each piece, shelled, on a cutting board in front of you, with the outer curve of the shrimp closest to you. Using a paring knife, slice horizontally from the thick end of the shrimp to $1/2$ inch from the tail. With the tip of the knife, separate and cut away the dark vein. Rinse.

ROAST STUFFED EGGPLANT WITH SPICY TOMATO SAUCE

A longtime favorite appetizer at Union Square Cafe, this colorful dish is an eggplant version of twice-baked potatoes. Once the baby eggplants are stuffed, you can hold them, refrigerated and well covered, for up to two days before sprinkling on the Parmigiano and finishing them under the broiler. Minus the tomato sauce, the Roast Stuffed Eggplant makes a delicious accompaniment for roast chicken, lamb, or veal.

SERVES 4

6 baby eggplants, 5 to 7 inches long
3 tablespoons olive oil
2 teaspoons minced garlic
4 ounces leeks, white and light green parts only, washed and cut into 1/8-inch rounds (1 1/2 cups)
5 ounces shiitake mushrooms, stemmed and sliced
1 red bell pepper, roasted, peeled, and sliced into thin strips
1 yellow bell pepper, roasted, peeled and sliced into thin strips
2 anchovy fillets, minced (optional)
1 teaspoon kosher salt
Pinch of cayenne
Freshly ground black pepper
1/3 cup finely grated Parmigiano-Reggiano
2 cups Tomato Coulis (optional, page 319)

1. Preheat the oven to 350 degrees F.

2. Rub the eggplants with 1 tablespoon of the olive oil and roast on a cookie sheet, uncovered, for 45 minutes to 1 hour, until soft. Allow

Gigondas, California Syrah, and Rosso di Montalcino come to mind as good choices for this richly flavored dish.

the eggplants to cool before splitting them lengthwise. Remove the flesh with a spoon, taking care not to tear the skins. Reserve 8 of the 12 eggplant skins. Coarsely chop the flesh and set aside.

3.   In a 2-quart ovenproof skillet, heat the remaining oil over medium heat and cook the garlic for 30 seconds. Add the leeks and continue cooking until wilted, about 3 minutes. Add the shiitake mushrooms and cook 3 minutes longer, until softened. Stir in the peppers, anchovy, and chopped eggplant. Season with the salt, cayenne, and pepper. Cover and bake in the oven for 20 minutes.

4.   Remove the eggplant stuffing from the oven and stir in half the cheese. When cool enough to handle, fill the reserved eggplant skins evenly, using all of the stuffing.

5.   Preheat the broiler. Heat the tomato sauce to a simmer. Sprinkle the stuffed eggplants with the remaining Parmigiano and brown under the broiler. Transfer to a serving platter and serve with the tomato sauce.

HOT GARLIC POTATO CHIPS

*A*lmost everyone who's ever eaten at Union Square Cafe has enjoyed these addictive chips at least once. But for a cook's serendipitous mistake, they never would have graced our menu. When the restaurant first opened, we served confit of duck every Monday night—accompanied by thick-cut garlicky cottage fries, browned in duck fat. One Monday, quite by accident, a new prep cook misadjusted the thickness of the mandoline slicer and the cottage fries became chips. The error eluded the eye of our *sous-chef*— until two diners commented that the potatoes were even better than the duck! The next day we changed our menu and gave the chips star billing in our side dish section, where they've been a best-seller ever since.

SERVES 6 TO 8

> 4 Idaho potatoes, peeled (3 to 3 1/2 pounds)
> 1 1/2 quarts vegetable oil for frying
> 3 tablespoons butter
> 1 tablespoon pressed garlic
> 2 tablespoons chopped parsley
> 1 teaspoon salt
> 1/8 teaspoon freshly ground black pepper

If you run out of beer, Champagne is a wonderful way to wash down these chips!

1. With a mandoline (vegetable slicer) or a sharp knife, slice the potatoes about 1/16-inch thick. You should have about 6 cups. Place the potato slices in a large bowl and rinse with cold water until the water runs clean. Thoroughly dry the potatoes, first in a salad spinner, then on paper towels. This is important because any moisture left on the potatoes will cause the oil to splatter.

2. Pour the oil into a 6-quart heavy bottomed, straight-sided saucepan, 8 to 10 inches in diameter. The oil should be 1 1/4 to 1 1/2 inches deep and the pan no more than a quarter full. This prevents any bubbling over when frying the potatoes. Heat the oil to 315 degrees F

on a deep-fat thermometer. (To check the temperature without a thermometer, drop a small piece of bread the size of a crouton into the oil. It should float to the surface and lightly brown in about 2 minutes.)

3. Carefully fry the potato slices in two to three batches until light brown and crisp. You will need to stir the potatoes with a slotted spoon almost constantly to ensure even cooking. Each batch should take 15 to 20 minutes to cook. (If the potatoes brown in much less time, the oil is too hot. This will result in a chip that is neither cooked through nor crisp.)

4. As you remove each batch of crisp potato chips, place them on a cookie sheet lined with paper towels. When all the potatoes are done, place them in a mixing bowl large enough to hold them comfortably.

5. Over a medium flame, heat the butter and garlic in a saucepan, without allowing the garlic to brown. Drizzle the butter and garlic over the potatoes, add the chopped parsley, salt, and pepper, and mix thoroughly with a rubber spatula. Be careful not to crush the chips. Serve hot.

NOTE: The chips can be made several hours in advance. Store in a tightly closed container and reheat in a 350-degree oven until hot. Toss with the seasoned garlic butter at the last minute.

COTECHINO WITH WINE-SOAKED CROSTINI

*T*his mouth-watering dish is perfect as a passed hors d'oeuvre or as an appetizer garnished with a vinegary salad. Italian grocers often make their own cotechino, a sweetly spiced fresh pork sausage whose origins are in Emilia-Romagna. The bread can be either fresh or stale without altering the recipe. Cooking the soaked bread is a bit like making French toast—though French toast and breakfast sausage never tasted this good. If you end up with more sausage than you need for your toasts, reheat the leftovers and serve with braised lentils and balsamic vinegar or spicy Dijon mustard.

SERVE 6 TO 8

1¼ pound cotechino sausage or saucisson a l'ail, or
   garlic sausage, 6 to 8 inches long
6 cups red wine
2 cups water
1 medium onion, peeled and quartered
3 celery ribs, cleaned and split in half
12 peppercorns
1 bay leaf
Sprig of fresh thyme
½ teaspoon kosher salt
6 to 8 slices sourdough peasant bread, ¾ inch thick
   and halved
¼ cup olive oil
2 tablespoons chopped parsley

This dish is made to be washed down with a slightly chilled glass of Beaujolais, Dolcetto d'Alba, or Lambrusco.

1. Lightly prick the sausage with a fork or the tip of a small knife in three or four places. (This prevents the casing from bursting when heated.) Place the cotechino in a saucepan just large enough to accommodate it and add all the other ingredients except the bread,

oil, and parsley. Bring to a boil, immediately lower to a simmer, and poach the sausage, covered, for 50 minutes. Remove from the heat and allow the sausage to cool in its cooking liquid. (The dish can be prepared up to 2 days ahead at this point. Store the cotechino refrigerated and covered in its liquid and bring back to a simmer before serving.)

2.   Preheat the oven to 200 degrees F.

3.   Peel the cotechino and discard the casing. Slice the sausage into $1/4$-inch-thick rounds. Set aside, covered, in the oven.

4.   Dip each slice of bread in the sausage cooking liquid until it becomes thoroughly soaked, about 15 seconds a side. Gently squeeze the bread to remove any excess liquid and transfer to a plate until ready to cook.

5.   Heat the olive oil over a medium flame in a large skillet. Sauté the bread until brown, 2 to 3 minutes a side. Place the toasts on a warm serving platter and top each one with a slice or two of the warm sausage. Sprinkle with chopped parsley and serve.

RATATOUILLE-STUFFED ZUCCHINI BLOSSOMS

*C*apturing the flavors and colors of summer, these stuffed squash blossoms are marvelous as an appetizer, served with Tomato Coulis. Alternatively, you can serve them alongside a dressed salad of crisp mesclun.

SERVES 4

1/2 medium eggplant, split lengthwise
2 tablespoons extra-virgin olive oil
1 cup sliced zucchini
1/2 cup peeled and sliced onion
1/2 yellow bell pepper, cored, seeded, and sliced
1 1/2 tablespoons peeled and sliced garlic
1 tablespoon fresh thyme leaves
1/2 teaspoon kosher salt
1/8 teaspoon freshly ground black pepper
1 tablespoon bread crumbs
1 tablespoon minced parsley
16 large zucchini blossoms, preferably open for
    easier stuffing

1. Preheat the oven to 400 degrees F.

2. Place the eggplant half, cut side down, on a baking sheet. Roast for 30 minutes, or until very tender. When cool enough to handle, scoop out and coarsely chop the flesh.

3. Heat the olive oil in a medium skillet over moderate heat. Add the zucchini, onion, bell pepper, garlic, and thyme. Cook, stirring frequently, until the vegetables have softened, about 5 minutes. Stir in the chopped eggplant, season with salt and pepper, and cook an

We'd serve a chilled fruity rosé to complement the Provençal flavors in the stuffed blossoms. Try Cassis, Sancerre, Tavel, or any rosé made from grenache.

additional 10 to 15 minutes. Mix in the bread crumbs and minced parsley. Remove from the heat and set aside to cool.

4.   Purée the cooled vegetables in a food processor until smooth.

5.   Fit a pastry bag with a large open tip. Spoon the eggplant stuffing into the bag and carefully insert the tip into a zucchini blossom. Squeeze the bag gently to fill the flower three-quarters full. Twist the end of the blossom to seal in the stuffing. Repeat with the remaining blossoms until they are all filled. The blossoms may be stuffed several hours ahead up to this point and held, covered and refrigerated.

6.   Just before serving, lay the stuffed blossoms in a vegetable steamer. Cover and steam over boiling water for 2 to 3 minutes, or until warmed through. Serve immediately or at room temperature.

PAPPARDELLE OF ZUCCHINI

A pasta dish without the pasta! This favorite signature recipe debuted on Union Square Cafe's opening night menu. The zucchini and yellow squash are cut into long thin strips to mimic the shape of the classic pappardelle noodle. The trick to this easy-to-prepare dish is to have all the ingredients at hand when you begin cooking. Cook the squash quickly, so it doesn't give off too much water and dilute the sauce.

SERVES 4

1 pound (2 medium) zucchini, washed, ends trimmed
1 pound (2 medium) yellow squash, washed, ends trimmed
2 tablespoons olive oil
2 tablespoons white wine
2 tablespoons minced garlic
1/2 teaspoon kosher salt
Freshly ground black pepper
1/2 cup basil, cut into thin ribbons
2 medium tomatoes, peeled, seeded, and diced
2 cups Basic Tomato Sauce (page 317)
2 tablespoons heavy cream
1/4 cup finely grated Parmigiano-Reggiano

Crisp, fruity whites like Tocai Friulano and Sancerre do well with the pappardelle, as would lightly chilled reds like Dolcetto d'Alba or Beaujolais.

1.   Slice the zucchini and squash lengthwise into 1/8-inch strips on a mandoline. (If you don't have a mandoline, the backside of a spatula-shaped cheese slicer is just as effective.) Be sure the zucchini slices are not stuck together.

2.   Heat the olive oil over high heat in a large skillet. Just before the olive oil begins to smoke, add the cut squash and stir. Continue stirring for 3 to 4 minutes, or until the squash strips are barely wilted. Add the white wine, garlic, salt, and pepper. Toss in the basil and tomatoes. Stir in the tomato sauce, heavy cream, and half the Parmigiano. Bring to a boil. Serve immediately with the remaining Parmigiano sprinkled on top.

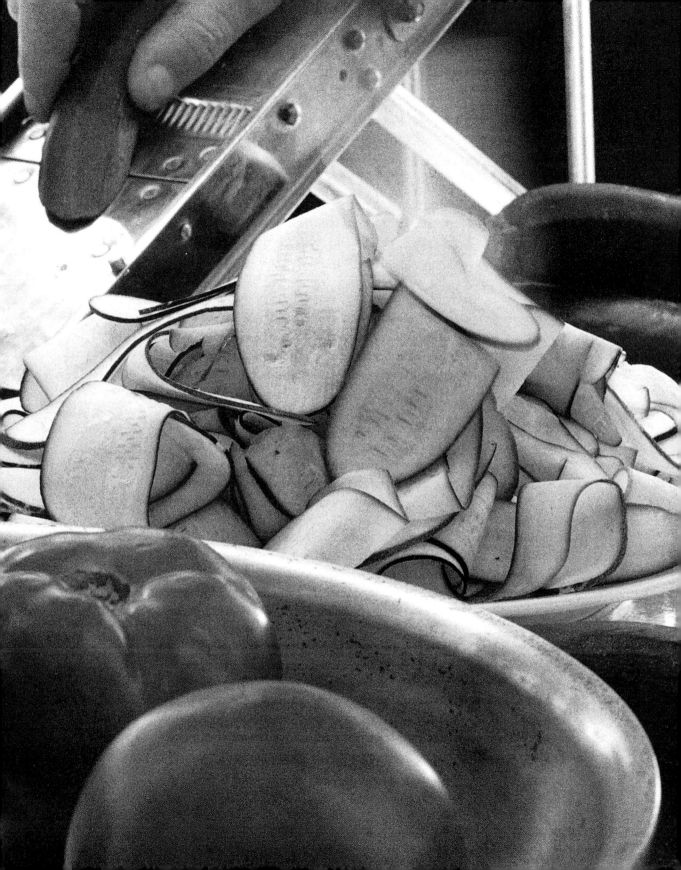

BOMBOLOTTI AL MODO MIO

*W*hen Danny worked as a tour guide in Rome in the late seventies, he surprised many of the groups by showing them more neighborhood trattorias than classic Roman sights. His favorite trattoria, nestled just across the bridge from the Castel Sant'Angelo, was La Taverna da Giovanni. It was there that he learned to speak and eat Italian, and thanks to a wonderfully warm family and staff, it became his Italian home away from home. Chef Claudio was generous enough to share his signature pasta dish—loosely translated as *bombolotti* "My Way." Outside Rome, *bombolotti* is referred to as *mezza-rigatoni*. The short, wide-mouthed pasta tubes are perfect for carrying the creamy chunks of sausage. If you cannot find fennel sausage, use fresh Italian pork sausage and add $1/4$ teaspoon fennel seeds.

SERVES 4 TO 6

$1/2$ cup grated Pecorino Romano (2 ounces)
$1/4$ cup grated Parmigiano-Reggiano (1 ounce)
$1/2$ pound Italian fresh sweet fennel sausage
1 tablespoon olive oil
$1/2$ cup Cognac or brandy
$1/2$ cup white wine
1 tablespoon plus $1/4$ teaspoon kosher salt
3 cups heavy cream
$1/4$ teaspoon freshly ground white pepper
$1/4$ teaspoon dried red pepper flakes
1 pound bombolotti pasta (mezza-rigatoni shape)
$1/3$ cup firmly packed basil leaves, cut lengthwise into thin ribbons
2 tablespoons finely chopped parsley

The creamy sauce, dotted with rich fennel sausage and hot peppers, is well matched with a slightly tannic, spicy wine like Zinfandel, Nebbiolo d'Alba, or Montepulciano d'Abruzzo.

1. Combine the Pecorino and the Parmigiano cheeses in a bowl.

2. Cut open the fennel sausage and remove the meat from the casing. Discard the casing and coarsely chop the meat.

3.   In a sauté pan, heat the olive oil over a moderate flame and add the sausage pieces. Sauté the sausage, stirring frequently, until just cooked through, 2 to 3 minutes. Remove the cooked sausage from the pan and set aside. Drain and discard the fat.

4.   Holding the pan away from the flame, pour in the brandy and wine. Return to the heat to cook the alcohol. If the brandy flames, simply allow it to burn away. Reduce over high heat to one third the original volume. As the brandy and wine reduce, scrape up any cooked bits of sausage stuck to the bottom of the pan to incorporate into the liquid.

5.   Add the cream to the pan along with a third of the cheese mixture, white pepper, pepper flakes, and fennel seeds if you are using them. Cook the sauce, stirring occasionally, until it coats the back of a spoon. Add $1/4$ teaspoon salt and the reserved fennel sausage and set the sauce aside while the pasta cooks.

6.   In a large pot, bring 1 gallon of water to a rolling boil and add 1 tablespoon salt.

7.   Cook the bombolotti just until al dente and drain in a colander. Sprinkle the steaming pasta with half the remaining cheese mixture so the cheese melts directly onto it. Transfer the sauce to the empty pasta pot and bring to a boil. Add the cooked pasta and basil and combine thoroughly. Serve in warm bowls, sprinkled with the parsley and remaining cheese.

LINGUINE WITH SPINACH, GARLIC, AND OLIVE OIL

*T*his is inspired by the classic Roman *aglio e olio*. We've simply added fresh chopped spinach to the recipe, making it even more colorful and nutritious. While the recipe calls for linguine, it would be equally good with spaghetti or spaghettini. Freshly grated Pecorino Romano brings out the best in this dish.

SERVES 4 TO 6

BREAD CRUMB TOPPING

4 tablespoons homemade bread crumbs
   (grated day-old dry bread)
1 1/2 teaspoons finely grated Pecorino Romano
2 tablespoons chopped parsley
1 teaspoon olive oil
1/8 teaspoon kosher salt
Freshly ground black pepper

PASTA

1 tablespoon kosher salt
2/3 cup extra-virgin olive oil
6 garlic cloves, peeled and cut into thin slivers
1 teaspoon dried red pepper flakes
1 pound spinach, stemmed, thoroughly cleaned, and
   coarsely chopped
3/4 pound linguine
1 cup reserved pasta cooking water
1/4 cup finely grated Pecorino Romano

1.   Combine topping ingredients in a small bowl and reserve.

2.   In a large pasta pot, bring 4 quarts of water to a boil and add 1 tablespoon salt. Preheat the broiler.

A crisp white wine with mineral flavors will complement the spinach. We'd suggest Vernaccia di San Gimignano, Vouvray sec, or Bordeaux blanc.

3.   In a large skillet, heat the olive oil and garlic over a low flame. Cook the garlic slivers until they turn a light golden brown. This should be a slow process in which the oil becomes infused with the garlic's fragrance. When the slivers are golden, remove them with a slotted spoon and discard. (Some cooks claim the garlic should be left in the dish. We disagree.)

4.   Add the red pepper flakes to the oil and cook approximately 30 seconds to impart their warmth to the oil. Toss the spinach in the oil and cook until limp, turning often with tongs or a kitchen fork. Remove the pan from the heat and reserve until pasta is done.

5.   Plunge the pasta into the boiling water and cook until al dente. Just before draining the pasta, ladle 1 cup of its cooking water into the spinach and oil and place the pan over moderate heat. Drain the linguine and sprinkle the cheese directly onto the steaming pasta. Add the linguine to the pan with the spinach and oil and toss well. Transfer the pasta to an ovenproof serving platter and sprinkle with the bread crumb mix. Broil until the crumbs are golden brown and serve immediately.

Malloreddus alla Campidanese

*D*on't be put off by the tongue-twister name of this Sardinian classic. In Sardinian dialect, *malloreddus* is a ridged, narrow pasta shell, often flavored with saffron. In case you can't find authentic malloreddus, substitute cavatelli. When Michael learned this recipe in the Sardinian town of Pula, he observed a technique applicable to other recipes that call for small, toothsome pasta shapes. The pasta is drained before it is even al dente, and the cooking is completed in the sauce itself, adding starchy richness in the process. Since this is an involved recipe, we've given amounts to make twice as much sauce as you will need for six appetizer servings. Freeze half to enjoy sometime when you don't feel like spending hours in the kitchen.

SERVES 6, ENOUGH SAUCE FOR 12

3 pounds canned plum tomatoes, drained (5 cups)

2 tablespoons plus 2 teaspoons olive oil

$1/2$ cup peeled and diced onion

$1/2$ cup peeled and diced carrot

$1/2$ cup diced celery

2 tablespoons minced garlic

Pinch of saffron

$1/4$ cup chopped fresh basil

2 tablespoons chopped parsley

2 tablespoons plus $1^1/4$ teaspoons kosher salt

$1/4$ teaspoon freshly ground black pepper

$1/4$ cup white wine

2 large tomatoes (1 pound), peeled, seeded, and diced

1 pound fresh Italian fennel sausage, or sweet pork
    sausage and $1/4$ teaspoon fennel seeds

2 ounces coppa (Italian salami from pork shoulder),
    diced ($1/2$ cup)

pinch of dried red pepper flakes

Flavored with saffron, fennel, and herbs, this sauce calls for an exotically perfumed wine. Try a Rhone-style white, a Provençal rosé, the Sardinian white, Vermentino di Gallura, or red, Cannonau.

1/2 cup Oven-Dried Tomatoes, halves cut into quarters
   (page 318), or oil-packed sun-dried tomatoes
1 cup finely grated Pecorino Romano
1 pound malloreddus or cavatelli pasta

1.   Purée the drained plum tomatoes through a food mill to remove their seeds and skins. There should be 4 cups of tomato purée. Set aside.

2.   Heat 2 tablespoons of the olive oil in a 3-quart saucepan over medium heat. Add the onion, carrots, celery, and garlic; cook for 10 minutes, stirring occasionally to soften.

3.   Add the saffron, basil, and parsley to the vegetables and season with salt and pepper. Cook an additional 2 minutes. Add the white wine and reduce by half over a high flame. Add the puréed tomatoes and diced fresh tomatoes, lower the flame, and simmer for 30 minutes.

4.   While the sauce is simmering, remove the sausage meat from its casing. Break the meat apart and sauté in a skillet with 2 teaspoons olive oil until the sausage has lost its red color, but is still moist and somewhat underdone. Drain well.

5.   Stir in the sausage, coppa, pepper flakes, oven-dried tomatoes, and $2/3$ cup of the cheese. Simmer for another 30 minutes. Stir frequently to prevent the cheese from sticking to the pan. Season with additional salt and pepper. Remove from the stove and reserve half the sauce for future use. The sauce may be prepared ahead to this point.

6.   Bring 4 quarts water to a boil and add 2 tablespoons salt. Cook the pasta to just before it reaches al dente and drain. Combine with half the sauce and over medium heat continue cooking the pasta until al dente. Transfer to a warm platter, sprinkle with the remaining Pecorino Romano, and serve.

ORECCHIETTE WITH BROCCOLI RABE AND TOMATOES

*T*his dish originates in Puglia, the heel of Italy's boot, and the birthplace of Michael's paternal grandparents. He remembers his grandmother painstakingly shaping each orecchietta, piece by piece, early Sunday mornings. The toothsome pasta holds its own with the heady flavor of the broccoli rabe.

Be sure to choose broccoli rabe that has a vibrant green color, absolutely no yellowing in the florets, and tender, not woody stalks.

SERVES 4 TO 6

1 1/2 pounds broccoli rabe, cleaned and stems removed
2 medium tomatoes (1 pound)
1/4 cup olive oil
1 teaspoon minced garlic
1/8 teaspoon red pepper flakes
1 tablespoon plus 1/2 teaspoon kosher salt
1/8 teaspoon freshly ground black pepper
3 cups Basic Tomato Sauce (page 317)
1/2 cup water
1/2 pound orecchiette
1/2 cup finely grated Pecorino Romano (2 ounces)

Try Vernaccia di San Gimignano or one of the new breed of sprightly white table wines from Italy's southernmost regions, including Sicily, Puglia, and Campania.

1. Separate the leaves and florets from the tough bottom stems of the broccoli rabe and discard the stems. Cut the florets from the leaves and tear the largest leaves into 2- to 3-inch pieces. Set aside.

2. Cut the tomatoes in half and squeeze out the seeds. Chop the tomatoes into 3/4-inch pieces. Set aside.

3. Combine the olive oil, garlic, and red pepper flakes in a 3-quart saucepan or a skillet large enough to hold all the broccoli rabe. Cook over moderately high heat for 45 seconds to flavor the oil, but do not allow the garlic to brown. Add the broccoli rabe. Cook 2 to 3 minutes to wilt, turning constantly with tongs or a kitchen fork. Season with $1/2$ teaspoon salt and the black pepper. Add the chopped tomatoes, tomato sauce, and water; return to a simmer. Cook an additional 3 to 5 minutes to a brothy consistency. Set aside.

4. Bring 1 gallon of water to a boil in a large pot. Add 1 tablespoon salt and cook the pasta until al dente. While the pasta is cooking, return the broccoli rabe and tomato sauce to a simmer. Drain the pasta, and while still in the colander, sprinkle with half the cheese. Toss the pasta with the broccoli rabe. Combine well and serve sprinkled with the remaining cheese.

BUCATINI ALL'AMATRICIANA

A staple on the menu of most Roman *trattorias,* this dish origi-
nated in the small town of Amatrice, just 90 miles outside the Eternal
City. The classic pasta choice is bucatini—a thick, hollow spaghetti
whose toothsomeness holds up to the bacony sauce. If you can't find
bucatini, look for perciatelli. Each of these takes a longer time to
cook than most other pastas, so be sure to check the package for
cooking times. When fresh red chili peppers are not available, you
can use jalapeño instead.

SERVES 4

> 3 pounds fresh or canned tomatoes, coarsely chopped
> 1 tablespoon olive oil
> 1 pound pancetta, cut into pieces $1/4$ inch thick by
>   1 inch long
> 1 cup diced onion
> 1 cup white wine
> $2^1/2$ tablespoons minced fresh red chili pepper, seeds
>   removed (3 medium)
> 1 teaspoon dried red pepper flakes
> $1/2$ cup sliced fresh basil leaves
> $1^1/2$ cups finely grated Pecorino Romano
> 1 tablespoon plus 1 teaspoon kosher salt
> Freshly ground black pepper
> $3/4$ pound bucatini or perciatelli

Romans are
perfectly satisfied
to quaff a refreshing
carafe of Frascati
with their bucatini.
Additionally, we'd
recommend Soave
Classico or Vernaccia
di San Gimignano.

1.   In a 3-quart nonreactive saucepan, heat the tomatoes over
medium heat until juicy, about 5 minutes. Pass the tomatoes through
a food mill to remove their seeds and skins. You will have about 5
cups of tomato purée. Reserve.

2.   Wipe the saucepan clean and return to medium heat. Add the
olive oil and the pancetta, stirring until the pancetta is crisp, about 15
minutes. Remove the pancetta with a slotted spoon and reserve.

3. Pour off all but about 2 tablespoons of fat from the pan. Add the onions and cook over medium heat until golden, about 5 minutes. Pour in the white wine and reduce by three-fourths. Add the puréed tomatoes, chili pepper, and red pepper flakes. Simmer gently for 30 minutes, stirring occasionally with a wooden spoon.

4. Add the reserved pancetta, basil, and all but $1/4$ cup of the Pecorino Romano. Season with 1 teaspoon salt and pepper. Simmer for an additional 15 minutes, stirring occasionally to prevent the cheese from sticking to the bottom of the pan. (May be prepared ahead up to this point and frozen for future use.)

5. Bring 1 gallon of water to a boil and add 1 tablespoon of salt. Cook the bucatini until al dente. Toss with the sauce, transfer to a warmed bowl, and serve, sprinkled with the remaining cheese.

NOTE: In Rome, Amatriciana sauce is typically made with *guanciale*, or pork cheeks cured like prosciutto. We have found pancetta to be the best substitute, since *guanciale* may be difficult to find in the United States.

PENNE WITH ASPARAGUS AND RED PEPPERS

Stir-frying asparagus in butter gives them a nutty taste. In this recipe, partially cooked penne is finished right in the chicken stock, enriching the sauce with its starch.

SERVES 4 TO 6

4 tablespoons butter
1 pound medium asparagus, peeled, tough ends
  snapped, and stalks cut into 2-inch pieces
2 yellow bell peppers, charred, peeled, and diced
2 red bell peppers, charred, peeled, and diced
1 teaspoon minced garlic
1 1/2 cups Chicken Stock (page 312)
1 tablespoon plus 1 teaspoon kosher salt
3/4 pound penne
1 1/2 tablespoons minced fresh thyme
2/3 cup finely grated Parmigiano-Reggiano
1/8 teaspoon freshly ground black pepper

To suit the sweet peppers and asparagus, try a lightly chilled fruity red wine such as a California Grenache or Piedmont's Dolcetto or Barbera d'Alba.

1.   In a 10-inch skillet over medium heat, melt 2 tablespoons of the butter. Add the asparagus and cook, stirring, until tender and lightly browned, 5 to 7 minutes. Stir in the peppers and garlic and toss to heat through, 1 minute. Add the chicken stock, bring to a boil, and set aside.

2.   Bring 1 gallon of water to a boil and add 1 tablespoon kosher salt. Add the pasta, cook to just before it reaches al dente, and drain.

3.   Return the skillet to medium heat and add the penne and fresh thyme. Stir to combine the ingredients and simmer 5 to 7 minutes, or until the pasta is al dente. Stir in half the Parmigiano and the remaining butter, salt, and pepper. Transfer to a warm bowl, sprinkle with the remaining cheese, and serve.

PENNE WITH GORGONZOLA, BEETS, AND TOASTED WALNUTS

*T*he flavors and textures in this dish are a wonderful combination. The inspiration for this pasta was a colorful salad we used to serve that featured romaine, Gorgonzola, walnuts, and beets. If it tasted that good as a salad, why not try it cooked on pasta? Quill-shaped penne is a good choice for this dish as its holes lap up the delicious Gorgonzola cream sauce. Follow this rich appetizer with a simple, nonsauced main course such as Grilled Veal Lombatina or Seared Rib Steak.

SERVES 4

2 medium beets (1 pound), scrubbed
2 teaspoons olive oil
1 tablespoon minced garlic
1 1/2 cups sliced red onion
1 cup white wine
2 cups heavy cream
1/4 pound Gorgonzola, crumbled
1 tablespoon plus 1/2 teaspoon kosher salt
Freshly ground white pepper
3/4 pound penne
3/4 cup toasted walnuts
2 tablespoons finely grated Pecorino Romano
2 tablespoons chopped parsley

1. Trim the tops and root ends of the beets (save the green leaves if they are fresh—they're delicious cooked like spinach). Cook the beets, unpeeled, in lightly salted water until they are easily pierced by a paring knife, about 45 minutes. Cool, peel away the loosened skin, and cut into strips as long as the penne and 1/4 inch thick. Reserve.

The sweet-salty flavors in the cream sauce work well with fruity red wines bolstered by a good dose of tannin. Look for a youthful bottle of Valpolicella Classico, Barbera d'Alba, or Salice Salentino.

2.   Heat the olive oil over medium heat in a saucepan or skillet large enough to hold all the cooked pasta. Cook the garlic and onions to soften but not color, 5 to 7 minutes. Pour the wine into the pan and raise the heat. Reduce the wine until syrupy.

3.   Stir in the heavy cream, lower to a simmer, and reduce the sauce until it very lightly coats the back of a spoon. Strain over a bowl, pressing the onions and garlic with a ladle. Return the strained sauce to the saucepan and bring back to a simmer. Reduce the heat and slowly whisk in the Gorgonzola until it is completely melted. Season with $1/2$ teaspoon each salt and pepper and set aside.

4.   Bring 4 quarts of water to a boil and add 1 tablespoon salt. Cook the pasta until al dente and drain. Return the sauce to a simmer over a medium flame and add the pasta, stirring until coated. Toss in the beets and the walnuts, mixing lightly just until the sauce turns pink. Transfer the pasta to a warm bowl, sprinkle with the Pecorino and parsley, and serve.

Penne with Eggplant and Roasted Pepper

*M*ichael's inspiration for this recipe came from a small trattoria in Sicily—a region whose people never seem to tire of cooking with eggplant. Make sure to use good-quality *ricotta salata* sheep's milk cheese—white, firm, and not too dry—available in most Italian specialty stores.

SERVES 4

1 medium eggplant (1 pound), peeled
3 tablespoons olive oil, plus more for baking sheet
Kosher salt
Freshly ground black pepper
2 medium red bell peppers
1 teaspoon minced garlic
4 cups Basic Tomato Sauce (page 317)
$^1/_4$ cup grated Pecorino Romano
$^3/_4$ pound penne
$^1/_2$ cup coarsely grated ricotta salata cheese
1 tablespoon minced parsley

1. Preheat the oven to 400 degrees F. Lightly oil a baking sheet.

2. Cut the eggplant in half lengthwise, then slice each half lengthwise into thirds. Keep the slices together to retain the original shape of the eggplant. (This prevents the eggplant from drying out when cooking.) Slice across the eggplant at $^1/_2$-inch intervals. With a wide spatula, carefully lift the cut eggplant onto the baking sheet. Drizzle the eggplant with 1 tablespoon of olive oil and season with salt and pepper. Cover with foil and roast in the oven for 45 minutes. When done, the eggplant should be very tender and soft to the touch. (Unlike green beans or other vegetables that can be eaten al dente or

There's lots of lusty play here between sweet and salty flavors, and it's hard to go wrong with any refreshingly crisp and fruity Italian white. Since this is a southern Italian dish, why not try a white from Sicily, Puglia, or Campania?

even raw, eggplant is unpleasant and difficult to digest if not well cooked.) Set aside, loosely covered.

3.   Preheat the broiler.

4.   Cook the red peppers under the broiler until their skins blacken. Be sure to turn them every few minutes to color evenly. Alternatively, spear each pepper on a kitchen fork and hold over an open flame until charred. Place the charred peppers in a paper bag or a covered container until they are cool enough to handle. (This step completes the cooking of the peppers and facilitates removing the skin.) Rub away the skins (never run them under water, which washes away the flavorful oils) and discard the seeds. Cut the peppers into $1/2$-inch strips and set aside.

5.   Bring 1 gallon of water to a boil and add 1 tablespoon salt.

6.   In a 3-quart saucepan, heat the remaining 2 tablespoons olive oil over a low flame. Add the garlic and sauté 1 minute without browning. Add the roasted eggplant and peppers and cook for 1 minute. Stir in the tomato sauce and cheese and bring to a simmer.

7.   Cook the pasta until al dente and drain. Toss well with the sauce to combine all the ingredients. Serve in a warm bowl sprinkled with the ricotta salata and parsley.

PORCINI GNOCCHI WITH PROSCIUTTO AND PARMIGIANO CREAM

In Rome, gnocchi are traditionally made on Thursdays, and each trattoria seems to have a devoted following loyal to its family recipe. Gnocchi making is typically left to Mama (while Papa bastes the roast), possibly since light and pillowy gnocchi rely on a very gentle touch—which Papa obviously lacks. Most Roman gnocchi are unadorned potato dumplings sauced with fresh tomatoes, olive oil, and sharp Pecorino Romano. This unusual recipe—flavored with porcini mushrooms—has developed quite a following at Union Square Cafe, where we make gnocchi every day. We've even found a few Papas on our staff who have the gentle touch! Making gnocchi takes time and patience, but be assured it gets easier with practice and the rewards make the effort worth it.

SERVES 4 TO 6

GNOCCHI

2 cups boiling water

1 ounce dried porcini mushrooms (1 cup loosely packed)

2 medium Idaho potatoes (1 1/4 pounds), skin on and scrubbed

1/3 cup finely grated Parmigiano-Reggiano

1 large egg

2 1/2 teaspoons kosher salt

1/2 teaspoon freshly ground black pepper

1 cup all-purpose flour

PARMIGIANO CREAM

3 tablespoons butter

3/4 cup sliced red onion

2 tablespoons minced garlic

An earthy Barbaresco or a Loire Valley cabernet franc—such as Chinon or Saumur-Champigny—will complement the mushroomy richness of the gnocchi.

5 ounces shiitake mushrooms, sliced, stems removed and
    reserved (2 cups)
$^1/_4$ cup parsley stems
1 cup dry white wine
1 cup reserved porcini liquid (from the gnocchi)
2 cups heavy cream
2 ounces prosciutto, cut into thin strips 1 inch long
    ($^1/_4$ cup)
1 cup cleaned, stemmed, and chopped red or green swiss
    chard or spinach
$^1/_4$ cup grated Parmigiano-Reggiano ($^3/_4$ ounce)
1 tablespoon plus $^1/_2$ teaspoon kosher salt
$^1/_8$ teaspoon freshly ground black pepper
2 tablespoons chopped parsley

1. Pour the boiling water over the porcini and soak until fully reconstituted, about 15 minutes. Lift the mushrooms out of the water with a slotted spoon and set aside. Strain the liquid through a coffee filter to remove any grit and dirt. Reserve the liquid to use later in the sauce. Squeeze the mushrooms with your hands until very dry and purée to a completely smooth paste in a food processor.

2. Boil the potatoes in water to cover with 1 teaspoon salt until easily pierced with the point of a knife. When the potatoes are cooked but still warm, peel them and immediately pass through a food mill or ricer onto a large cookie sheet. It is important to move the food mill over the cookie sheet so the potatoes fall evenly in one layer. Above all, do not move the potatoes around; the less they are handled at this point, the better the texture of the finished gnocchi. Refrigerate until cool, about 15 minutes.

3. Transfer the cooled potatoes to a clean work surface, create a mound, and form a well in the center. Add the porcini purée, cheese, egg, $^1/_2$ teaspoon salt, and $^1/_4$ teaspoon pepper to the well. With your fingertips, combine these ingredients with the potato, stirring to form a rough dough. Sprinkle the flour over the potato mix and combine gently. Knead the dough, using a downward press and

(continued)

quarter turn motion with the heel of your hand, until it is smooth, uniformly colored, and elastic. This should take 8 to 10 minutes.

4. Form the dough into a rectangular loaf, 8 × 4 inches, and slice into 8 pieces. Be sure both your work space and your hands are clean of any flour or dough. Begin pressing each piece of dough onto the table while simultaneously rolling it back and forth between your spread-out fingers and palms. This requires a delicate touch and some practice, but is not at all difficult. You will be forming a cylinder about 18 inches long, as thick as your index finger. Move the cylinder away from the work area and dust lightly with flour. Repeat with the remaining pieces.

5. Line up 4 of the 8 cylinders horizontally. With a sharp knife, cut across them to form $1^1/_4$-inch dumplings. Repeat with the remaining 4 cylinders. Form the dumplings into the traditional gnocchi crescent shape: hold a fork backside up in one hand; with the thumb of your other hand, press each dumpling against the back of the fork forming an indentation while simultaneously rolling it down over the tines. This makes a decorative ribbed pattern on one side and a pocket to hold the sauce on the other.

6. Lay the gnocchi in a single layer on a cookie sheet so they don't stick together. Cover and refrigerate until ready to cook.

7. For the sauce, melt half the butter in a 2-quart nonreactive saucepan over medium heat. Add the onions, garlic, mushroom stems, and parsley stems. Cook until wilted but not browned, about 4 minutes. Add the wine and the porcini liquid. Bring to a boil and reduce to a third of its original volume. Add the heavy cream and boil, reducing until it coats the back of a spoon. Strain the sauce and set aside.

8. In a medium sauté pan, heat the remaining butter over medium-high heat until it begins to brown. Add the sliced shiitake mushrooms and sauté for 2 to 3 minutes.

9. Return the cream sauce to a medium flame and stir in the sautéed mushrooms, prosciutto, chopped Swiss chard, and half the cheese. Cook over medium heat for 3 to 4 minutes. Season with $^1/_2$ teaspoon salt and the pepper.

10. Bring 4 quarts of water to a boil and add 1 table-spoon salt. Add all the gnocchi at once. With a slotted spoon, remove each dumpling as it floats to the surface and drain in a colander. Continue until all of the gnocchi have risen to the top. When all the gnocchi are cooked and drained, place them in the cream sauce and warm over medium heat. Spoon into a warm bowl, sprinkle with chopped parsley and the remaining cheese, and serve immediately.

NOTE: If you are not planning to cook the gnocchi the same day you make them, freeze in a single layer, covered, for up to one week.

RISOTTO WITH CHICKEN LIVERS, MOSCATO D'ASTI, AND MUSHROOMS

Chicken livers and sparkling Moscato d'Asti may never become as famous a gastronomic pairing as foie gras and Sauternes, but to our taste and for a lot less money, the combination works extremely well. The success of this risotto recipe does not depend on the wine's bubbles, so feel free to use Moscato from an opened bottle you may have enjoyed for a previous dessert, or find a bottle of any good California or French wine made from the muscat grape.

SERVES 4 TO 6

>   5 to 6 cups Chicken Stock (page 312)
>   1 pound chicken livers, trimmed
>   1 teaspoon kosher salt
> $1/4$ teaspoon freshly ground black pepper
>   3 tablespoons olive oil
>   2 tablespoons minced shallots
>   1 teaspoon minced garlic
> $1/4$ pound shiitake mushrooms, stemmed and sliced
>   (2 cups)
> $1^1/2$ cups peeled and sliced carrots
> $1^3/4$ cups arborio rice
> $1^1/2$ cups Moscato wine
> $3/4$ cup ($2^1/2$ ounces) snow peas, stemmed and cut
>   into thirds
>   2 tablespoons butter
> $1/2$ cup finely grated Parmigiano-Reggiano

Piedmont's lightly sweet and sparkling Moscato d'Asti is an obvious match for this risotto, but Alsatian Gewürztraminer, Tokay Pinot Gris, or Riesling would also be excellent choices.

1.   Bring the chicken stock to a simmer.

2.   Season the chicken livers with $1/2$ teaspoon salt and freshly ground black pepper. In a 3-quart heavy-bottomed skillet, heat the

olive oil over a high flame and sear the livers, browning both sides, 3 to 4 minutes. While they are still rare, remove the livers from the pan with a slotted spoon and reserve.

3. Add the shallots and garlic to the pan and cook over a medium flame for 1 to 2 minutes, stirring to prevent browning. Stir in the shiitakes and carrots and cook 3 minutes. Add the rice and stir with a wooden spoon until coated with the oil.

4. Reserve 2 tablespoons of the Moscato and add the remainder to the pan. Stir constantly over medium heat until the wine has been absorbed by the rice.

5. Ladle $1/2$ cup of hot chicken stock into the pan and stir until it is absorbed. Continue with the rest of the stock, adding $1/2$ cup at a time and letting each addition be absorbed completely by the rice before adding more liquid. The constant stirring allows the rice to release its starch into the cooking liquid, resulting in the characteristic risotto creaminess. The grains of rice should be al dente. Count on 20 to 25 minutes for the rice to cook.

6. When all the stock has been used, stir in the snow peas and chicken livers and heat through. Swirl in the butter, the reserved 2 tablespoons Moscato, half the cheese, and the salt and pepper. Spoon the risotto into a warm serving bowl, sprinkle with the remaining cheese, and serve immediately.

PUMPKIN RISOTTO

*H*ere is a comforting risotto, perfect for a brisk autumn or winter day. While many recipes for pumpkin risotto call for diced pumpkin simmered in chicken broth, we use a sweet-spiced pumpkin broth to capture the elusive and delicate pumpkin flavor.

SERVES 6

PUMPKIN BROTH

1 tablespoon butter

1 medium onion, peeled and thinly sliced

2 carrots, peeled and thinly sliced

1 celery rib with leaves, washed and sliced

*1 leek, washed and thinly sliced, white and light green
  parts only*

2 cups canned pumpkin purée

8 cups Chicken Stock (page 312)

1 bay leaf

1/2 teaspoon whole black peppercorns

4 allspice berries

1/4 teaspoon freshly grated nutmeg

1/4 cinnamon stick

2 tablespoons pure maple syrup

RISOTTO

1/4 cup olive oil

1 3/4 cups arborio rice

*1 1/2 cups diced (1/2 inch) fresh pumpkin, butternut, or
  other firm-fleshed squash*

1/2 cup dry white wine

6 to 7 cups pumpkin broth

1 tablespoon minced fresh sage

2 cups arugula, washed and chopped

1/3 cup diced fresh mozzarella

Try to find an intensely fruity Chardonnay, Pinot Blanc, or Chenin Blanc for this richly flavored risotto.

1 teaspoon kosher salt
¹/₄ teaspoon freshly grated black pepper
¹/₄ cup freshly grated Parmigiano-Reggiano (³/₄ ounce)
3 tablespoons butter

1. In a large saucepan or stockpot, melt the butter over medium heat. Add the onion, carrots, celery, and leek; sauté until tender and moist, about 10 minutes. Stir in the pumpkin purée and continue cooking for 2 to 3 minutes. Add the chicken stock, bay leaf, spices, and maple syrup. Reduce the heat and simmer, covered, for 45 minutes. Pour the broth through a fine-mesh strainer. To avoid ending up with a thick purée rather than a broth, take care not to mash the vegetables through the strainer.

2. In the same saucepan, heat the pumpkin broth to a simmer.

3. Heat the olive oil over medium heat in a separate, 3-quart heavy saucepan or skillet. Toss in the rice and diced pumpkin and stir with a wooden spoon until the rice is coated with the oil. Add the white wine and stir constantly until all the wine has been absorbed by the rice. Ladle ¹/₂ cup of hot pumpkin broth into the pan and stir until it is absorbed. Continue with the rest of the broth, adding ¹/₂ cup at a time and letting each addition be absorbed completely by the rice before adding more liquid. The constant stirring allows the rice to release its starch into the cooking liquid, resulting in the characteristic risotto creaminess. The grains of rice should be al dente. Count on 20 to 25 minutes for the rice to cook.

4. Finish by stirring in the sage, arugula, mozzarella, salt, pepper, and half the cheese. Swirl in the butter. Spoon into warm bowls, sprinkle with the remaining cheese, and serve immediately.

RISOTTO D'ORO

*T*his golden-colored risotto looks convincingly like *risotto alla milanese*—the saffron-infused Lombardy classic. But appearance is where the similarity ends. Substituting fresh carrot and celery juices for the standard chicken stock adds a gentle sweetness to this summery, all-vegetable risotto. A vegetable juicer makes this recipe convenient to prepare, but fresh vegetable juices are widely available in health food stores.

SERVES 4 TO 6

3 cups carrot juice
3 cups celery juice
1/4 cup olive oil
1 3/4 cups arborio rice
1/2 teaspoon minced garlic
1/2 cup white wine
1/2 cup sliced carrots, split lengthwise
1/2 cup green beans, in 1-inch pieces
1/2 cup sliced zucchini, split lengthwise
1/2 cup of asparagus, tough ends discarded,
     in 1/2-inch pieces
1/2 cup sliced red bell pepper
1/2 cup fresh shelled peas
1/3 cup sliced scallions
4 tablespoons butter
3/4 cup finely grated Parmigiano-Reggiano
1 teaspoon kosher salt
1/8 teaspoon freshly ground black pepper
1 tablespoon chopped parsley

Choose a white wine with lots of fruit to stand up to the sweetness of the carrot and celery juices. Ripe Chardonnays from Australia and California will do the trick.

1. In a saucepan, combine the carrot and celery juices and bring to a simmer.

2. In a 3-quart skillet, heat the olive oil over medium heat. Add the rice and garlic and stir together until the rice is coated with the oil. Add the white wine and bring to a boil, stirring constantly until the wine is absorbed by the rice. Add the carrots and green beans to the rice.

3. Ladle $1/2$ cup of the hot juice mixture into the saucepan and stir until it is absorbed. Continue with the rest of the juice, adding $1/2$ cup at a time and letting each addition be absorbed completely into the rice before adding more liquid. The constant stirring allows the rice to release its starch into the cooking liquid, resulting in the characteristic risotto creaminess. When three-quarters of the juice has been used, after 15 to 20 minutes, stir in the remaining vegetables. Continue ladling and stirring in the remaining juice, about 10 additional minutes. The grains of rice should be al dente.

4. Swirl in the butter and $1/2$ cup of the cheese and season with the salt and pepper. Serve the risotto sprinkled with parsley and the remaining cheese.

SHRIMP RISOTTO WITH CUCUMBER AND JALAPEÑO

*L*ike Risotto d'Oro, this dish relies on vegetable juice instead of stock. The cucumber flavor is a sweet complement to the shrimp and softens the punch of the spicy jalapeño.

SERVES 4 TO 6

6 cups cucumber juice, or 8 cucumbers, peeled,
    blended, and strained to yield 6 cups juice
2 tablespoons olive oil
3/4 pound medium shrimp, cleaned and split lengthwise
1/4 cup minced seeded jalapeño
1 teaspoon kosher salt
1/8 teaspoon freshly ground black pepper
1 tablespoon minced shallots
1 3/4 cups arborio rice
1 cup white wine
2 tablespoons butter
3/4 cup chopped cilantro
Juice of 1 lime

Ripe, herbaceous Sauvignon Blanc or Sémillon from Australia, New Zealand, or California works well with this risotto.

1. In a small saucepan, bring the cucumber juice to a simmer, remove from the heat, and reserve.

2. In a 3-quart saucepan or skillet, heat 1 tablespoon of the olive oil. Add the shrimp and jalapeño, season with half the salt and pepper and sauté 2 minutes over high heat. Remove from the pan and reserve.

3. Return the pan to a medium flame, add the remaining tablespoon of oil, and cook the shallots, scraping up any cooked bits from the bottom of the pan. Toss in the rice and stir with a wooden spoon

until the rice is coated with oil. Add the white wine and stir constantly over medium heat until all the wine has been absorbed by the rice. Ladle $1/2$ cup of the warm cucumber juice into the pan and stir until it is absorbed. Continue with the rest of the juice, adding $1/2$ cup at a time and letting each addition be absorbed completely by the rice before adding more liquid. The constant stirring allows the rice to release its starch into the cooking liquid, resulting in the character- istic risotto creaminess. The grains of rice should be al dente. Count about 20 to 25 minutes for the rice to cook.

4. Add the shrimp and jalapeño and swirl in the butter. Season with the remaining salt and pepper. Finish by stirring in the chopped cilantro and lime juice. Serve immediately.

NOTE: Named for the Lombardian valley town where it is grown, arborio has become a generic catch-all name for the short-grained rices of Italy. Two other varieties worth seeking out are Vialone nano and Carnaroli, either of which provide the essential starchiness for making creamy risotto, provided you don't rinse the rice before cooking. Unfortunately, brown rice, basmati, and other domestic long-grain rices are not suitable for risotto.

RISOTTO WITH SNAILS, PANCETTA, AND RED WINE

*T*his savory risotto is inspired by the countryside cooking of Italy's Lombardy region, where both rice and snails abound. It offers a delicious way to enjoy snails as something other than a vehicle for garlic butter.

SERVES 4 TO 6

SNAILS

1 4¹/₂-ounce can snails, drained and rinsed (1 cup)
1 celery rib, quartered lengthwise
1 medium onion, peeled and quartered
1 carrot, peeled and quartered
1 sprig of fresh thyme
Reserved parsley stems (see below)
6 whole black peppercorns
1 bay leaf
6 cups Chicken Stock (page 312)
¹/₂ teaspoon kosher salt

RISOTTO

3 ounces lean pancetta, cut into 1 × ¹/₂-inch pieces (¹/₂ cup)
2 tablespoons olive oil
2 leeks, white and light green parts only, split lengthwise, sliced into ¹/₄-inch pieces, and thoroughly washed (1 cup)
2 teaspoons minced garlic
1³/₄ cups arborio rice
1 cup red wine
2 tablespoons butter
¹/₄ cup grated Parmigiano-Reggiano (³/₄ ounce)

Try the Lombardian Franciacorta Rossa or a Rhone red like Gigondas or Côte-Rôtie to complement the bacony flavor of the risotto.

¹/₂ teaspoon kosher salt
¹/₄ teaspoon freshly ground black pepper
2 tablespoons chopped parsley (reserve the stems)

1.   In a 2-quart saucepan, combine the snails with the remaining ingredients. Bring to a boil, reduce the heat, and simmer, covered, for 1 hour. The snails should be very tender.

2.   Strain, return the liquid to the saucepan, and set aside; you should have 6 cups broth. Discard the vegetables and reserve the snails until ready to use in the risotto. (This can be done up to 2 days ahead. In that case, store the snails in their strained cooking liquid, covered and refrigerated, until ready to use.)

3.   Bring the snail broth to a simmer. In a heavy 3-quart saucepan cook the pancetta over low heat until very crisp and brown. Remove the pancetta and all but 1 tablespoon of fat from the pan. Combine the olive oil with the reserved fat, add the leeks and minced garlic, and sauté 1 minute over a low flame until softened but not brown. Pour the rice into the pan and stir with a wooden spoon until rice is well coated with the oil.

4.   Raise the flame to medium, add the red wine, and stir constantly until all the wine has been absorbed. Ladle ¹/₂ cup of hot snail broth into the pan and stir until it has been absorbed. Adjust the heat so the mixture barely simmers. Continue with the rest of the broth, adding ¹/₂ cup at a time and letting each addition be absorbed completely before adding more liquid. The constant stirring allows the rice to release its starch into the cooking liquid, resulting in the characteristic risotto creaminess. Along with the final ladle of broth, add the snails and pancetta and allow them to heat thoroughly. Count on 20 to 25 minutes for the rice to be al dente.

5.   Swirl in the butter, half the cheese, and salt and pepper. Spoon onto a warm platter, sprinkle with the remaining cheese and the chopped parsley, and serve immediately.

Cracked Wheat "Panzanella"

Sourdough Panzanella

Endive, Radicchio, and Arugula Salad with Oregano Vinaigrette

Crunchy Fava Bean Salad with Frisée, Peppers, and Pecorino

Red Oakleaf and Bibb Salad with Gruyère, Garlic Croutons,
   and Dijon Vinaigrette

Summer Tomato and Goat Cheese Salad

Haricots Verts, Mâche, Beet, and Goat Cheese Salad

Frisée Salad with Shrimp, Fennel, and Clementines

$\mathcal{U}$nion Square Cafe has always featured a varied lineup of appetizer-size salads, often using specialty lettuces, baby greens, vegetables, cheeses, homemade croutons, and flavored vinaigrettes. Salads provide a wonderful opportunity to enjoy a variety of textures, flavors, and colors, depending on the lettuces, oil, and vinegar you choose. Since the ingredients are most often eaten raw, their freshness and the way they've been handled is paramount. Greens are at their flavorful best when just plucked from the garden, with vibrant colors, firm leaves, a sweet fragrance, and the bright look of being alive. Look for as many of these just-picked qualities as you can when selecting greens at your grocer or farmer's market. If you're fortunate enough to have a source for organic or pesticide-free greens, make them your first choice.

Dressing salads provides the opportunity to bring out your best extra-virgin olive oil and wine vinegar. Their complex aromas and fruity flavors will be enjoyed unmasked and won't be broken down by cooking. With leafy salads, a good way to start is to actually "dress" your empty

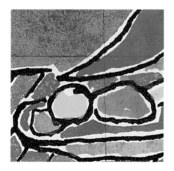

salad bowl with the prepared dressing and only then add the lettuces. With your hands, gently toss the salad, picking up a little of the dressing from the bottom with each turn. You will be entirely in control of how much actually coats the lettuces. This is the best way to toss a salad gently enough to avoid bruising the lettuces while still coating them evenly.

CRACKED WHEAT "PANZANELLA"

*T*his is a zesty Middle Eastern variation on Tuscany's bread and tomato salad—we add mint and substitute cracked wheat for leftover bread. The panzanella makes a wonderful appetizer salad served over a bed of such spicy greens as arugula, mizuna, or baby mustard greens. It's also a nice room-temperature accompaniment for Grilled Veal Lombatina or Stuffed Chicken Breasts with Herbed Goat Cheese. We serve the salad on the day it's made, but next-day leftovers are also delicious, with a softer texture and more intense flavors.

SERVES 4

1 cup medium-grain bulgur wheat
2 cups water
$^1/_8$ teaspoon each cayenne, ground cumin,
*   and ground cinnamon*
Pinch of ground cloves
$1^1/_4$ teaspoons kosher salt
1 roasted red pepper, peeled and diced
1 roasted yellow pepper, peeled and diced
2 medium tomatoes, cored and diced
$^1/_2$ cup peeled and thinly sliced celery
$^1/_2$ cup thinly sliced red onion
$^1/_4$ cup pitted niçoise olives, roughly chopped
2 tablespoons sliced basil leaves
2 tablespoons coarsely chopped parsley
3 tablespoons coarsely chopped mint
2 tablespoons toasted pine nuts
2 tablespoons balsamic vinegar
2 tablespoons Italian red wine vinegar
$^1/_2$ cup extra-virgin olive oil
$^1/_4$ teaspoon freshly ground black pepper

Serve with a fruity Italian white like Vernaccia di San Gimignano, Pigato di Albenga, or Ribolla Gialla.

1. Pour the cracked wheat into a large mixing bowl. Bring the water to a boil with the cayenne, cumin, cinnamon, cloves, and $\frac{1}{4}$ teaspoon salt. Pour the boiling water over the wheat and let stand until plumped and tender, 30 to 40 minutes.

2. In another large bowl, combine the roasted peppers, tomatoes, celery, onion, olives, basil, parsley, mint, and pine nuts. Toss with the vinegars and olive oil and season with the remaining salt and pepper.

3. Drain the wheat of any excess liquid in a fine-mesh strainer. Transfer to the bowl with the seasoned vegetables and stir to combine. Adjust the seasoning to your taste and serve.

SOURDOUGH PANZANELLA

*T*here are probably as many different versions for this bread salad as there are households in central Italy. Originally a peasant recipe designed to use up leftover bread, panzanella has moved into the sophisticated culinary mainstream. It's not uncommon to come across salads with anchovies, capers, or small chunks of mozzarella cheese; once you get our recipe down, you can experiment endlessly with this thrifty delight. We also serve it with our roast chicken, and it becomes a replacement for the "stuffing" Americans love with their roast fowl. Panzanella is also great as a first course salad or as a refreshing light lunch.

SERVES 8

1 pound 2-day-old sourdough or
*   whole wheat peasant bread*
2 red bell peppers
Ice water (see note)
4 ripe tomatoes, split crosswise, squeezed to remove
*   seeds and juice, and diced*
1 cup peeled and thinly sliced celery
1 cup peeled, halved, and thinly sliced red onion
1/3 cup coarsely chopped pitted gaeta or niçoise olives
1/3 cup washed, dried, and sliced basil leaves
1/4 cup toasted pine nuts
3/4 cup extra-virgin olive oil
1/4 cup balsamic vinegar
1 tablespoon kosher salt
1/4 teaspoon freshly ground black pepper

Crisp whites wines from Italy's Friuli-Venezia-Giulia region—such as Tocai Friulano, Sauvignon Blanc, and Ribolla Gialla—go beautifully with panzanella.

1.   Cut the stale bread into $^3/_4$-inch slices. If the bread is not completely hard, leave it out longer or place in a 200-degree oven until you have the desired texture.

2.   Preheat the broiler. Roast the peppers under the broiler, turning them from side to side, until their skins blacken. Place the charred peppers in a covered container or paper bag until cool. Remove the skins by rubbing the peppers with a paper towel or by peeling them with a small knife. Discard the seeds. (To avoid losing flavor, never peel roast peppers under running water.) Cut the flesh into $^3/_4$-inch dice and set aside.

3.   Soak the bread in ice water to cover for 5 minutes, or just until soft. Drain the water and, with your hands, squeeze out all the excess water from the bread. Over a large bowl, rub the bread between the palms of your hands until it crumbles into small pieces.

4.   Combine the bread with the peppers, tomatoes, celery, onion, olives, basil, and pine nuts. Season with the olive oil, balsamic vinegar, salt, and pepper and continue to mix well. Serve.

NOTE: When soaking the stale bread, make certain to use ice water. If the water is anything but ice cold, the stale bread will turn into an unappealing mush instead of a tender crumb that holds its own with the other ingredients.

ENDIVE, RADICCHIO, AND ARUGULA SALAD WITH OREGANO VINAIGRETTE

*T*his is our version of *insalata tricolore*—a salad that has become quite popular in one form or another at New York's Italian restaurants. We have chosen the sweet flavors of fresh oregano, garlic, and fruity olive oil as a balancing contrast to the trio of bitter greens used in the salad.

SERVES 4

VINAIGRETTE

1/2 teaspoon salt

1/4 teaspoon freshly ground black pepper

1 tablespoon chopped fresh oregano leaves

1 teaspoon minced garlic

2 tablespoons Italian red wine vinegar (see note)

5 tablespoons extra-virgin olive oil

SALAD

1 hard-boiled egg, sieved

1 tablespoon minced parsley

2 endives, any discolored outer leaves removed

1/4 pound arugula, stemmed, washed, and dried

1 small head of radicchio (1/4 pound), washed, dried, and cut or torn into 2-inch pieces

Kosher salt

Freshly ground black pepper

This salad is complemented by a crisp Sauvignon Blanc from California, Italy, or the Loire Valley.

1. Combine the vinaigrette ingredients in a jar. Close the lid tightly and shake vigorously. Let the vinaigrette sit for 15 minutes to develop the flavors. Taste again before serving for any adjustments to the seasoning. This dressing can be made several hours in advance.

2. Combine the sieved hard-boiled egg with the chopped parsley. This mixture is called "mimosa" and makes a lovely garnish when sprinkled over salads and chilled vegetables.

3. Cut the bottoms of the endives and peel off at least 12 of the long outer leaves to garnish the plates. Cut the rest of the endive across the length of the spear into ½-inch pieces. Pour all but 2 tablespoons of the vinaigrette into a bowl. Add the cut endive, arugula, and radicchio; toss lightly to coat evenly. Taste the salad and add more salt and pepper if necessary.

4. Toss the endive spears with the remaining vinaigrette. Place three spears in a spoke pattern around each plate. Place equal amounts of the dressed arugula, radicchio, and endive in the center of each plate, forming light, full bunches. Sprinkle an equal amount of the mimosa over each salad and serve.

NOTE: The distinctive flavor and high acidity level of Italian red wine vinegar—approximately 7.5 percent compared to the 5 percent or 6 percent of other vinegars—lend an assertive edge, essential to the taste of this vinaigrette.

CRUNCHY FAVA BEAN SALAD WITH FRISÉE, PEPPERS, AND PECORINO

*F*resh fava beans, when they make their all-too-brief appearance in the spring, are a special treat, well worth the trouble of shelling and peeling. Look for firm, full beans that have a bright green color. In Italy, young fava beans are enjoyed raw and unpeeled, simply accompanied with a glass of the local red wine. Favas also have an affinity for the sharp bite of aged sheep's milk cheese. Try garnishing this salad with paper-thin slices of the same cheese you used for grating.

SERVES 4

> 3 to 4 pounds fresh fava beans
> 1/2 cup extra-virgin olive oil
> 1 1/4 cups sliced celery
> 1 1/2 cups leek rounds, white and light green
>   parts only, washed
> 1 yellow pepper, sliced into 1/4-inch-wide strips
> 1 teaspoon kosher salt
> Freshly ground black pepper
> 1/4 cup lemon juice
> 2 teaspoons lemon zest
> 1 teaspoon minced garlic
> 4 cups frisée, washed and dried
> 1/4 cup finely grated Pecorino Romano

Vino Nobile di Montepulciano, Barbera d'Alba, and Chianti Classico match well with the sharp cheese and meaty beans.

1.   Remove the fava beans from their pods. Bring a medium pot of lightly salted water to a boil and add the beans. Cook for 3 to 4 minutes, until tender but not mushy. Refresh the beans in ice water. Drain and peel the beans. You will have about 2 cups of peeled fava beans.

2.   Heat 2 tablespoons of the olive oil in a medium skillet. Over high heat, cook the celery and leeks for 3 to 4 minutes, stirring occasion-

ally. The vegetables should retain some crispness. Add the yellow pepper and cook 1 to 2 minutes more. Add the fava beans and season with half the salt and fresh black pepper to taste. Remove from the heat and set aside to cool.

3. To make the vinaigrette, place the lemon juice, zest, remaining salt, fresh black pepper, garlic, and remaining olive oil in a jar. Close the lid tightly and shake vigorously to combine.

4. To assemble the salad, pour the vinaigrette into a large bowl. Add the cooked vegetables, frisée, and Pecorino and toss lightly to coat evenly. Adjust the seasonings if necessary, and serve.

Red Oakleaf and Bibb Salad with Gruyère, Garlic Croutons, and Dijon Vinaigrette

*N*amed for the picturesque Swiss district in which it is made, authentic, aged Gruyère is as versatile as it is delicious—great for eating, grating, or melting. This is a simple bistro salad, made with tender lettuces and enhanced by the nutty richness of grated Gruyère and a mustardy vinaigrette.

SERVES 4

VINAIGRETTE

1/8 teaspoon kosher salt

Freshly ground black pepper

2 teaspoons water

1 teaspoon minced shallots

4 teaspoons Dijon mustard

1 tablespoon French red wine vinegar

1/2 cup grapeseed oil or vegetable oil

SALAD

1 cup 1/2-inch bread cubes

1 garlic clove, unpeeled and smashed

*2 heads Bibb lettuce, washed, dried, and gently torn
    into 2-inch pieces (about 3 cups)*

*5 ounces red oakleaf lettuce, stems cut away, washed
    and dried*

1/2 cup shredded Gruyère cheese (2 ounces)

Kosher salt

Freshly ground black pepper

Light reds like Beaujolais, Pinot Noir, and Grenache go beautifully with this salad.

1. Preheat the oven to 350 degrees F for the croutons.

2. Combine the vinaigrette ingredients in a jar, close tightly with a lid, and shake vigorously until the mixture develops a creamy consistency.

3. Spread the bread cubes on a cookie sheet and bake in the oven until lightly toasted, about 5 minutes. When done, flavor the hot croutons by tossing in a bowl with the smashed garlic clove.

4. To assemble the salad, pour the vinaigrette into a large bowl. Add the lettuces, half the shredded Gruyère, and the croutons. Season with salt and pepper if necessary. Mix thoroughly. Garnish with the remaining Gruyère and serve.

SUMMER TOMATO AND GOAT CHEESE SALAD

This is a delightfully simple summer salad that takes advantage of ripe tomatoes and soft goat cheese. The addition of yellow tomatoes, if available, makes this a particularly colorful presentation, but the salad tastes just as good if you use red tomatoes exclusively. Soaking the paper-thin raw onion slices in water will rid them of their excess pungency and crisp them nicely for the salad.
(SERVES 4 TO 6)

2 large red tomatoes
2 large yellow tomatoes
Kosher salt
Freshly ground black pepper
1 cup thinly sliced red onions, soaked in ice water for
   20 minutes
$1/4$ cup thinly sliced basil leaves
5 ounces fresh soft goat cheese, crumbled
4 teaspoons Italian red wine vinegar
$1/4$ cup extra-virgin olive oil

Sancerre, California Sauvignon Blanc, and crisp Italian whites are perfect with this tangy salad.

1. Core and slice the tomatoes $1/4$-inch thick.

2. Arrange the tomatoes on a large platter in concentric circles, overlapping alternating red and yellow slices. Season with salt and pepper to taste.

3. Drain the onions well and lay them over the tomatoes. Sprinkle evenly with basil and crumbled goat cheese. Season the goat cheese with salt and pepper to taste. Drizzle the vinegar and the olive oil over the salad. Serve.

HARICOTS VERTS, MÂCHE, BEET, AND GOAT CHEESE SALAD

*T*his colorful French-inspired salad makes a wonderful lunch entrée or a light starter. If you are unable to find mâche (also known as lamb's lettuce), you can substitute another soft, green lettuce, such as Bibb, Boston, or oakleaf.

SERVES 4, OR 2 AS A MAIN COURSE

VINAIGRETTE

1 teaspoon Dijon mustard
$1/4$ teaspoon salt
Freshly ground black pepper
2 tablespoons French red wine vinegar
1 teaspoon raspberry vinegar
6 tablespoons walnut oil

SALAD

2 medium beets ($1/2$ pound), unpeeled,
* roots trimmed to $1/2$ inch*
1 teaspoon kosher salt
$1/2$ pound haricots verts, cleaned
1 ounce mâche, trimmed and washed
$1^1/2$ teaspoons minced shallots
Freshly ground black pepper
$1/4$ cup crumbled fresh, mild goat cheese
$1/4$ cup walnut pieces, toasted

Sancerre, Vouvray, and Beaujolais are natural matches for this bistro-style salad.

1. Combine the vinaigrette ingredients in a jar. Close the lid tightly and shake vigorously. Reserve.

2.   In a small saucepan, cover the beets with water, add $\frac{1}{4}$ teaspoon salt, and simmer until a knife pierces the beets easily, about 30 minutes. When the beets are cool enough to handle, trim the ends and gently rub off their skins with a paper towel. Rubbing off the skin, instead of peeling it with a knife, allows the beets to keep their natural shape, so you'll end up with attractive, round slices. Cut into $\frac{1}{4}$-inch slices and set aside.

3.   Bring $1\frac{1}{2}$ quarts water to a boil and add the remaining salt. Cook the haricots verts until they are crisp but not too resistant to the tooth. Drain the cooked beans and refresh by plunging them immediately into ice water. This will stop the cooking and preserve their bright green color. Drain and set aside.

4.   To assemble the salad, arrange the beet slices around the inside of a platter. Lightly drizzle the beets with a third of the vinaigrette. Pour the remaining vinaigrette into a bowl and lightly toss the cooked haricots verts, mâche, and shallots to coat evenly. Season with additional salt and pepper, if desired.

5.   Place the salad atop the beets in the center of the platter. Sprinkle with the crumbled goat cheese and toasted walnuts and serve.

FRISÉE SALAD WITH SHRIMP, FENNEL, AND CLEMENTINES

*T*his colorful winter salad combines enough bright flavors and textures to wake you from the cold-weather blues. We find the combination of clementines, fennel, and sherry wine vinegar irresistible! Follow it with something hearty like Braised Oxtails, Rustic Duck Stew, or Braised Lamb Shanks.

SERVES 10

1/3 cup plus 2 tablespoons sherry wine vinegar
1/2 teaspoon kosher salt
1/4 teaspoon freshly ground black pepper
1 cup plus 3 tablespoons olive oil
4 shallots, peeled and minced
1 pound shrimp, shelled, deveined, and split
   lengthwise
2 fennel bulbs, trimmed
Juice of 1 lemon
2 heads frisée or curly endive, washed
5 clementines (or mandarin oranges or tangerines),
   peeled and sectioned, with pith and pits removed

A good quality dry sherry works beautifully with the salad, as do Pouilly-Fumé and young Chablis.

1. In a glass jar, combine 1/3 cup of vinegar with half the salt and pepper. Add 1 cup of olive oil and the shallots. Cover tightly and shake vigorously until the dressing thickens. Set aside.

2. Season the shrimp with the remaining salt and pepper. In a large skillet, heat the 3 tablespoons olive oil over medium-high heat until very hot. Add the shrimp and sauté, stirring constantly, until cooked through, 2 to 3 minutes.

3. Transfer the shrimp to a bowl and toss with half the dressing.

4.   Over medium heat, deglaze the pan with the 2 tablespoons vinegar, scraping any solids from the bottom of the pan. Pour over the shrimp, cover the bowl, and set aside to marinate.

5.   Halve the fennel bulbs and cut into $1/4$-inch slices. Toss with the lemon juice in a large salad bowl. Combine the fennel, frisée, clementine sections, and remaining dressing and toss in the shrimp with its dressing. Serve immediately.

Black Bean Soup with Lemon and Sherry

Carrot–Red Lentil Soup with Asian Spices

Sweet Corn and Potato Vichyssoise

Mushroom Soup with Barley and Wild Rice

Creamless Mushroom Soup

Ratatouille Soup

Ribollita

White Bean and Broccoli Soup with Parmigiano
    and Prosciutto

$\mathcal{W}$e take our soups seriously and we take pride in doing them well. One thing our guests have counted on through the years is that no matter what time of day it is, we've always offered a selection of soups in the dining room or at the bar. Union Square Cafe's Black Bean Soup with Lemon and Sherry—our most popular soup—has garnered such a devoted following that we've never had the courage to remove it from the menu. However, we do simmer a different "chef's soup" every day, using seasonal ingredients.

Most soups continue to improve for a day or two after their initial cooking, and there's no reason you can't double our recipes and suc-

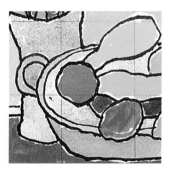

cessfully freeze the leftovers. Make sure to have good bread on hand when you serve soup. The only thing worse than using your fingers to wipe up the last drops of a great soup is leaving the drops in the bowl.

BLACK BEAN SOUP WITH LEMON AND SHERRY

*T*his smooth-textured black bean soup has been hugely popular since the day we opened. The smokiness of the bacon and the gentle infusion of dried thyme over the long cooking period are what make the soup so tasty. Cooking the soup in the oven gives it a wonderfully mellow, baked flavor that stove-top cooking doesn't achieve.

SERVES 4 TO 6

1 pound black beans (approximately 2 1/2 cups),
*   picked over*
1 cup peeled and sliced carrots
1 cup peeled and sliced onions
1 cup chopped celery
3 garlic cloves
2 teaspoons dried thyme
4 ounces slab bacon, cut crosswise into 1-inch pieces
1 teaspoon kosher salt
1/2 teaspoon freshly ground black pepper
4 to 6 slices of lemon
2 tablespoons minced parsley
1 1/2 ounces good quality dry sherry (optional)

Drink Sherry with the soup, or if you want an additional wine, try a young, light- bodied Rioja.

1.   Soak the beans overnight, or for at least 6 hours, in cold water.

2.   Preheat the oven to 300 degrees F.

3.   Rinse the beans well and place them in a pot with water to cover. Bring to a boil, then drain the beans, discarding the water. (This rids the beans of their bluish tint and bitterness.)

4. Place the beans in a 4-quart ovenproof pot with the carrots, onion, celery, garlic, thyme, and bacon. Cover with 2 quarts of water and add the salt and pepper. Bring to a boil, cover tightly, and place in the oven to cook for 4 hours.

5. Purée the contents of the pot in a food processor or blender. Depending on the size of your blender, you may need to do this in more than one batch. Adjust the seasoning to your taste. You can serve the soup as it is or pass it through a strainer if you prefer an even smoother texture.

6. To serve, dip one side of each lemon slice in minced parsley and float, parsley side up, on each portion of soup. Add a $^{1}/_{4}$-ounce shot of dry sherry to each bowl just before serving, if desired.

CARROT–RED LENTIL SOUP WITH ASIAN SPICES

*H*ere's a brightly colored and lively flavored soup that satisfies year-round. For the most vibrant flavor, use whole spices freshly ground in a spice mill.

SERVES 6

2 tablespoons butter
1 1/2 tablespoons grated fresh ginger
1/4 teaspoon cayenne
1/4 teaspoon allspice
1/4 teaspoon cumin
1/2 teaspoon curry
1/2 teaspoon ground coriander seeds
3/4 cup sliced onions
3/4 cup peeled and sliced parsnips
4 cups scrubbed and sliced carrots
1/2 cup sliced celery
1 1/2 teaspoons kosher salt
1/4 teaspoon freshly ground black pepper
1/4 cup red lentils
1/4 cup basmati rice
7 cups Vegetable Stock (page 316) or water
3/4 cup coconut milk
2 tablespoons lime juice

This soup is a natural with Alsatian whites like Gewürztraminer, Riesling, and Sylvaner.

1. In a 3-quart saucepan, melt the butter over a low flame. Stir in the ginger and spices and cook for 1 minute. Add the onions, parsnips, carrots, and celery. Season to taste with salt and pepper. Raise the flame to medium and cook for 10 to 12 minutes. Soften but do not brown the vegetables.

2. Stir in the lentils and basmati rice, mixing until well combined with the vegetables. Add the stock (or water) and bring to a boil. Lower the heat, cover the pot, and simmer for 30 minutes, until the vegetables and rice are tender. Purée the soup in a blender until smooth.

3. Return the soup to the saucepan, bring back to a boil, and stir in the coconut milk and lime juice. Cook for 1 more minute and serve.

SWEET CORN AND POTATO VICHYSSOISE

A refreshing variation on the classic vichyssoise, this soup combines the flavors of sweet summer corn and spicy cumin with the traditional chilled leek and potato soup.

SERVES 4

5 ears of corn
6 1/2 cups water
1 1/4 teaspoons kosher salt
1/8 teaspoon freshly ground white pepper
1 tablespoon butter
3/4 teaspoon ground cumin
1/4 teaspoon cayenne
1 1/2 cups sliced leeks, washed, white and light green
    parts only
1 1/2 cups sliced onions
1 1/2 cups diced potatoes
3/4 cup sliced celery
1 1/4 cups buttermilk, chilled
1 1/2 tablespoons minced chives

Try Macon-Villages, Viognier, or a dry Riesling with the soup.

1. Cut the corn kernels from the cobs and reserve. Chop the cobs into 1-inch pieces. Place the cob pieces in a 2-quart saucepan with the water and half the salt and pepper. Bring to a boil, lower to a simmer, and cook, covered, for 30 minutes. Strain and reserve the corn broth. Discard the cobs.

2. Melt the butter in the saucepan over medium heat. Add the cumin and cayenne and allow to sizzle for 1 minute, stirring. Stir in the corn kernels, leeks, onions, potatoes, and celery. Season with the remaining salt and pepper and cook until the vegetables are wilted, about 7 minutes.

3. Add the corn broth and simmer until the vegetables are tender, about 30 minutes.

4. While the soup is still hot, pour into a blender and purée until very smooth. It may be necessary to do this in more than one batch. Strain the soup through a fine strainer and chill in a bowl over ice.

5. When chilled, stir in the buttermilk and adjust the seasoning to taste. Serve in chilled soup bowls, sprinkled with chives.

NOTE: Use the remaining buttermilk to make your favorite buttermilk biscuit recipe. They'll be delicious with the Sweet Corn and Potato Vichyssoise!

MUSHROOM SOUP WITH BARLEY AND WILD RICE

*R*oot vegetables and Madeira give this mushroom and grain soup a sweet, woodsy flavor that makes it perfect for a brisk fall or winter afternoon. For a hearty dinner, follow the soup with Braised Oxtails with Red Wine and Onions, Orange-Fennel Osso Buco, or Roast Stuffed Leg of Lamb.

SERVES 4 TO 6

2 tablespoons butter
$^3/_4$ cup finely diced onions
$^3/_4$ cup sliced leeks, washed
$^3/_4$ cup scrubbed and sliced carrots
$^3/_4$ cup peeled and diced parsnips
1 teaspoon minced garlic
1 pound cleaned and sliced mushrooms
$1^1/_2$ teaspoons kosher salt
$^1/_4$ teaspoon freshly ground black pepper
2 teaspoons finely chopped fresh sage leaves
$^1/_4$ cup dry Madeira
$^1/_3$ cup wild rice
$^1/_4$ cup pearl barley
5 cups Vegetable Stock (page 316) or water
1 scallion, thinly sliced

Floral whites like Côtes-du-Rhône Blanc, Sauvignon Blanc, and Liguria's Pigato pair nicely with this soup.

1.   Melt the butter over medium heat in a 3-quart saucepan. Sauté the onions, leeks, carrots, parsnips, and garlic until softened, about 5 minutes. Add the mushrooms, salt, pepper, and sage. Cook until the mushrooms have softened.

2.   Add the Madeira and reduce by half over high heat. Stir in the rice, barley, and vegetable stock. Bring to a boil, reduce the heat, and simmer, covered, for 50 minutes, or until the rice is tender. Serve garnished with sliced raw scallions.

NOTE: To store the soup for serving the next day, strain the broth from the solids and refrigerate separately. Otherwise, all the liquid will be absorbed into the grains. When ready to serve, combine the broth and mushroom-grain base, heat, and serve.

CREAMLESS MUSHROOM SOUP

*O*ur guests love this full-flavored but surprisingly light mushroom soup. It gets its richness by slowly stewing and then puréeing the mushrooms and vegetables—rather than adding cream.
SERVES 6

2 tablespoons butter
1 cup peeled and sliced carrots
1 cup sliced onions
1 cup sliced leeks, washed, white and
*   light green parts only*
1/2 cup sliced celery
1 teaspoon fresh thyme leaves
2 pounds cleaned and sliced white mushrooms
6 cups Chicken Stock (page 312)
1 1/2 teaspoons kosher salt, or to taste
1/8 teaspoon freshly ground black pepper
4 teaspoons minced chives
3 tablespoons extra-virgin olive oil (optional)

Loire Valley Chenin Blancs like Vouvray and Savennieres taste wonderful with this soup.

1.   Melt the butter over medium heat in a large soup pot. Add the carrots, onions, leeks, and celery and cook until tender but not browned, about 10 minutes.

2.   Stir in the thyme and mushrooms and cook for 5 minutes, until the mushrooms have softened. Add the chicken stock, salt, and pepper and simmer, covered, for 30 minutes.

3.   Purée the soup in a food processor or blender in as many batches as necessary. Adjust seasoning to taste. Serve in warm bowls with a sprinkling of chives and a drizzle of extra-virgin olive oil, if desired.

RATATOUILLE SOUP

*T*he gutsy Provençal flavors of ratatouille lend themselves perfectly to soup. This version is equally delicious served either hot or
chilled. Ratatouille soup can be enjoyed year-round, but is at its best
when made with the sweet and juicy vine-ripened tomatoes of late
summer.

SERVES 4 TO 6

2 pounds ripe tomatoes
2 tablespoons olive oil
1/3 cup peeled and chopped onion
1 teaspoon minced garlic
3/4 cup chopped zucchini
3/4 cup peeled and chopped eggplant
3/4 cup chopped red bell pepper
2 tablespoons rinsed and sliced fresh basil leaves,
    plus 4 to 6 sprigs for garnish
1 teaspoon fresh thyme leaves, minced
2 cups Vegetable or Chicken Stock (pages 316 or 312)
Pinch of cayenne
1 teaspoon kosher salt
1/8 teaspoon freshly ground black pepper

Floral whites
like Côtes-du-Rhône
Blanc, Sauvignon
Blanc, and Liguria's
Pigato pair nicely
with this soup.

1. To peel the tomatoes, bring 2 quarts of water to a boil in a large
pot. Cut the core from the tomatoes with a paring knife and plunge
them into the boiling water for 30 seconds. Remove with a slotted
spoon and immediately immerse in ice water until cool. Use a knife
to gently peel the skin, which should be discarded.

2. Cut the tomatoes in half crosswise and squeeze them gently over
a mesh strainer to separate the seeds from the juice. Reserve the
juice.

3. Gently flatten the tomato halves on a cutting board and coarsely chop into 1-inch pieces. Place the chopped tomatoes and the reserved juice in a bowl and set aside.

4. Heat the olive oil over medium heat in a 3-quart saucepan. Add the onion and garlic and cook for 1 minute. Stir in the zucchini, eggplant, and red pepper, sautéing until softened but not browned, about 5 minutes.

5. Add the tomatoes and their juice, the basil, thyme, broth, cayenne, salt, and pepper. Bring to a boil, lower the heat to a simmer, cover, and cook until soft, about 15 minutes.

6. Carefully pour the hot soup into a blender or food processor and purée until smooth. Serve hot or chilled with a sprig of fresh basil as a garnish.

RIBOLLITA

*R*ibollita is a wonderful bread and vegetable soup proudly served by almost every cook in Tuscany. Italian for "reboiled," ribollita will change dramatically when you reheat it the next day— and that's exactly how the Tuscans love it. The first day's helping will be chunky and soupy, and the next day's reboiled serving should be thick and puddinglike, as the bread absorbs the broth. No matter which way you prefer your ribollita—soupy or thick—finish it with a drizzle of top quality extra-virgin olive oil and a sprinkling of Pecorino Romano.

SERVES 6 TO 8

1 cup dried cannellini or Great Northern beans
2 teaspoons kosher salt
4 tablespoons olive oil
2 cups diced zucchini (1 medium)
1¹/2 cups diced onions
²/3 cup diced celery
¹/2 cup scrubbed and diced carrots
¹/4 pound pancetta, diced (1 cup)
2 tablespoons minced garlic
¹/2 head savoy cabbage, washed and cut into 1-inch
    pieces
2 tomatoes, peeled, seeded, and chopped
¹/2 cup chopped basil
2 cups cleaned spinach leaves
¹/4 teaspoon freshly ground black pepper
4 cups cubed day-old sourdough bread
¹/2 cup grated Pecorino Romano
4 tablespoons extra-virgin olive oil

In addition to Chianti Classico Riserva, lesser-known Tuscan reds like Morellino di Scansano and Vino Nobile di Montepulciano are soulmates with ribollita.

1.   Rinse and cover the beans with cold water and soak overnight.

2.   Drain the beans and place them in a saucepan with 8 cups cold water. Cook, covered, for 1 hour. Add 1 teaspoon of the salt and continue cooking for an additional 30 minutes, or until the beans are tender. Set the beans aside with their liquid.

3.   Over a medium flame, heat the olive oil in a large soup pot. Over medium heat, sauté the zucchini, onions, celery, carrots, pancetta, and garlic until softened, about 10 minutes. Add the cabbage, tomatoes, basil, and spinach. Season with the remaining 1 teaspoon salt and pepper. Continue to cook, stirring occasionally, for another 10 minutes.

4.   Strain the beans, reserving their cooking liquid. Purée half the beans in a food processor. Add the puréed beans, the whole beans, and their cooking liquid (8 cups) to the soup pot and simmer over low heat for 20 minutes. If you don't have enough cooking liquid, add water to make up the difference.

5.   Add the diced sourdough bread to the soup and cook for 10 more minutes. Adjust the seasoning. Serve with the Pecorino Romano and a drizzle of extra-virgin olive oil.

White Bean and Broccoli Soup with Parmigiano and Prosciutto

*T*his hearty white bean soup is enlivened with broccoli, Parmigiano, and bits of prosciutto. The last-minute addition of balsamic vinegar adds a sweetly acidic balance to the richness of the soup. Cut the broccoli florets small enough to fit on your soup spoon. Don't discard the stalks—they make delicious "broccoli chips" when peeled, thinly sliced, and deep-fried at a low temperature (320 degrees) in vegetable or olive oil. You can prepare the soup a day ahead through step 4 of the recipe. Allow the beans and broth to cool, then cover and refrigerate.

SERVES 4

3/4 cup dried cannellini or Great Northern beans

1 teaspoon coriander seeds

1/4 teaspoon black peppercorns

1 fresh thyme sprig

4 parsley sprigs

1 bay leaf

1 tablespoon butter

3/4 cup sliced onions

3/4 cup sliced celery

3/4 cup sliced leeks, white and light green parts only, washed

1 teaspoon minced garlic

1 teaspoon kosher salt

2 ounces prosciutto, finely diced (1/2 cup)

4 cups broccoli florets (1/2 pound)

2 teaspoon balsamic vinegar

Freshly ground black pepper

1/4 cup shredded or coarsely grated Parmigiano-Reggiano

We recommend a fruity Italian red like Dolcetto d'Alba, Sangiovese, or Chianti Classico.

1. Soak the beans in water overnight or for at least 6 hours.

2. Make an herb bundle: In a small piece of clean cheesecloth, place the coriander seeds, peppercorns, thyme, parsley, and bay leaf. Close the bundle by tying with a piece of kitchen twine.

3. Melt the butter over a medium flame in a 3-quart saucepan; add the onions, celery, leeks, and garlic. Cook for 10 minutes, until the vegetables are softened but not browned. Add the herb bundle, beans, and 8 cups water.

4. Bring to a boil, lower the heat, and gently simmer, covered, for 1½ hours. Season with the salt and cook for an additional 30 minutes, or until the beans are tender.

5. Discard the herb bundle, add the prosciutto and the broccoli, and simmer 3 to 5 minutes, until cooked. Just before serving, stir in the balsamic vinegar and season with freshly ground black pepper to your taste. Pour the soup into warm bowls and garnish with the grated Parmigiano.

SANDWICHES, EGGS & LUNCH SALADS

B.L.T. Sandwich

Chicken Salad "Deluxe"

Crabmeat Frittata with Tomatoes and Herbs

Artichoke and Potato Frittata

Sweet Onion Frittata with Balsamic Vinegar

Sardinian Lobster Salad

Yellowfin Tuna Burgers with Ginger-Mustard Glaze

Tuna Club Sandwich

Uove al Forno (Baked Eggs)

*A*nyone who has ever eaten lunch at Union Square Cafe has surely felt the positive, electric energy generated daily between noon and 3:30, as editors, publishers, agents, advertising executives, and media types of all sorts gather to negotiate, close deals, sip wine, and network. The restaurant resembles a bustling clubhouse at lunchtime, as the same folks congregate several times per week, each "regular" claiming a favorite among our three dining rooms, and some even insisting on a single preferred table for every visit. Knowing what a herculean task it is to eat a big midday meal several times a week, we design our lunch menu with plenty of lighter dining options, which make sense for you at home as well.

Though some first-time guests seem surprised when they spot a hamburger, B.L.T., chicken salad, or frittata among Union Square Cafe's

noontime offerings, the goal of our lunch menu is to provide both sophisticated and casual choices for dining—at equal levels of excellence.

B.L.T. Sandwich

*L*ong a Union Square Cafe signature, this B.L.T. demonstrates how a simple sandwich can rise to new heights by using excellent ingredients. It's best enjoyed at the peak of late-summer tomato season. Present the B.L.T. open-faced, served with potato salad or Hot Garlic Potato Chips.

SERVES 4

> 12 thick slices of slab bacon
> 8 ¹/₄-inch slices of sourdough bread
> ¹/₃ cup mayonnaise
> 3 cups arugula, cleaned (1 4-ounce bunch)
> 2 to 3 ripe tomatoes, cut into 12 ¹/₄-inch slices
> Kosher salt
> Freshly ground black pepper

1. Preheat the oven to 375 degrees F.

2. Lay the bacon slices on a rack placed over a roasting pan and roast in the oven until crisp, 20 to 25 minutes.

3. Toast the sourdough bread.

4. Spread one side of each piece of toast with mayonnaise. Distribute the arugula evenly over each piece of toast. Lay 3 slices of tomato on each of 4 pieces of toast and season with salt and pepper. Arrange 3 pieces of bacon over each of the other 4 pieces of toast. Transfer to individual plates and serve.

Sauvignon Blanc and Riesling are excellent white wine accompaniments for the B.L.T. If you're in the mood for red, pair the sandwich with the bacony Syrah flavors of northern Rhone Valley reds like St. Joseph or Crozes-Hermitage.

CHICKEN SALAD "DELUXE"

*T*his chicken salad, stocked with crispy vegetables, has become a popular lunch dish at the restaurant. While we roast chickens daily for the salad, your results will be equally successful if you use next-day leftover chicken or turkey. If you can't find pancetta (unsmoked, cured pork belly), lightly smoked bacon is a suitable substitute.

SERVES 4

1/4 pound pancetta, sliced into paper
thin rounds (1 cup)
1 3 1/2-pound chicken, roasted
1 cup scrubbed and grated carrots
1 cup sliced celery
3/4 cup string beans, blanched, refreshed,
and cut into 1-inch pieces
1/2 cup grated radish
2 tablespoons seeded and minced jalapeño
1/2 cup mayonnaise
1 tablespoon fresh lemon juice
1/8 teaspoon cayenne
1 teaspoon kosher salt
Freshly ground black pepper
2 cups arugula, cleaned
2 medium tomatoes, cored and sliced 1/2-inch thick

Pouilly-Fumé, Chenin Blanc, and Alsace whites are refreshing accompaniments for the salad's smoky bacon flavor and piquant spices.

1. Preheat the oven to 375 degrees F.

2. Lay the pancetta slices on a baking sheet and bake until crisp, 20 minutes. Transfer to paper towels and set aside.

3. Separate the breast and legs from the chicken carcass. Remove the skin and discard. Remove the meat from the bones and dice into 1-inch cubes. The carcass and bones may be frozen and saved to make soup or stock.

4. In a large bowl, combine the diced chicken with the carrots, celery, cooked green beans, radish, jalapeño, mayonnaise, lemon juice, cayenne, salt, and pepper. Mix thoroughly.

5. Arrange a bed of arugula to cover a serving platter. Transfer the chicken salad to the center of the platter. Lay the tomato slices around the chicken salad and top with the crisped slices of pancetta.

NOTE: Before mincing jalapeños or other hot peppers, make sure to clear the seeds away from your cutting board. It's all too easy to lose control of your knife blade if it catches on a seed, causing it to swerve dangerously. Also, wash your hands thoroughly after handling hot peppers to avoid rubbing the burning-hot oils onto your face.

CRABMEAT FRITTATA WITH TOMATOES AND HERBS

*H*ere's a delightful open-faced omelet—perfect for brunch—that uses fresh crabmeat as its star ingredient. Serve with Red Oakleaf and Bibb Salad and toasted slices of sourdough, either buttered or drizzled with olive oil.

SERVES 4 TO 6

> 10 eggs
> 1 teaspoon kosher salt
> Freshly ground black pepper
> 2 teaspoons minced garlic
> 3 tablespoons minced shallots
> 1 tablespoon olive oil
> 2 tomatoes, peeled, seeded, and diced (1^1/$_2$ cups)
> ^{1}/$_3$ cup thinly sliced basil
> 2 teaspoons fresh thyme leaves
> ^{1}/$_2$ pound fresh lump or flake crabmeat, picked
>   over to remove cartilage

Serve with Sancerre, Rhone Valley whites, or Cassis rosé. Alternatively, a spicy Bloody Mary might hit the spot.

1.   In a bowl, whisk the eggs until frothy and season with half the salt and pepper.

2.   In a nonstick 10-inch skillet, cook the garlic and shallots in the olive oil for 1 minute over moderate heat. Add the tomatoes, basil, and thyme, raise the heat, and continue cooking until most of the water from the tomatoes has evaporated. Stir in the crabmeat, season with the remaining salt and pepper, and cook 1 minute to heat through.

3.   Stir the eggs into the skillet. Over high heat, continue stirring with a wooden spoon while simultaneously shaking the pan back and forth over the flame. The eggs will begin to form small curds. Continue stirring and shaking until the eggs are set but still somewhat soft on top.

4.   Loosen the frittata from the skillet with a rubber spatula and slide it onto a large dinner plate. Cover the frittata with another dinner plate and invert the plates. Slide the frittata back into the skillet and continue cooking over high heat to brown the other side, about 2 minutes. The cooked frittata should be golden brown on both sides. Carefully transfer the frittata to a large dinner plate, cut into wedges, and serve hot or at room temperature.

ARTICHOKE AND POTATO FRITTATA

*W*e prepare this open-faced omelet for lunch, but at home it would be perfect for a small brunch party. Serve with herbed focaccia and your favorite tossed salad on the side. As an alternative, you can let the frittata come to room temperature, then slice it into small wedges and serve as an hors d'oeuvre.

SERVES 4 TO 6

10 eggs
1/2 teaspoon kosher salt
1/8 teaspoon freshly ground black pepper
2 tablespoons grated Parmigiano-Reggiano
2 tablespoons olive oil
1 medium Idaho potato (1/2 pound), peeled, cut into 3/4-
 inch pieces, and boiled until just tender
1 medium tomato, peeled, seeded, and diced
2 teaspoons minced garlic
1/2 batch Braised Baby Artichokes, drained (page 220)
1/2 cup tightly packed chopped basil

Choose a wine with good fruit and acidity for the artichoke frittata. German Riesling, Viognier, and Rhone Valley rosés are good matches.

1.   In a large bowl, beat the eggs until the yolks and whites are thoroughly combined and frothy. Season with the salt, pepper, and Parmigiano. Set aside.

2.   In a 10-inch nonstick skillet, heat the olive oil over high heat and toss in the potatoes and the diced tomato. Cook 1 to 2 minutes to heat through. Add the garlic and cooked artichokes and heat through. Add the basil and stir to combine thoroughly.

3.   Stir the eggs into the skillet. Continue stirring with a wooden spoon over high heat while simultaneously shaking the pan back and forth over the flame. The eggs will begin to form small curds. Continue stirring and shaking until the eggs are set but still somewhat soft on top.

4. Loosen the frittata from the skillet with a rubber spatula and slide it onto a large dinner plate. Cover the frittata with another dinner plate and invert the plates. Slide the frittata back into the skillet and continue cooking over high heat to brown the other side, about 2 minutes. The cooked frittata should be golden brown on both sides. Carefully transfer the frittata to a large dinner plate, cut into wedges, and serve hot or at room temperature.

Sweet Onion Frittata with Balsamic Vinegar

*T*his oniony sweet frittata was inspired by a unique countryside trattoria Michael and Danny loved in the heart of Emilia-Romagna's balsamic vinegar region. The Osteria di Rubbiara in Nonantola serves a small wedge of the frittata to accompany its famous chicken stewed in Lambrusco wine. Of course the frittata is excellent on its own, drizzled with a few precious drops of aged *balsamico tradizionale,* as they do at the osteria.

SERVES 4 TO 6

3 tablespoons olive oil
8 cups sliced onions
1 teaspoon minced garlic
2 teaspoons minced fresh oregano
1¼ teaspoons kosher salt
⅛ teaspoon freshly ground black pepper
2 tablespoons balsamic vinegar
10 eggs
3 tablespoons finely grated Parmigiano-Reggiano
2 tablespoons minced parsley

Serve with chilled Lambrusco, Beaujolais, or Dolcetto d'Alba.

1. In a 10-inch nonstick skillet, heat 2 tablespoons of the olive oil over medium heat. Add the onions, garlic, oregano, and half the salt and pepper. Cook 25 to 30 minutes, stirring occasionally, until the onions are tender and browned.

2. Add the balsamic vinegar and 2 tablespoons water to the pan and stir well with a wooden spoon to incorporate any browned bits. Continue cooking to reduce the liquid and coat the onions. Remove from the heat. The onions can be prepared up to 1 day ahead to this point and held covered and refrigerated.

3. In a large bowl, beat the eggs until the yolks and whites are thoroughly combined and frothy. Season with the Parmigiano, parsley, and the remaining salt and pepper. Whisk in the cooked onions.

4. Stir the beaten eggs into the skillet with the cooked onions and combine well. (If the onions were prepared in advance, reheat them in the nonstick skillet before whisking in the eggs.) Over high heat, continue stirring with a wooden spoon or rubber spatula while simultaneously shaking the pan back and forth over the flame. The eggs will begin to form small curds. Continue stirring and shaking until the eggs are set but still somewhat soft on top.

5. Loosen the frittata from the skillet with a rubber spatula and slide it onto a large dinner plate. Cover the frittata with another dinner plate and invert the plates. Slide the frittata back into the skillet and continue cooking over high heat to brown the other side, about 2 minutes. The cooked frittata should be golden brown on both sides. Carefully transfer the frittata to a large dinner plate, cut into wedges, and serve hot or at room temperature.

SARDINIAN LOBSTER SALAD

*T*his is our variation of a wonderful recipe we found on the southern coast of Sardinia. The combination of roe, tomalley, tomatoes, and balsamic vinegar gives the sauce a lively flavor reminiscent of the seaside. Serve with a side dish of roasted peppers and a loaf of fresh, crusty bread.

SERVES 4 TO 6

1/2 cup black beans, soaked overnight
3 parsley sprigs
2 fresh thyme sprigs
1 bay leaf
2 cups peeled, seeded, and diced tomatoes (2 large tomatoes)
1 1/2 teaspoons plus a pinch of kosher salt
4 1 1/2-pound female lobsters
1 tablespoon minced garlic
2 tablespoons balsamic vinegar
1/4 cup extra-virgin olive oil
1/8 teaspoon freshly ground black pepper
2 tablespoons seeded, minced jalapeño
1/2 cup thinly sliced celery
4 cups arugula, stemmed, washed, and dried

Try to find a crisp Sardinian white like Vermentino di Gallura, or serve instead with Muscadet, Frascati, or Cassis rosé.

1. Drain the beans, rinse well, and transfer to a saucepan with cold water to cover. Add the parsley, thyme, and bay leaf, bring to a boil, and cook, covered, for 45 minutes. Add a pinch of salt and cook an additional 15 minutes, until tender. Allow the beans to cool in their cooking liquid, then drain the liquid and reserve the beans.

2. While the beans are cooking, put 1 1/2 cups of the diced tomatoes in a colander placed over a bowl; sprinkle with 1/2 teaspoon salt to remove their excess moisture. Allow the juice to drain. Set aside the drained tomatoes; discard the drained juice.

3. Bring a large pot of water to a boil and add the lobsters. Cover the pot immediately and cook the lobsters for 8 minutes. Drain and set aside to cool.

4. When the lobsters are cool enough to handle, remove the claw and tail meat from the shell. Cut the meat into $1/4$-inch slices. Remove the tomalley (green liver) and the red roe from the body and the tail and set aside.

5. To make the sauce, combine the tomalley, coral roe, garlic, balsamic vinegar, and the remaining $1/2$ cup tomatoes in a blender. Purée until smooth and, with the motor running, slowly add $1/4$ cup extra-virgin olive oil. Season with the remaining salt and pepper.

6. Combine the lobster, drained tomatoes, jalapeño, celery, and black beans in a large bowl. Pour in the sauce and mix thoroughly. Season with additional salt and pepper to taste and serve on a platter, layered with a bed of arugula.

YELLOWFIN TUNA BURGERS WITH GINGER-MUSTARD GLAZE

*I*f necessity is the mother of invention, then Union Square Cafe's tuna burger is one of our menu's most successful children. Thanks to the overwhelming popularity of our Fillet Mignon of Tuna—which we butcher only from the front, fat end of the tuna—we've always had an enormous supply of expensive, delicious, but oddly shaped tuna tail meat left over. We needed to figure out a way to sell the back end of the tuna to avoid doubling our menu price for the fillet mignon. For years, we floundered with experimental tuna recipes that tasted better than they looked. We came up with such unmemorable ideas as sashimi niçoise, tuna sloppy joes, and tuna chili. None of them worked. Then one day, our friend Pierre Franey asked if we had ever considered doing tuna burgers. We worked up the following recipe, which has been a signature lunch dish ever since. The tuna burger is so popular that we actually now need to cut into our fillet mignon supply just to have enough tuna to meet the demand.

SERVES 4

GINGER-MUSTARD GLAZE

> *1/3 cup teriyaki sauce*
> *2 teaspoons minced ginger*
> *1/2 teaspoon minced garlic*
> *1 tablespoon honey*
> *1 tablespoon Dijon mustard*
> *1/2 teaspoon white wine vinegar*

TUNA BURGERS

> *1 1/2 pounds yellowfin tuna, free of any skin or gristle*
> *2 teaspoons minced garlic*
> *3 tablespoons Dijon mustard*
> *1/2 teaspoon cayenne*

To complement the sweet-hot tuna burger flavors, choose a fruity white like Vouvray, or California Sauvignon Blanc. It's also great with an ice-cold glass of beer!

1 teaspoon kosher salt
¼ teaspoon freshly ground black pepper
¼ cup olive oil
4 fresh hamburger buns with seeds
¼ cup Japanese pickled ginger, available in Japanese
  specialty food shops (optional)

1. Combine all the ginger-mustard glaze ingredients in a 1-quart saucepan and bring to a boil. Lower the heat and simmer until the glaze coats the back of a spoon, about 5 minutes. Strain through a sieve and reserve in a warm place until tuna burgers are cooked. Can be prepared up to 2 days ahead and stored, covered, in the refrigerator.

2. Grind the tuna in a meat grinder or chop with a large sharp knife to the texture of hamburger meat. Do not use a food processor, which will shred the tuna rather than chop it.

3. Transfer the ground tuna to a bowl and combine with the garlic, mustard, cayenne, salt, and pepper. Mix thoroughly. Divide the tuna into four equal portions. Using your hands, roll each part into a smooth ball and then flatten into a compact patty.

4. Heat the olive oil in a large skillet over medium-high heat and sear the tuna burgers until browned and medium rare, 3 to 4 minutes a side. Serve each burger on a buttered toasted bun and spread with a tablespoon of warm glaze. Garnish the burgers with equal amounts of pickled ginger slices.

TUNA CLUB SANDWICH

*T*he secret of this Dagwood-size sandwich is that it's stuffed with the best tuna salad you're likely to taste anywhere. Serve a heaping bowl of our Hot Garlic Potato Chips to accompany the sandwiches. Use any leftover lemon-pepper aïoli as a dressing for sliced steak sandwiches, grilled fish, or steamed vegetables.

SERVES 4

LEMON-PEPPER AÏOLI

2 egg yolks

1½ tablespoons lemon juice

2 teaspoons red wine vinegar

1 tablespoon Dijon mustard

½ teaspoon kosher salt

2 teaspoons finely minced garlic

1½ cups olive oil

¾ teaspoon coarsely ground black pepper

TUNA SALAD

1 small onion, coarsely chopped (½ cup)

1 scrubbed carrot, coarsely chopped (⅓ cup)

1 celery rib, sliced (⅓ cup)

1 bay leaf

3 whole black peppercorns

1 pound yellowfin tuna, skinless, cut into 2-inch pieces

2 tablespoons diced red pepper

2 tablespoons diced yellow pepper

¼ cup minced red onion

1 tablespoon julienned basil

1 teaspoon mint

1 teaspoon toasted fennel seeds

¾ teaspoon kosher salt

Freshly ground black pepper to taste

This calls for a racy Sauvignon Blanc or an herbaceous rosé.

Fresh lemon juice to taste
12 slices of sourdough, white, or whole wheat bread
2 ¹/₂ cups arugula, trimmed, washed, and dried
8 ¹/₄-inch-thick slices of slab bacon, cooked until crispy

1.   To make the aïoli, combine the egg yolks, lemon juice, vinegar, mustard, salt, and garlic in a food processor. Start the motor and slowly add the olive oil in a constant stream until all the oil is absorbed and the mixture has the consistency of mayonnaise. Add the pepper and mix for an additional 10 seconds. Transfer the aïoli to a bowl, cover, and reserve in the refrigerator.

2.   Combine 4 cups water, onion, carrot, celery, bay leaf, and peppercorns in a 2-quart saucepan over high heat. Bring to a boil, lower to a simmer, and cook for 15 minutes, covered. Add the tuna pieces and simmer until they are cooked through, approximately 10 minutes.

3.   Remove the tuna from the cooking liquid (the liquid can be strained and saved, refrigerated or frozen, to be used again). While the tuna is still warm, flake it into small pieces with a fork or with your fingers. It is best to flake the tuna while warm because as it cools and firms up, it takes much more effort to break apart, resulting in a less appealing texture. Set aside, loosely covered, to cool.

4.   Mix together the flaked tuna, red and yellow peppers, red onion, herbs, fennel seeds, salt, and ¹/₂ cup of aïoli. Combine well and taste for seasoning, adding salt, pepper, or lemon juice if you like. The tuna salad can be made ahead to this point and stored, covered and refrigerated, until the next day.

5.   Spread a slice of bread first with some of the aïoli, then with a spoonful of the tuna salad. Top with a few leaves of arugula, and one slice of the bacon. Repeat with a second slice of bread. Stack one layer on the other and finish by topping with a third slice of bread. Repeat to make three more club sandwiches. Slice each sandwich into halves or thirds and skewer each piece with a toothpick.

Uove al Forno
(Baked Eggs)

*H*ere's a delicious Italian-inspired version of shirred eggs that's a meal in itself. Coppa is a spicy Italian salami made from whole pork shoulder rather than ground meat. If you are unable to find it, substitute soppressata or Genoa salami. Serve the eggs with slices of herbed focaccia or toasted peasant bread.

SERVES 4

3 tablespoons olive oil
1 teaspoon minced garlic
1/8 teaspoon dried red pepper flakes
8 cups mixed greens, cleaned and cut into 1- to 2-inch
*   pieces (choose from mustard greens, Swiss chard, dan-*
*   delion, spinach)*
1/4 cup water
1/4 pound thinly sliced coppa
1/2 pound fresh mozzarella, thinly sliced
8 large eggs
1/8 teaspoon kosher salt
Freshly ground black pepper

1. Preheat the oven to 450 degrees F.

2. In a skillet large enough to hold all the greens, combine the olive oil, garlic, and red pepper flakes. Cook over moderately high heat for about 45 seconds to flavor the oil, but do not allow the garlic to brown. Add the greens and the water and cook, stirring constantly, until the greens have wilted, 3 to 4 minutes.

3. Transfer the greens to a shallow, 10-inch ovenproof gratin dish or casserole. Arrange the coppa atop the greens in a circle around the

Drink a refreshingly crisp Pinot Bianco, Tocai Friulano, or chilled Lambrusco as a counterpoint to the bitter greens and salty sausage.

outside of the gratin dish, leaving the center open for the eggs. Lay the mozzarella slices on top of the coppa. Carefully crack the eggs onto the greens in the center of the dish. Some of the eggs may overlap the coppa and mozzarella. Sprinkle the eggs with salt and pepper. Bake for 10 to 12 minutes, or until the whites are set and the yolks still slightly runny. Serve immediately in the gratin dish.

"Carpaccio" of Black Sea Bass al Forno

Polenta-Crusted Sea Bass with Corn and Tomatillo Salsa

Cod with Radicchio, White Beans, and Lemon Vinaigrette

Seared Salmon with Sweet Corn, Shiitake Mushrooms,
    and Balsamic Vinegar Butter Sauce

Grilled Trout with Warm Rosemary Vinaigrette

Grilled Swordfish with Tomato and Roast Pepper Compote

Pan-Roasted Salmon with Citrus-Balsamic Vinaigrette

Grilled Marinated Fillet Mignon of Tuna

Red Snapper with Tomato-Onion Compote

Seared Curried Whitefish with Raïta

Salt Cod, Onion, and Squash Gratin

Shrimp with "Gazpacho" Sauce

Seared Sea Scallops with Lemon Vinaigrette, Broccoli Rabe,
    and Roast Tomatoes

Sizzled Soft-Shell Crabs with Spicy Carrot Sauce

Lobster Shepherd's Pie

Lobster–Sweet Corn Chowder

Cacciucco di Pesce

Herb-Roasted Chicken

Mama Romano's Baked Lemon Chicken

Grilled Marinated Chicken Breast with Yogurt and Asian Spices

Stuffed Chicken Breasts with Herbed Goat Cheese

Roast Lemon-Pepper Duck with Red Wine Vinegar Sauce

Rustic Duck Stew with Rigatoni

Seared Filet Mignon with Tomato-Anchovy Sauce

Seared Rib Steak with Rosemary and Arugula

Roast Breast of Veal with Spinach, Mushroom, and Rice Stuffing

Grilled Veal Lombatina

Roast Leg of Veal with Shiitake Mushroom and Goat Cheese Sauce

Orange-Fennel Osso Buco

Braised Oxtails with Red Wine and Onions

Roast Peppered Rack of Venison with Dried Cherry and Pearl Onion Sauce

Grilled Lamb Chops "Scotta Dita"
Braised Lamb Shanks with Garlic and Herbs
Roast Stuffed Leg of Lamb
Vegetable and Goat Cheese Lasagne al Forno
Roman Roast Pork Loin Arista di Maiale
Seared Calf's Liver with Sprouted Mustard Seeds
Seared Sweetbreads with Mushrooms and Frisée

Straightforward, seasonal, amply portioned, and generously flavored, Union Square Cafe's eclectic main course recipes draw their
inspiration primarily from the rustic traditions of Italy, France, America,
and the home cooking we grew up with. Sometimes we're influenced by
the rich culinary traditions of the Orient and Middle East. In this chapter

you'll find mostly fish and poultry recipes, with
a few easy-to-prepare meat dishes.

You can change the flavors of our main
courses in subtle but interesting ways by alternating the vegetable garnishes you choose to
accompany them. Have fun experimenting
with our side-dish and wine suggestions, just as
our guests love to do in the restaurant.

"CARPACCIO" OF BLACK SEA BASS AL FORNO

*T*his is a take-off on the standard carpaccio of thinly sliced raw beef. We've replaced the meat with thin slices of fish that are quickly broiled and then napped with a savory emulsified vinaigrette. Sautéed Spinach is an ideal partner for this dish. For a sauce that uses no dairy products, the herbed champagne vinaigrette is satisfyingly rich.

SERVES 4

4 6-ounce fillets of black sea bass or flounder
Olive oil for coating foil
1 medium zucchini
1 scallion
3 cups Fish Stock (page 313)
4 teaspoons champagne vinegar or other good quality
   white wine vinegar
1/2 cup extra-virgin olive oil
1/2 cup grapeseed oil
1 ripe medium tomato, peeled, seeded, and finely diced
1 1/2 teaspoons each finely chopped parsley, chives, tarragon, and chervil
3/4 teaspoon kosher salt
1/8 teaspoon freshly ground white pepper

1. Place each fillet between two sheets of plastic wrap and gently flatten to a thickness of 1/8 inch with a meat pounder or cleaver. Try not to tear the fillets. Lightly oil a sheet of aluminum foil large enough to hold all the fish without overlapping. Transfer the fish to the foil and refrigerate, covered, until ready to cook.

Here's a dish that calls for an elegant, full-bodied white from Graves, Burgundy's Côte de Beaune, or even Champagne.

2. Cut the ends from the zucchini. Slice lengthwise into quarters and then cut across the lengths into $1/8$-inch slices. Clean and slice the entire scallion into $1/8$-inch slices.

Reserve $1/3$ cup of the fish stock. In a small saucepan, reduce the remaining $2\,2/3$ cups of stock over high heat until only $1/2$ cup remains (reducing the stock provides the essential viscosity for a good emulsion). Place the reduced hot stock and vinegar in a blender. Combine the two oils in a measuring cup with a spout. Cover the blender and turn on the motor. Uncover and very slowly add $1/4$ cup of the oil. As the oil blends into the hot liquid, a creamy emulsion will start to form. Slowly add a quarter of the reserved fish stock to loosen the sauce. Alternate between the fish stock and the oil until both are used up.

3. Preheat the broiler.

4. Pour the finished sauce into a $1\,1/2$-quart saucepan. Over medium heat, add the tomatoes, zucchini, scallion, and herbs. Season with the salt and pepper. Heat the sauce enough to warm the vegetables, but avoid boiling or the emulsion will separate. Keep the sauce warm.

5. Place the foil with the fish fillets under the broiler. Cook the bass on one side only just until it becomes opaque, 1 to $1\,1/2$ minutes. With a wide spatula, transfer the fillets to four heated plates. Spoon the sauce and vegetables over the fish and serve immediately.

POLENTA-CRUSTED SEA BASS WITH CORN AND TOMATILLO SALSA

A polenta coating gives the fish a crackling, nutty-tasting outer crust, leaving the flesh juicy and tender. The corn and tomatillo salsa is also delicious as an accompaniment to barbecued chicken or pork, or as a dip for chips.

SERVES 4

1 ear of corn in the husk
6 tomatillos, husks removed, rinsed (^{1}/2 pound)
^{1}/3 cup peeled, seeded, and diced tomato
2 tablespoons seeded and minced jalapeño pepper
^{1}/3 cup peeled, seeded, and diced cucumber
^{1}/3 cup peeled and diced red onion
^{1}/3 cup diced red bell pepper
2 tablespoons coarsely chopped fresh cilantro
1 tablespoon lime juice
1^1/2 teaspoons kosher salt
^{1}/4 teaspoon freshly ground black pepper
^{1}/4 cup olive oil
^{1}/2 cup buttermilk
^{1}/2 cup medium-ground polenta or cornmeal
4 6-ounce fillets of sea bass, red snapper, or catfish

This dish requires a fruity white wine with lots of crisp acidity. Try an American Sauvignon Blanc or a Loire Valley Muscadet.

1.   Preheat the oven to 400 degrees F.

2.   Pull back the corn husk just enough to expose the silk. Remove the silk and close the husk back over the ear of corn. Roast the corn for 10 minutes. Remove from the oven and, when cool enough to handle, peel the husk and cut the kernels from the cob.

3. Place the tomatillos in a small saucepan with enough water to barely cover. Bring to a boil, lower the heat, and simmer until soft but not falling apart, about 5 minutes. Drain the tomatillos and purée in a blender until completely smooth.

4. In a bowl, combine the puréed tomatillos, roasted corn, tomatoes, jalapeño, cucumber, red onion, red pepper, cilantro, and lime juice. Season with 1 teaspoon salt and $1/8$ teaspoon pepper. Set aside while you prepare the fish. The salsa may be prepared 6 to 8 hours ahead to this point and kept covered in the refrigerator.

5. Heat the olive oil in a 12-inch skillet over medium heat.

6. Pour the buttermilk into a shallow bowl and sprinkle the polenta onto a dinner plate. Season the fish fillets with the remaining salt and pepper. Dip the fillets into the buttermilk then dredge in the polenta.

7. Sauté the fish until lightly browned, 3 to 4 minutes a side. Transfer the fillets to a warm platter and serve with the room-temperature salsa on the side.

COD WITH RADICCHIO, WHITE BEANS, AND LEMON VINAIGRETTE

*T*his recipe is a complete meal in one, with the sautéed cod nestled against a warm salad of radicchio, celery, white beans, and leeks. The tangy lemon vinaigrette brings out the cod's flavor. Since cod is so flaky, try these tips to prevent the fish from breaking apart as you cook it. Make sure the oil is quite hot before putting the fish in the pan. After a few seconds, give the pan a gentle shake to see if the fish has stuck to the bottom. Use a wide spatula to scrape any stuck parts and to support the fish while you turn it over.

SERVES 4

LEMON VINAIGRETTE

1 tablespoon finely chopped lemon zest
$^1/_4$ cup lemon juice
1 tablespoon minced garlic
1 teaspoon kosher salt
$^1/_4$ teaspoon freshly ground black pepper
1 cup extra-virgin olive oil
3 tablespoons coarsely chopped parsley

COD AND BEAN SALAD

2 cups cooked white beans (see Fagioli alla Toscana, steps 1 and 2, page 253)
4 tablespoons extra-virgin olive oil
$1^1/_2$ cups peeled and thinly sliced celery
2 cups leek rounds, white and light green parts only, washed
3 heads radicchio, quartered, cored, and leaves separated

Chenin Blanc grown in cool climates has a crisp, citrusy flavor that's perfect with the cod. From France's Loire Valley, try Savennières or a dry Vouvray.

¹/₂ teaspoon kosher salt
¹/₄ teaspoon freshly ground black pepper
4 6-ounce cod fillets
1 tablespoon flour

1. Combine the vinaigrette ingredients in a jar. Close the lid tightly and shake vigorously. Set aside.

2. In a small saucepan, bring the cooked beans to a simmer. Heat 2 tablespoons olive oil in a large skillet over medium heat. Add the celery and leeks and stir with a wooden spoon until the vegetables are softened but not colored, 4 to 5 minutes. Raise the heat to high and toss in the radicchio leaves. Cook an additional 3 to 4 minutes, stirring constantly, to wilt the leaves. Season with half the salt and pepper.

3. Transfer the cooked vegetables to a large bowl and, while still warm, toss with the beans and 1 cup of the lemon vinaigrette. Set aside.

4. Season the cod fillets with the remaining salt and pepper. Lightly dredge both sides of the fish in the flour. Heat the remaining 2 tablespoons olive oil over high heat in a large skillet. Sauté the cod until golden, 4 to 5 minutes a side. Arrange the cod fillets on a platter around the radicchio and white bean salad. Spoon the remaining vinaigrette over the cod and serve.

SEARED SALMON WITH SWEET CORN, SHIITAKE MUSHROOMS, AND BALSAMIC VINEGAR BUTTER SAUCE

*T*his signature dish returns to Union Square Cafe's menu for about eight weeks each summer when sweet corn makes its all-too-brief appearance in the Greenmarket. Sautéed spinach is our favorite accompaniment, and you might precede the salmon with Summer Tomato and Goat Cheese Salad.

SERVES 4

1/2 pound (2 sticks) plus 4 tablespoons butter, chilled
3/4 pound shiitake mushrooms, stems removed and
    reserved, caps thinly sliced
3/4 cup peeled and sliced red onions
1 1/2 teaspoons peeled and sliced garlic
1 medium tomato, coarsely chopped (about 1 cup)
3/4 teaspoon black peppercorns
1 bay leaf
1/4 cup balsamic vinegar
3/4 teaspoon kosher salt, plus to taste
1/8 teaspoon freshly ground black pepper, plus to taste
4 cups fresh sweet corn kernels, cut from 6 to 8
    medium ears
4 6-ounce skinless salmon fillets
2 tablespoons olive oil
3 tablespoons minced chives

This dish calls for a ripe, buttery Chardonnay from California, Australia, or Burgundy's Côte de Beaune.

1.   Cut the 1/2 pound butter into 1/2-inch pieces and reserve in the refrigerator.

2. To make the sauce, melt 1 tablespoon of the remaining butter over moderate heat in a medium saucepan. Add the mushroom stems, onions, garlic, tomato, peppercorns, and bay leaf. Cook, stirring occasionally, until the vegetables are softened, about 7 minutes.

3. Add the balsamic vinegar and $1/4$ cup water, raise the heat, and reduce until syrupy.

4. Reduce the heat to low and slowly whisk in the chilled butter, a few pieces at a time. Allow each addition of butter to be absorbed into the sauce before adding more. The sauce should remain just below a simmer during the whole process. After all the chilled butter has been added, strain the sauce through a fine-mesh strainer into the top of a double boiler set over low heat. Season with $3/4$ teaspoon salt and $1/8$ teaspoon pepper and keep warm.

5. Preheat the oven to 200 degrees F.

6. To cook the corn and mushrooms, melt the remaining 3 tablespoons butter in a large skillet over medium-high heat. Cook the sliced mushrooms for 4 to 5 minutes, until tender. Stir in the corn and cook an additional 4 to 5 minutes. Season with salt and pepper to taste, transfer to a platter, and keep warm in the oven.

7. Season the salmon with salt and pepper to taste. Heat the olive oil in a large skillet over high heat. Sear the salmon until golden, 3 to 5 minutes. Turn over with a spatula and cook an additional 2 to 3 minutes for medium rare, or longer if desired.

8. Transfer the cooked salmon to the platter with the corn and mushrooms, arranging the fillets around the vegetables. Nap the salmon with the warm balsamic vinegar sauce, sprinkle with the chives, and serve.

GRILLED TROUT WITH WARM ROSEMARY VINAIGRETTE

Rosemary lovers will enjoy this emulsified vinaigrette, which is creamy in texture yet contains no dairy. While any hot barbecue will cook your trout properly, a closed-lid charcoal-burning pit will add a delicious smoky flavor. This vinaigrette also works well with salmon or red snapper. Though fish stock is easy enough to make, it's becoming more widely available these days in seafood and fish markets. Precede the trout with Bruschetta Rossa, Artichoke and Potato Ragout, or Linguine with Spinach, Garlic, and Olive Oil.

SERVES 4

4 cups Fish Stock (page 313)
$^1/_2$ cup rosemary sprigs
1 tablespoon white wine vinegar
$^1/_2$ cup plus 2 tablespoons olive oil
$^1/_2$ cup grapeseed oil
1 teaspoon kosher salt
$^1/_4$ teaspoon freshly ground black pepper
4 12-ounce brook trouts, boned, head and tail intact

Try the trout with Sauvignon Blanc, Rhone Valley whites, or a good bottle of rosé.

1. Reserve $^1/_2$ cup of the fish stock and combine the remaining 3 $^1/_2$ cups and the rosemary sprigs in a saucepan. Reduce over medium-high heat to $^1/_2$ cup. Strain.

2. Combine the reduced hot stock and vinegar in a blender. Combine $^1/_2$ cup of the olive oil and the grapeseed oil in a pourable measuring cup. Cover the blender and turn on the motor. Uncover and *very* slowly add $^1/_4$ cup of the oil. As the oil blends into the hot liquid, a creamy emulsion will start to form. Slowly add a quarter of the reserved fish stock to loosen the sauce. Alternate between the fish stock and the oil until both are used up. Season with $^1/_2$ teaspoon salt and $^1/_8$ teaspoon black pepper. Transfer to a saucepan and set aside.

3.   Preheat a grill, grill pan, or outdoor barbecue to very hot.

4.   Brush the trout with 2 tablespoons of olive oil. Season with the remaining salt and pepper. Grill the trout 4 to 5 minutes a side. While the trout is cooking, warm the sauce over very low heat, never allowing the sauce to boil. Transfer the cooked trout to a platter and serve with the rosemary vinaigrette.

Grilled Swordfish with Tomato and Roast Pepper Compote

*T*his is a light and refreshing way to enjoy barbecued swordfish steaks. The colorful compote includes the best of summer's bounty and adds a Sicilian twist with the sweet raisins and toasted pine nuts. Precede with Endive, Radicchio, and Arugula Salad and serve with steamed ears of corn.

SERVES 4

COMPOTE

1/2 cup raisins

1/4 cup white wine

2 red bell peppers

1 yellow bell pepper

3 medium tomatoes, peeled, seeded, and diced

1 1/2 cups leek rounds, white and light green parts only, washed

1/3 cup extra-virgin olive oil

1 cup chopped zucchini

1 1/2 teaspoons minced garlic

1/4 cup pine nuts, lightly toasted

1/3 cup tightly packed basil, cut into thin strips

2 tablespoons balsamic vinegar

1 tablespoon kosher salt

1/4 teaspoon freshly ground black pepper

SWORDFISH

4 6-ounce swordfish steaks (3/4 inch thick)

2 tablespoons olive oil

1/2 teaspoon kosher salt

1/4 teaspoon freshly ground black pepper

4 large basil sprigs

Sauvignon Blanc's smokiness and fruity herbaceousness stand up to the grilled fish and compote.

1.   Combine the raisins and the white wine in a small saucepan and bring to a simmer over medium heat. Remove immediately from the heat and set aside to plump.

2.   Preheat the broiler.

3.   Cook the red and yellow peppers under the broiler, turning often, until their skins blacken. Alternatively, spear each pepper with a kitchen fork or skewer and hold it over an open flame until charred. Place the charred peppers in a paper bag or in a closely covered container until they are cool enough to handle. (This step completes the cooking of the peppers and facilitates removing the skin.) Rub off the skins (never run them under water, which washes away the flavorful oils) and discard the seeds. Cut the peppers into 1-inch dice, combine in a bowl with the diced tomatoes, and set aside.

4.   In a small sauté pan over low heat, cook the leeks in 2 teaspoons of the olive oil until they are tender, stirring frequently, 5 to 7 minutes. Add to the peppers and tomatoes.

5.   In the same pan, heat 2 teaspoons of olive oil and cook the zucchini over medium heat until softened but not limp, 3 to 4 minutes. Combine with the other compote ingredients.

6.   Drain the raisins, discarding any remaining wine, and add to the compote, along with the garlic, pine nuts, basil, balsamic vinegar, and remaining olive oil. Season with the salt and pepper and mix well. Reserve at room temperature.

7.   Preheat a grill, grill pan, or barbecue to very hot. Brush the swordfish steaks with the olive oil and season with salt and pepper. Cook 3 to 4 minutes a side. Transfer to a warm platter, garnish with the basil sprigs, and serve with the compote.

Pan-Roasted Salmon with Citrus-Balsamic Vinaigrette

In this recipe, the salmon is seared on one side while the other side is flash-roasted in a hot oven. The richness of the fish is set off by the tangy and slightly sweet vinaigrette made with orange juice, balsamic vinegar, and herbs. A perfect accompaniment for this dish is Three-Grain Pilaf with Almonds and Shiitake Mushrooms.

SERVES 4

SAUCE

³/4 cup fresh orange juice
¹/2 cup balsamic vinegar
2 tablespoons extra-virgin olive oil
1 anchovy fillet, very finely minced (optional)
2 tablespoons finely minced onion
2 teaspoons each coarsely chopped parsley, basil, and mint
2 tablespoons finely minced orange zest
¹/8 teaspoon kosher salt
Freshly ground black pepper

SALMON

4 6-ounce skinless fillets of salmon
Kosher salt
Freshly ground black pepper
2 tablespoons olive oil

1. Preheat the oven to 450 degrees F.

2. Combine all the sauce ingredients in a glass jar, cover tightly, and shake vigorously. Reserve.

Alsace whites like Riesling, Tokay Pinot Gris, and Sylvaner have enough refreshing fruit and body to stand up to this recipe.

3. Season the salmon with salt and pepper to taste. In a skillet large enough to hold all the salmon, heat the olive oil over high heat. Place the salmon in the pan with its original skin side down. Transfer the pan to the oven and roast for 8 to 10 minutes, until medium rare, or longer if desired. Transfer the cooked salmon to a serving platter and keep warm while finishing the sauce.

4. Wipe out any olive oil remaining in the skillet and add the sauce. Heat through for a few seconds over high heat, spoon the sauce over the salmon, and serve.

GRILLED MARINATED FILLET MIGNON OF TUNA

Since the day we opened in 1985, no dish has ever outsold the Fillet Mignon of Tuna at Union Square Cafe. Scores of our guests have yet to try anything else on our menu, no matter how often they've returned. The biggest trick to making this taste like ours is to convince your fishmonger to cut the tuna steaks into 3-inch cubes, 8 to 10 ounces each, from the reddest possible tuna, so they look just like filet mignon steaks. Serve with Eggplant Mashed Potatoes, grilled vegetables, or Spicy Gingered Asian Slaw.

SERVES 4

MARINADE

> 2 cups teriyaki sauce
> 1/2 cup dry sherry
> 4 tablespoons finely chopped fresh ginger
> 1/2 cup chopped scallions
> 2 garlic cloves, thinly sliced
> 1/2 teaspoon cayenne
> 2 teaspoons freshly ground black pepper
> Juice of 2 lemons

TUNA

> 4 yellowfin tuna steaks, 8 to 10 ounces each,
>   cut into 3-inch cubes
> 2 tablespoons olive oil
> 1/4 cup Japanese pickled ginger
>   (available at Asian markets)

1. Combine all the marinade ingredients in a bowl large enough to hold the tuna. Place the tuna steaks in the marinade and refrigerate for 3 hours, turning every hour.

Through the years, our guests have tried practically every imaginable wine with this tuna recipe. Two favorites have been Cornas— a smoky-spicy Rhone red—and Tokay Pinot Gris—a full-bodied Alsace white. They hold their own with the intense ginger flavors. A chilled beer also pairs well with the tuna.

2. Thirty minutes before cooking, drain the tuna and bring to room temperature. Preheat a grill, grill-pan, or outdoor barbecue to very hot.

3. Brush the tuna with the olive oil. Grill the steaks for 1 to 2 minutes on each of their six sides. The outside of the tuna should be nicely charred and the center should be barely warm and quite rare. Cooked this way, the tuna will remain moist and flavorful.

4. Top each steak with pickled ginger and serve.

RED SNAPPER WITH TOMATO-ONION COMPOTE

*H*ere's a simple preparation Michael learned as a young apprentice in the kitchen of Michel Guérard. The dish is at its best when made with the vine-ripened tomatoes of late summer and served with Tomato Coulis. As an accompaniment, we recommend Basil Mashed Potatoes or spinach.

SERVES 6

8 medium tomatoes
¹/4 cup extra-virgin olive oil
3 cups sliced onions
1 teaspoon sherry vinegar
1 tablespoon minced tarragon
³/4 teaspoon kosher salt
¹/8 teaspoon freshly ground black pepper
6 6-ounce red snapper fillets, skin on
Flour for dredging
Tomato Coulis (optional) (page 319)

Inspired by the cooking of southern France, this dish does well with herbaceous Provençal rosés and Rhone Valley whites.

1.   Preheat the oven to 350 degrees F.

2.   Core the tomatoes and cut them in half crosswise. Place them cut side down on a lightly oiled baking sheet. Place the baking sheet on the oven's upper rack and roast until the skin blisters and begins to curl away from the tomatoes, 30 to 40 minutes. When the tomatoes are cool enough to handle yet still warm, gently lift the skin from the tomato and squeeze out the seeds.

3.   In a skillet, heat 2 tablespoons of the olive oil over moderate heat. Add the sliced onions and cook, stirring occasionally, until completely tender and sweet, about 30 minutes. If any of the onions stick

to the bottom of the pan, stir in a few tablespoons of water. This will simultaneously release the onions and dissolve the caramelized bits adhering to the pan. Set the pan aside.

4. Combine the tomatoes with the cooked onions. Add the sherry vinegar and simmer over moderate heat, stirring occasionally, until slightly thick. Stir in the minced tarragon, $1/4$ teaspoon salt, and half the pepper; remove from the heat. The compote can be prepared up to 1 day ahead to this point and stored, covered and refrigerated.

5. Dredge the skin side of the snapper in the flour and season both sides with the remaining salt and pepper.

6. Heat the remaining olive oil in a large skillet over medium heat. Sauté the snapper skin side down for 4 to 5 minutes. Turn the fish over with a spatula and cook an additional 1 to 2 minutes. While the fish is cooking, return the compote to a simmer. When the fish is done, transfer the compote to a serving platter and arrange the snapper fillets on top. Spoon the warm Tomato Coulis over the fillets and serve.

SEARED CURRIED WHITEFISH WITH RAÏTA

*T*his recipe combines a delicately flaky fish with the pungent spices of Indian cooking. If you can't find whitefish, substitute flounder, fluke, or sole. If the whitefish fillets are longer than your skillet is wide, cut them in half before cooking for easier handling. The Red Lentil–Basmati Rice Pilaf is an excellent accompaniment for the whitefish. The chilled raïta is a refreshing balance for the curried whitefish, and also stands alone as a terrific hors d'oeuvre served with warmed pita wedges.

SERVES 4

RAÏTA

1 medium cucumber (about $^1/_2$ pound)
1$^1/_4$ teaspoons kosher salt
1$^1/_2$ cups plain whole-milk or low-fat yogurt
$^1/_4$ cup peeled and finely diced red onion
$^1/_4$ teaspoon ground coriander
$^1/_8$ teaspoon dried red pepper flakes
4 teaspoons fresh lemon juice
3 tablespoons chopped fresh mint
$^1/_8$ teaspoon freshly ground black pepper

CURRIED WHITEFISH

4 teaspoons curry powder
$^1/_4$ cup all-purpose flour
4 6-ounce whitefish fillets, with skin
$^3/_4$ teaspoon kosher salt
$^1/_8$ teaspoon freshly ground black pepper
1 tablespoon vegetable oil
1 tablespoon butter

As it is for most spicy Indian cuisine, a full-flavored beer would be a delicious thirst-quenching match for the whitefish. You could also choose an off-dry white like Vouvray demi-sec or a spätlese-quality German Riesling.

1. Peel the cucumber and split it lengthwise. Remove the seeds and split each half again lengthwise. Cut the quartered cucumber into $1/8$-inch-thick slices. Place the slices in a colander and toss with 1 teaspoon of the salt. Set aside to drain for 30 minutes.

2. In a medium bowl, combine the cucumber with the yogurt, red onion, coriander, red pepper flakes, lemon juice, mint, the remaining $1/4$ teaspoon salt, and pepper. Cover and refrigerate. The raïta can be prepared up to 1 day in advance.

3. To prepare the whitefish, combine the curry powder and flour on a large plate. Season the whitefish fillets with the salt and pepper and dredge in the curried flour.

4. Heat the oil and butter in a 12-inch skillet over high heat. Place the fish in the pan, skin side up, and sear until golden brown, about 3 minutes. Carefully turn the fish over with a large spatula and cook for an additional 2 minutes. Transfer the fillets to a serving platter and serve the raïta on the side.

SALT COD, ONION, AND SQUASH GRATIN

*F*or salt cod aficionados, here's an elegantly presented alternative to the more traditional New England cod balls or French *brandade de morue*. The amount of time you'll need to soak the cod will depend on how dried and salty it is to start. Precede with Red Oakleaf and Bibb Salad and serve with a crusty baguette of French bread.

SERVES 4

2 fillets of salt cod, cut into four pieces
  (1 1/2 to 1 3/4 pounds)
5 tablespoons extra-virgin olive oil
2 teaspoons minced garlic
7 cups sliced onions
Flour for dredging
1/4 teaspoon freshly ground black pepper
1 tablespoon each minced fresh thyme, oregano,
  and basil
1 medium zucchini, washed and cut into 1/8-inch
  rounds (about 2 cups)
1 medium yellow squash, washed and cut into 1/8-inch
  rounds (about 2 cups)
6 fresh plum tomatoes, cut into 1/4-inch slices
1/2 teaspoon kosher salt

Try a heady Châteauneuf-du-Pape Blanc or Bordeaux Blanc or a fragrant rosé made from the grenache grape.

1.   Twenty-four to 36 hours before serving, place the salt cod in a bowl with enough cold water to cover. Refrigerate and change the water several times over the course of the day to remove excess salt. The reconstituted cod should feel like fresh fish and not taste overly salty.

2. Heat 2 tablespoons of the olive oil in a medium skillet over moderate heat. Add the garlic and onions and cook, stirring occasionally, until the onions are tender and browned, about 30 minutes. Transfer to a 9 × 11-inch gratin dish, spread in an even layer and set aside.

3. Remove the salt cod from the water and pat dry with paper towels. Dredge the fish in flour and shake off the excess. Wipe the skillet clean and return to moderate heat with 1 tablespoon olive oil. When the oil is almost to the smoking point, brown the salt cod fillets on both sides. Transfer to the gratin dish and arrange over the onions in one even layer. Season with $1/8$ teaspoon pepper and half the herbs.

4. Preheat the oven to 400 degrees F.

5. Arrange the slices of zucchini, edges overlapping, in a row across the width of the gratin dish. Repeat with a row of yellow squash, just below the zucchini, and with a row of tomatoes just below the yellow squash. Continue alternating rows until the entire surface of the gratin dish is covered.

6. Sprinkle with the remaining herbs and drizzle evenly with the remaining olive oil. Season with the salt and $1/8$ teaspoon pepper. Cover the gratin dish with foil.

7. Place in the oven and bake for 15 minutes, covered, to soften the vegetables. Continue baking, uncovered, an additional 40 minutes, or until the vegetables are lightly brown. Let rest 5 minutes, cut into even portions with a spatula, and serve on warm plates.

SHRIMP WITH "GAZPACHO" SAUCE

*T*his recipe uses every ripe ingredient from the summer vegetable garden to give a lively and spicy flavor to seared shrimp. Serve with boiled white rice, couscous, or orzo.

SERVES 4

¹/₃ cup extra-virgin olive oil
1¹/₂ teaspoons minced garlic
¹/₄ cup peeled and sliced onion
¹/₂ cup cored, seeded, and chopped red bell pepper
¹/₂ cup peeled, chopped cucumber
1 tablespoon chopped jalapeño with seeds
1 ¹/₄ teaspoons kosher salt
1 cup cored and chopped tomato (¹/₂ pound)
2 parsley sprigs
³/₄ cup coarsely chopped fresh cilantro
¹/₄ teaspoon freshly ground black pepper
1¹/₂ pounds medium shrimp, shelled and deveined

1. In a medium saucepan, heat ¹/₂ tablespoon of the olive oil over moderate heat. Add the garlic, onion, red pepper, cucumber, jalapeño, and ¹/₄ teaspoon of the salt. Cook, stirring, for 3 to 4 minutes.

2. Add the tomato, parsley, and ¹/₂ cup of the cilantro. Bring to a simmer, cover, and cook for 10 minutes. Transfer to a blender, purée, and strain through a fine-mesh strainer.

3. Return the gazpacho sauce to the saucepan. With the sauce over low heat, whisk in 3 tablespoons of the olive oil. Season with ³/₄ teaspoon salt and half the pepper. Set aside.

Serve a fruity German Riesling, an herbaceous California Sauvignon Blanc, or an Alsace Gewürztraminer to balance the sweet-spicy shrimp sauce.

4.   Season the shrimp with the remaining salt and pepper. Heat the remaining olive oil over high heat in a 10-inch skillet. Add the shrimp and cook for 2 minutes, stirring occasionally, until they begin to turn pink. Lower the heat to medium, add the gazpacho sauce and remaining chopped cilantro, and toss with the shrimp. Simmer 1 minute to finish cooking the shrimp. Serve on a warm platter.

SEARED SEA SCALLOPS WITH LEMON VINAIGRETTE, BROCCOLI RABE, AND ROAST TOMATOES

*W*e love the unlikely combination of flavors and textures in this dish. Be sure to buy the freshest sea scallops available—their bright color, firm texture, and clean smell assure a sweet, nonfishy taste. The delicate scallops work beautifully with the bitter crunchiness of the broccoli rabe. Start this meal with Black Bean Soup or Creamless Mushroom Soup.

SERVES 4

> 2 cups fish stock (page 313)
> 1 tablespoon minced shallots
> ^{1}/2 teaspoon minced garlic
> 2 tablespoons lemon juice
> 1 teaspoon minced fresh rosemary
> 1 ^{3}/4 teaspoons kosher salt
> ^{1}/4 teaspoon freshly ground black pepper
> ^{3}/4 cup plus 3 tablespoons extra-virgin olive oil
> 1 cup Oven-Dried Tomatoes (page 318)
> 1 recipe Sautéed Broccoli Rabe (page 224)
> 1^1/2 pounds large sea scallops, cleaned

1. In a small saucepan over medium heat, reduce the fish stock to ^{1}/4 cup.

2. Combine the shallots, garlic, lemon juice, rosemary, 1 teaspoon salt, and ^{1}/8 teaspoon pepper in a mixing bowl. Add the warm reduced fish stock. Slowly pour in ^{3}/4 cup olive oil, whisking until the oil is completely incorporated and the sauce somewhat thick.

Choose a Chenin Blanc, Mendocino Sauvignon Blanc, or Friuli's Ribolla Gialla to complement the citrusy flavors in this dish.

3. Preheat the oven to 200 degrees F.

4. Add the oven-dried tomatoes to the skillet with the cooked broccoli rabe and, over medium heat, toss to heat through. Transfer to a serving platter and keep warm in the oven.

5. Pat the scallops dry with paper towels and season with the remaining salt and pepper. Wipe the skillet clean and heat the remaining olive oil over medium-high heat. Add the sea scallops and sauté until golden brown, 3 to 5 minutes. Turn the scallops over and cook 1 additional minute. The scallops are done when browned and slightly firm to the touch.

6. Transfer the scallops to the center of the serving platter with the broccoli rabe and tomatoes. Drizzle with the lemon–olive oil sauce and serve.

SIZZLED SOFT-SHELL CRABS WITH SPICY CARROT SAUCE

*H*ere's a colorful way to serve one of spring and summer's culinary treats. The carrot sauce highlights the sweetness of the crabs, while the assertive spices add a balancing warmth.

SERVES 4

1 teaspoon butter
1 scallion, thinly sliced
2 tablespoons peeled and minced fresh ginger
1 teaspoon minced jalapeño, seeded
2 teaspoons minced garlic
$1/8$ teaspoon ground cumin
$1/8$ teaspoon ground coriander seeds
$1/8$ teaspoon ground mustard seeds
$2 1/4$ teaspoons curry powder
2 tablespoons lime juice
1 tablespoon cornstarch
1 tablespoon honey
2 cups carrot juice
$1/3$ cup flour
$1/2$ teaspoon kosher salt
$1/8$ teaspoon freshly ground black pepper
8 medium-size soft-shell crabs, cleaned
$1/4$ cup olive or vegetable oil
2 tablespoons chopped parsley or cilantro

Sauvignon Blanc, Gewürztraminer, or Riesling is delicious with the spicy carrot sauce. Ice-cold beer would also be a refreshing option.

1. Melt the butter in a 2-quart saucepan over medium heat. Add the scallion, ginger, jalapeño, and garlic; cook until wilted, 3 to 4 minutes. Stir in the cumin, coriander, mustard seeds, and $1/4$ teaspoon of the curry powder. Cook an additional minute, stirring with a wooden spoon to develop the flavor of the spices. Reserve.

2. In a large bowl, combine the lime juice, cornstarch, and honey, mixing with your fingers to form a paste. Whisk the carrot juice into the paste until combined thoroughly.

3. Transfer the carrot juice to the saucepan with the spiced vegetables, and return to a medium flame. Bring to a boil, whisking frequently, until the sauce thickens. Keep warm.

4. Combine the flour, salt, pepper, and remaining curry powder in a soup bowl. Dry the crabs thoroughly on a paper towel. Dredge the crabs in the flour and curry mixture, shaking off the excess. Transfer to another plate.

5. Heat the oil over medium-high heat in a 12-inch skillet. Sauté the crabs, shell side down, in one layer. You may need to do this in batches to avoid crowding the pan, causing the crabs to steam rather than sauté. Cook until golden, 4 to 5 minutes on each side. If cooking the crabs in more than one batch, keep them warm in a 200-degree oven while you prepare the second (or third) batch.

6. To serve, ladle the warm carrot sauce onto four warm dinner plates and place 2 crabs on each plate. Sprinkle with the parsley or cilantro and serve.

LOBSTER SHEPHERD'S PIE

*T*his succulent recipe is a variation on the British classic designed to use up leftover mutton and potatoes. Preceded by a tossed green salad, it is a complete meal in itself. We guarantee you'll hear an unending chorus of raves to reward your hard work.

SERVES 4 TO 6

SAUCE

4 1 1/2-pound live lobsters
4 tablespoons olive oil
2 medium tomatoes, cored and coarsely chopped
2 tablespoons tomato paste
3/4 cup peeled and chopped carrots
1 cup peeled and thinly sliced onion
1 tablespoon chopped garlic
Stems from 1/2 pound mushrooms (see below)
1/2 teaspoon dried red pepper flakes
2 cups white wine
5 cups heavy cream
1 teaspoon lemon juice
1/2 teaspoon kosher salt
1/8 teaspoon ground white pepper
Pinch of cayenne

PIE

3 cups peeled and thinly sliced carrots
1/2 cup water
3 tablespoons unsalted butter
1 teaspoon kosher salt
3/8 teaspoon freshly ground white pepper
3 tablespoons olive oil
2 pounds spinach, stems removed, washed
1/2 pound white mushrooms, wiped clean, stemmed
   (reserve the stems), and thinly sliced

Lobster Shepherd's Pie calls for an opulent, buttery Chardonnay. Look for a rich example from the Napa Valley or celebrate with a luscious Meursault or Puligny-Montrachet.

1 tablespoon chopped tarragon
3 1/2 cups lobster sauce (see above)
1 recipe Mashed Potatoes (page 232)

1.   Preheat the oven to 500 degrees F.

2.   Place a lobster belly side down on a cutting board and hold it firmly at its midsection. Place the point of a large kitchen knife about midway down the head of each lobster, blade side facing toward the head. With one strong motion, pierce downward and then slice forward with the knife, splitting the top portion of the lobster's head and killing it instantly. Set aside and repeat with the remaining lobsters.

3.   In a roasting pan large enough to hold the lobsters in one layer, spread 2 tablespoons of the olive oil. Heat the pan in the oven until the oil is to the smoking point. Position the lobsters on their backs in the hot pan and roast for 10 minutes. Remove the lobsters and cool. Carefully extract all the meat from the lobsters' tails and claws and set aside, covered, in the refrigerator. Reserve the bodies, tail shells, and pan juices.

4.   In a heavy-bottomed 5-quart saucepan over a high flame, heat 2 tablespoons olive oil to the smoking point. Toss in the reserved lobster shells and stir until they are bright red. Add the tomatoes, tomato paste, carrots, onion, garlic, mushroom stems, and red pepper flakes. Stir well and cook 5 minutes. Add the white wine and reduce by half. Pour in the reserved lobster pan juices and the cream. Reduce the heat to low and simmer, stirring occasionally, for $1^{1}/_{2}$ hours. Strain first through a colander, pressing down well on the lobster carcasses to extract a maximum of sauce, and then through a fine-mesh strainer. Season with the lemon juice, salt, pepper, and cayenne. You will have about $3^{1}/_{2}$ cups of sauce. The recipe can be done up to 1 day ahead to this point.

5.   Place the sliced carrots, water, 2 tablespoons of the butter, $^{1}/_{2}$ teaspoon salt, and $^{1}/_{8}$ teaspoon white pepper in a $1^{1}/_{2}$-quart skillet. Cook over a medium-low flame until the carrots are glazed with the butter and tender, about 10 minutes. Transfer the carrots to a bowl and reserve.

(continued)

6.   Wipe the skillet clean and heat 1 tablespoon of the olive oil over high heat. Cook the spinach until wilted, stirring constantly. Season with $1/4$ teaspoon salt and $1/8$ teaspoon pepper. Drain the spinach in a colander and set aside.

7.   Wipe the skillet clean and return to a medium flame. Heat the remaining 2 tablespoons olive oil and 1 tablespoon butter until the butter "sings" and begins to turn nut-brown. Toss in the sliced mushrooms and sauté until tender, 3 to 4 minutes. Season with $1/4$ teaspoon salt and $1/8$ teaspoon white pepper. Drain the mushrooms in a colander and set aside.

8.   In a large bowl, stir together the cooked carrots, mushrooms, chopped tarragon, and $1/2$ cup of the lobster sauce.

Preheat the oven to 350 degrees F. Butter a 10-inch soufflé dish that is about $2 1/2$ inches deep.

9.   Set aside 4 lobster claws and cut the remaining lobster meat on the bias into $1/4$-inch slices. Form an even layer of spinach on the bottom of the soufflé dish. Arrange half the carrot and mushroom mixture on top of the spinach, pressing to form an even layer. Distribute the sliced lobster evenly atop the carrots and mushrooms. Finish with a second layer of carrots and mushrooms.

10.   With a flexible spatula, spread the mashed potatoes evenly over the top of the assembled pie. Place the soufflé dish on a cookie sheet and bake to heat through, about 50 minutes.

11.   Bring the lobster sauce to a simmer and preheat the broiler. Arrange the reserved lobster claws atop the layer of mashed potatoes and brown the pie under the broiler. Spoon the lobster sauce around each portion of pie as it is served.

LOBSTER-SWEET CORN CHOWDER

A wonderful recipe to celebrate the last gasp of summer when corn is at its sweetest. Boiling the cobs along with the lobster shells imparts an intense corn flavor and thickens the chowder base. Try to use female lobsters, whose roe provides additional flavor and turns the chowder a lovely shade of pink when cooked.

SERVES 4 TO 6

Chardonnay, Vouvray, and Tokay Pinot Gris are recommended with the rich lobster chowder.

4 1^1/$_2$-pound live lobsters, preferably female

^{1}/$_4$ cup olive oil

4 ounces pancetta, cut into ^{1}/$_2$-inch dice (1 cup)

1 cup leek rounds, washed, white and light parts only

1 cup peeled and diced onions

1 cup sliced celery

1 cup peeled and sliced carrots

2 fresh thyme sprigs

^{1}/$_4$ teaspoon cumin seeds

^{1}/$_4$ teaspoon coriander seeds

^{1}/$_2$ teaspoon cayenne

^{1}/$_4$ teaspoon black peppercorns

2 cups white wine

2 cups heavy cream

4 ears of corn, kernels removed and reserved and cobs
  cut into 1-inch pieces

1 teaspoon kosher salt

^{1}/$_8$ teaspoon freshly ground black pepper

1^1/$_2$ cups diced red potatoes

1 red pepper, roasted and diced

2 teaspoons seeded and minced jalapeño

2 tablespoons chopped parsley or cilantro

1. Place a lobster belly side down on a cutting board and hold it firmly at its midsection. Place the point of a large kitchen knife about

(continued)

midway down the head of each lobster, blade side facing toward the head. With one strong motion, pierce downward and then slice forward with the knife, splitting the top portion of the lobster's head and killing it instantly. Set aside and repeat with the remaining lobsters.

2.   Separate the tails from the bodies and remove the claws. Cut each tail into 4 even pieces. Split the heads and remove the light green liver (tomalley) and the dark green roe (from the female lobsters). Set aside the tails, claws, and heads. Using a rubber spatula, pass the tomalley and roe through a strainer into a small bowl. Cover the bowl and refrigerate.

3.   Heat the olive oil over moderate heat in a Dutch oven or soup pot. Add the pancetta and cook, stirring occasionally, until brown. Add the leeks and cook until wilted, about 2 minutes. Remove the leeks and pancetta and reserve.

4.   Raise the heat to high and add the lobster tail pieces, claws, and heads. Cook, stirring frequently, for 5 to 7 minutes, until bright red. Remove the lobsters from the pan and set aside to cool.

5.   Add the onions, celery, carrots, thyme, cumin, coriander, cayenne, and black peppercorns to the pan. Lower the heat to medium and cook 10 minutes, until the vegetables are softened but not browned. Remove the pan from the heat.

6.   Crack open the lobster tails and claws, remove the meat, and return the shells and heads to the pan. Cut the lobster tail meat and claws into bite-size pieces and reserve, covered.

7.   Pour the white wine into the pot and cook over medium heat until reduced by half. Add cream, corn cob pieces, and 2 cups water. Lower the heat and simmer, covered, for 50 minutes. Strain in a colander, pressing the solids to extract the maximum amount of liquid. Season with salt and pepper.

8. Return the chowder base to the pot and add the potatoes, red pepper, jalapeño, corn kernels, reserved leeks, and pancetta. Simmer gently until the potatoes are cooked, 7 to 10 minutes. Add the reserved lobster meat to the chowder.

9. Ladle a small amount of the hot chowder into the bowl with the tomalley-roe mixture to warm slightly. Slowly stir the warmed roe back into the chowder. Heat over low heat, stirring, until the roe turns the chowder light pink. Do not boil the chowder once the roe has been added or the roe will separate. Ladle into warm bowls, sprinkle with chopped parsley or cilantro, and serve.

CACCIUCCO DI PESCE

*H*ere's our version of *cacciucco*—a fragrant seafood stew enjoyed in the western coast towns of Italy's Tuscany and Liguria regions. It's a refreshing alternative to the French bouillabaisse, substituting orange zest for saffron. Precede the cacciucco with an Endive, Radicchio, and Arugula Salad, and serve with fresh homemade garlic bread.

SERVES 6 TO 8

BROTH

2 tablespoons olive oil

Reserved shrimp shells (see below)

2 tablespoons minced garlic

2 cups peeled and sliced onions

2 teaspoons aniseed

$^1/_2$ teaspoon dried red pepper flakes

$^1/_2$ teaspoon kosher salt

$^1/_8$ teaspoon freshly ground black pepper

2 tablespoons tomato paste

$^3/_4$ cup dry white vermouth

2 pounds fresh tomatoes, cored and chopped

2 tablespoons chopped parsley

2 fresh thyme sprigs

1 bay leaf

4 cups Fish Stock (page 313)

SEAFOOD

2 tablespoons olive oil

$1^1/_2$ cups sliced leeks, white and light green parts only, washed

2 cups cored and sliced fennel bulb

$1^1/_2$ cups sliced zucchini or yellow squash

1 tablespoon minced garlic

Italy's Liguria region produces a delightful, flowery white wine, Pigato di Albenga, that complements the cacciucco beautifully. You might also try the Provençal wine produced in and around (and named for) the town of Cassis, in either its white or rosé versions.

18 littleneck, manila, or other small clams
1 pound monkfish or other firm-fleshed white fish,
  filleted and cut into 2-inch chunks
18 small mussels, beards removed and scrubbed
$1/2$ pound medium shrimp, cleaned, shells reserved
  for the broth
$3/4$ pound cleaned calamari, cut into $1/4$-inch rings
1 teaspoon minced orange zest
1 teaspoon kosher salt
$1/4$ teaspoon freshly ground black pepper
2 tablespoons chopped parsley

1.   Heat the olive oil in a large soup pot over high heat, add the shrimp shells, and stir well for 3 to 4 minutes. Lower the heat to medium and stir in the garlic, onions, aniseed, and red pepper flakes. Cook until the onions are tender, 5 to 7 minutes. Season with the salt and pepper.

2.   Stir in the tomato paste and cook for 1 minute to dissolve. Add the vermouth and reduce by half. Add the tomatoes, parsley, thyme, and bay leaf and cook 3 to 5 minutes. Pour in the fish stock, bring slowly to a boil, and skim any foam from the surface with a small ladle. Lower the heat and simmer, covered, 30 minutes. Strain in a colander set over a bowl, pressing the solids to extract the maximum amount of broth. The broth can be prepared several days ahead up to this point and held, covered and refrigerated, or up to 2 months frozen.

3.   To prepare the seafood, heat the olive oil over moderate heat in the soup pot and sauté the leeks, fennel, zucchini, and garlic until softened, 2 to 3 minutes.

4.   Pour in the reserved fish broth and bring to a simmer. Add the clams and monkfish and cook 5 to 6 minutes, or until the clams open. Add the mussels, shrimp, calamari, and orange zest and simmer 3 to 5 minutes, or until the mussels open. Season with salt and pepper. Ladle the stew into a warm soup tureen, sprinkle with chopped parsley, and serve.

HERB-ROASTED CHICKEN

*T*he secret to this deliciously moist chicken is seasoning it up to a day before roasting. This allows the salt and pepper to penetrate the chicken and flavor it in a way that last-minute seasoning cannot. If roasting a kosher chicken, use only pepper since it has already been salted. At Union Square Cafe we accompany the chicken with Creamy Polenta and Panzanella. You could also serve spinach, Mashed Potatoes, or turnips with satisfying results.

SERVES 4

1 4- to 5-pound chicken
$1/2$ teaspoon kosher salt
Freshly ground black pepper
2 tablespoons butter, at room temperature
4 thyme sprigs
2 tablespoons coarsely chopped parsley
1 tablespoon coarsely chopped tarragon
$1/2$ cup sliced carrots
$1/2$ cup sliced celery
$1/2$ cup sliced onions
2 cups Chicken Stock (page 312)

Look for light, fruity reds such as Beaujolais, Pinot Noir, or Dolcetto d'Alba to go with the roast chicken.

1. The day before roasting the chicken (or at least 8 hours ahead), season inside and out with salt and pepper. Cover and refrigerate.

2. Preheat the oven to 425 degrees F.

3. Truss the chicken, tying its legs together tightly with kitchen twine. Rub the butter all over the chicken. Place breast side down on a roasting rack set in a roasting pan. Transfer the pan to the oven and roast for 30 minutes.

4. Remove the chicken from the oven and place the thyme, parsley, tarragon, carrots, celery, and onions in the pan under the rack. Turn

the chicken over onto its back and continue to roast breast side up for another 35 to 40 minutes, or until the skin is browned. To check doneness, place a meat thermometer in the thickest point of the thigh, being careful not to pierce through to the cavity. It should read 170 degrees. If you don't have a thermometer, tilt the chicken forward on the rack until juices run from the cavity. They should be clear with no trace of pinkness.

5.   Transfer the chicken to a platter. Allow to rest in a warm place for 15 minutes before carving. Remove the rack, tilt the roasting pan, and pour off the fat, leaving the vegetables and herbs in the pan. Place the pan over a medium-high flame and pour in the chicken stock as well as any juice that has accumulated on the platter. Cook for 4 to 5 minutes, scraping up any browned bits with a wooden spoon. Strain.

6.   Carve the chicken and serve with the hot herbed pan juices.

MAMA ROMANO'S BAKED LEMON CHICKEN

*M*ichael's mother frequently cooked this dish, and it was a family favorite. This homestyle recipe has also pleased hundreds of Union Square Cafe diners looking for a rustic and comforting meal. We precede the chicken with a red-sauced pasta like Bucatini all'Amatriciana or Pappardelle of Zucchini. Serve broccoli rabe alongside the lemon chicken.

SERVES 4

1 3 1/2-pound chicken, cut into 10 pieces
1 teaspoon kosher salt
1/4 teaspoon freshly ground black pepper
Flour for dredging
2 tablespoons olive oil
3 cups thinly sliced onions
1 1/2 tablespoons thinly sliced garlic
8 fresh thyme sprigs
1 1/2 cups chicken stock
2 lemons

The lemony sauce will be complemented by coarse, rustic reds from Italy's southern regions. Try Salice Salentino, Aglianico del Vulture, or one of the outstanding vini da tavola being made in Sicily.

1. One hour before cooking, season the chicken pieces with half the salt and pepper.

2. Preheat the oven to 400 degrees F.

3. Dredge the chicken in flour.

4. In a 10-inch ovenproof skillet or Dutch oven, heat 1 tablespoon of the olive oil over medium heat. Sauté the chicken pieces to a rich golden brown. Transfer to a plate and reserve.

5. Discard the fat from the skillet and add the remaining olive oil. Add the onions and garlic and cook over moderate heat for 25 minutes, stirring occasionally, until very soft and lightly browned. Season with the remaining salt and pepper. Remove from the heat.

6. Spread the thyme sprigs over the onions and garlic. Arrange the browned chicken pieces side by side over the onions in the skillet. Add the chicken stock.

7. Cut 1 lemon into 10 slices, removing the seeds, and place 1 slice atop each piece of chicken. Squeeze the other lemon into a strainer over the chicken. Return the skillet to the heat and bring the stock to a simmer. Cover and place in the oven.

8. After 15 minutes, baste the chicken with the cooking liquid. Continue cooking uncovered, for an additional 35 to 40 minutes, basting every 10 minutes. When done, the chicken and lemon slices will be nicely browned. Let rest 5 minutes, transfer to a deep-welled platter, and serve.

GRILLED MARINATED CHICKEN BREAST WITH YOGURT AND ASIAN SPICES

*Y*ogurt has long been used in eastern cookery as a tenderizer and flavor enhancer. Goat's milk yogurt, if available, adds a distinctive tanginess that works well with the spicy marinade. For chicken skin that's cooked through and crisp—without being burned—cover the breasts with an inverted baking pan while you grill the skin side. Serve with spinach, Red Lentil–Basmati Pilaf, and toasted pita bread.

SERVES 4

CHICKEN

*1 cup goat's milk yogurt, or whole-milk
    or low-fat plain yogurt*
1 tablespoon minced garlic
$1/2$ teaspoon ground cumin
$1/2$ teaspoon curry powder
$1/4$ teaspoon cayenne
$1/4$ teaspoon dry mustard
$1/8$ teaspoon celery seeds
$1/8$ teaspoon ground ginger
$1/8$ teaspoon ground cinnamon
$1/8$ teaspoon grated nutmeg
1 teaspoon kosher salt
2 boneless chicken breasts, split

SAUCE

2 tablespoons olive oil
$1/2$ tablespoon minced garlic
$1/2$ cup diced red onion
$1/2$ cup peeled and diced cucumber

Rich, ripe Sauvignon Blanc and Sémillon from Australia, New Zealand, and California pair nicely with this aromatic chicken recipe.

¹/₈ teaspoon curry powder
¹/₈ teaspoon ground cumin
¹/₈ teaspoon cayenne
2 cups cored and chopped tomatoes (1 pound)

1. In a nonreactive bowl, combine the yogurt with all the remaining ingredients except the chicken. Stir to blend well, add the chicken breasts, and marinate, covered and refrigerated, at least 3 hours, or overnight for richer flavor.

2. For the sauce, heat the olive oil in a medium saucepan over moderate heat. Sauté the garlic, onion, and cucumbers until softened, about 5 minutes. Stir in the curry, cumin, and cayenne. Add the tomatoes and simmer until juicy, about 10 minutes.

3. Preheat a broiler grill, grill pan, or outdoor grill.

4. Remove the chicken from the marinade and set aside. Add ¹/₂ cup of the marinade to the tomato sauce. Bring to a boil, lower the heat, and simmer 1 minute.

5. Purée the sauce in a blender or food processor. Strain through a sieve into a nonreactive saucepan and season with ¹/₂ teaspoon salt. Keep the sauce warm.

6. Cook the chicken breasts over a hot grill until cooked through but still juicy, about 5 minutes a side. Alternatively, cook the chicken breasts under a preheated broiler, 4 to 5 minutes a side.

7. Transfer the chicken breasts to a platter and serve with the warm sauce.

STUFFED CHICKEN BREASTS WITH HERBED GOAT CHEESE

*B*oneless chicken breasts lend themselves beautifully to stuffing, and we've enjoyed using this summery mixture of fresh goat cheese and herbs. This simple recipe works equally well on a barbecue pit, accompanied by ears of sweet corn. Our Peach-Fig Chutney is a must with the stuffed chicken breasts.

SERVES 4

4 ounces fresh, soft goat cheese ($^1/_2$ cup)
1 tablespoon each minced tarragon, basil, parsley,
*   and chives*
2 tablespoons extra-virgin olive oil
$^1/_4$ teaspoon kosher salt
Freshly ground black pepper
4 boneless chicken breasts, with a 3-inch-long pocket cut
*   into the thickest part—have your butcher do this for you*
1 tablespoon butter

Sancerre, in any of its guises—white, rosé, or red—would be a perfect match for the stuffed chicken.

1. In a bowl, thoroughly combine the goat cheese, herbs, 1 table-spoon olive oil, and half the salt and pepper.

2. Using your fingers or a small spoon, stuff a quarter of the filling into each breast. Close each pocket with a toothpick. Season the breasts with the remaining salt and pepper, cover, and refrigerate for 1 hour or up to a day ahead.

3. Heat the butter and remaining olive oil over medium-high heat in a 10-inch skillet. Place the stuffed chicken breast skin side down in the pan. Sauté 5 to 6 minutes, until golden brown. Using a spatula, turn over and cook an additional 3 to 5 minutes, or until the chicken is somewhat firm to the touch. Transfer the breasts to a warm platter, remove the toothpicks, and serve.

Roast Lemon-Pepper Duck with Red Wine Vinegar Sauce

*A*fter Fillet Mignon of Tuna, this is our most popular dish. The lemon-pepper mix is carefully stuffed between the skin and the meat before the duck is roasted, imbuing the bird with its tangy-spicy flavor. An advantage of this recipe is that you can serve perfectly cooked and crisped duck while avoiding last-minute struggles with carving. You can vary the recipe by substituting a different sauce based on the season. In spring try Rhubarb and Dried Cherry Chutney; in summer, Peach-Fig Chutney. Serve with Three-Grain Pilaf or Parsnip Pancakes.

SERVES 4 TO 6

2 ducks, with neck, giblets, and livers removed
2 tablespoons minced lemon zest
1 teaspoon minced fresh thyme leaves
1 teaspoon coarsely ground black pepper
1 teaspoon kosher salt
^{1}/$_3$ cup chopped bacon (1 ounce)
1 tablespoon chopped garlic
^{1}/$_2$ cup peeled and sliced shallots
1 sprig each thyme, rosemary, and sage
2 anchovy fillets (optional)
1 tablespoon all-purpose flour
^{1}/$_2$ cup red wine vinegar
2^1/$_2$ cups Veal Stock (page 314)
^{1}/$_4$ teaspoon kosher salt
^{1}/$_8$ teaspoon freshly ground black pepper

The tangy sauce and peppery flavor make youthful, spicy red wines ideal matches for the roast duck. Try Zinfandel, California Cabernets, and Côte Rôtie.

1. Preheat the oven to 425 degrees F.

2. Remove the neck, giblets, and livers from the inside cavity of the duck. Cut the wings at the first joint. Reserve the cut wing tips, livers, and giblets for the sauce.

3. Combine the lemon zest, thyme, pepper, and salt in a small bowl. Beginning at the tip of the breastbone and working back toward the legs and thighs, use your fingers to create a pocket between the meat and skin, gently separating the skin from the body of the duck. Tuck the lemon-pepper mixture evenly into the pocket, covering each breast, leg, and thigh. Tie the legs together with kitchen twine.

4. Heat a roasting pan with a rack in the oven for 10 minutes. Place the prepared ducks breast side up on the rack and cook for 1 hour and 10 minutes. Remove the ducks from the pan and bring to room temperature. The ducks can be roasted to this point up to 1 day ahead and held, covered and refrigerated.

5. To make the sauce, brown the bacon over medium heat in a 2-quart saucepan. Pour off all but 1 tablespoon of the bacon fat, leaving the bacon in the pan. Add the duck livers, wing tips, giblets, garlic, shallots, herbs, and anchovies and brown over moderate heat, 8 to 10 minutes. Sprinkle with the flour and cook, stirring, until golden brown. Deglaze the pan with the red wine vinegar, stirring to incorporate the flour into the liquid, and boil for 1 minute. Add the veal stock, lower the heat, and simmer, uncovered, 45 minutes to 1 hour. Strain the sauce in a colander, pressing the solids to extract the maximum amount of sauce. Season with salt and pepper and keep warm.

6. Preheat the oven to 450 degrees F.

7. Cut the duck breasts and legs from the carcasses. Trim off any excess fat around the breast and leg. Heat an ovenproof skillet over high heat and add the duck pieces skin side down. Cook over high heat until the skin begins to sizzle, about 1 minute. Lower the heat and gently crisp the duck skin for 5 to 7 minutes. Drain off any excess fat. Cover tightly with a lid or with aluminum foil and place in the oven. Cook for 10 minutes until the skin is crisp and the meat cooked through and moist. Transfer the duck to a warm platter and serve with the sauce.

RUSTIC DUCK STEW WITH RIGATONI

*A*n often overlooked stew ingredient, duck holds up well to long, slow cooking and it delivers plenty of robust flavor. As with most stews, this one improves over time and can be made a day in advance.
SERVES 10

3 5-pound ducks, each cut into 8 pieces
Kosher salt
Freshly ground black pepper
4 fresh thyme sprigs
3 bay leaves
$1/2$ pound pancetta, cut into $1 \times 1/4$-inch pieces
3 large onions, peeled and coarsely chopped (6 cups)
1 head garlic, cloves peeled and minced
1 2-ounce jar or can of anchovy fillets, drained and
minced (optional)
1 pound carrots, peeled and cut into $1/4$-inch slices (3 cups)
$1/3$ cup all-purpose flour
2 cups white wine
1 cup pitted and coarsely chopped niçoise or gaeta
black olives
1 teaspoon cayenne
$1/4$ cup balsamic vinegar
1 16-ounce can peeled tomatoes, drained and crushed
6 cups Chicken or Veal Stock (page 312 or 314)
1 tablespoon kosher salt
2 pounds rigatoni or wide-mouthed maccheroni
1 cup grated Parmigiano-Reggiano

This is an ideal dish for the hearty wines of southern France. Châteauneuf-du-Pape, Hermitage, and Bandol are big enough to handle the richly flavored duck meat, black olives, herbs, and spices.

1.   Thirty minutes before cooking, sprinkle the duck pieces with salt and pepper on both sides. Tie the thyme sprigs and bay leaves together with a piece of kitchen string.

2. Heat a large, heavy Dutch oven or saucepan over medium heat. Add the pancetta and cook, stirring occasionally, until golden brown. Remove with a slotted spoon and set aside to drain.

3. In the same pot, brown the duck pieces on both sides over high heat, a few pieces at a time. Transfer each batch to drain in a colander. Pour out all but $^1/_4$ cup duck fat and reduce the heat to medium.

4. Add the onions and garlic to the pot and cook, stirring, until translucent. Stir in the anchovies and carrots and cook for 2 to 3 minutes. Add the flour and cook for 3 to 4 minutes, stirring until the flour absorbs the duck fat. Stir in the wine and olives and increase the heat to medium-high.

5. Return the duck pieces to the pot. Add the crisp pancetta, thyme and bay leaf, cayenne, balsamic vinegar, tomatoes, and stock. Stir well and bring to a boil. Reduce the heat to a low simmer, cover, and cook for 45 minutes. Remove the lid and continue cooking an additional 30 minutes, stirring occasionally, until the duck is fork tender. Remove from the heat and skim as much duck fat as possible from the top of the pot, using a bulb-baster or ladle. Remove the thyme and bay leaves and discard. Adjust the seasoning, return the pot to low heat, and keep warm. If made a day in advance, you can eliminate skimming the fat. Transfer the stew to a large bowl, bring to room temperature, cover tightly, and refrigerate. The fat will rise to the top and harden, making it easy to remove before you reheat.

6. In a large pot, bring 1 gallon of water to a rolling boil and add 1 tablespoon salt. Add the pasta and cook until al dente. Drain and pour into a warm serving bowl. Immediately toss with the Parmigiano. Transfer the duck to a warm, deep-welled platter. Serve the duck and its sauce with the pasta.

SEARED FILET MIGNON WITH TOMATO-ANCHOVY SAUCE

*T*hough beef and fish may seem like an odd couple, anchovy adds a subtle tanginess and body to this simple sauce. Avoid using a non-stick skillet when searing the steaks—the tasty bits left in the pan will add a wonderful flavor to the tomato-anchovy sauce when absorbed into the vinegar.

SERVES 4

> 4 6-ounce filets of beef
> 1 teaspoon kosher salt
> $1/4$ teaspoon freshly ground black pepper
> 3 tablespoons extra-virgin olive oil
> 3 tablespoons minced shallots
> 1 teaspoon minced garlic
> 2 tablespoons minced anchovy fillets
> 3 cups peeled, seeded, and diced tomatoes
>   (3 to 4 tomatoes)
> 2 tablespoons Italian red wine vinegar
> 2 tablespoons minced parsley

Select a young, racy red wine from Châteauneuf-du-Pape, Bandol, or Italy's Friuli-Venezia-Giulia to complement the filet's zesty sauce.

1. Season the beef with half the salt and pepper. Heat the olive oil in a 10-inch skillet over medium-high heat. Sear the filets until browned and medium-rare, about 5 minutes a side. Remove from the pan and set aside on a warm serving plate.

2. Add the shallots and garlic to the pan and cook over medium heat until softened, about 1 minute. Stir in the minced anchovy with a wooden spoon. Raise the heat to high, add the tomatoes, and cook 4 to 5 minutes until somewhat thickened. Add the vinegar and cook an additional 1 to 2 minutes. Sprinkle with the parsley and season with the remaining salt and pepper. Spoon the sauce over the filets and serve.

SEARED RIB STEAK WITH ROSEMARY AND ARUGULA

Inspired by *tagliata* (literally "cut" or "carved")—the well-loved specialty of Milan's trattorias—this is a succulent way to enjoy "roast beef" for two. As the Italian name signifies, the trick here is to thinly slice the steak before drizzling with the aromatic infused oil. The arugula, wilted under the heat of the steak, does double-duty as both a salad and vegetable accompaniment. Serve with Basil Mashed Potatoes.
SERVES 2

> *1/2 cup plus 1 tablespoon extra-virgin olive oil*
> *2 tablespoons coarsely chopped fresh rosemary*
> *2 tablespoons balsamic vinegar*
> *1/2 teaspoon kosher salt*
> *1/4 teaspoon freshly ground black pepper*
> *1 1-pound boneless beef rib-eye steak, trimmed of excess fat*
> *1/4 pound arugula, stemmed, washed, and dried*
> *1 lemon, quartered lengthwise*

Serve with a Cabernet Franc, either from northern Italy, California, or France's Loire Valley.

1. In a small saucepan, combine 1/2 cup olive oil with the rosemary. Bring to a simmer over low heat and remove from the heat. Let rest 10 minutes. Strain through a sieve, reserving both the infused oil and the chopped rosemary.

2. In a small jar, combine the balsamic vinegar with the reserved rosemary oil and half the salt and pepper. Cover tightly and shake vigorously. Set aside.

3. Preheat the oven to 400 degrees F.

4. Season the rib steak with the remaining salt and pepper. Heat 1 tablespoon olive oil in a medium ovenproof skillet over high heat. Sear the steak 2 to 3 minutes. Turn the steak over and place the pan in the oven. Cook for an additional 5 to 7 minutes for rare to medium-rare. Transfer the steak to a cutting board and let rest 4 to 5 minutes.

5. Arrange the arugula on a serving platter. With a long sharp knife, cut the steak on the bias into thin slices. Arrange the slices atop the arugula, drizzle with the reserved rosemary oil, and sprinkle with the reserved chopped rosemary. Serve with the lemon quarters.

Roast Breast of Veal with Spinach, Mushroom, and Rice Stuffing

*H*ere's a hearty and comforting roast to satisfy a group of hungry friends. The breast is one of the least expensive yet most flavorful cuts of veal. Long, slow roasting will assure the fall-off-the-bone tenderness that makes this dish so appealing. A green salad is about the only accompaniment you'll need for the hearty stuffed veal breast. The breast of veal can also be served cold the next day, sliced very thin.

SERVES 6 TO 8

3 tablespoons butter

³/4 cup minced onion

¹/2 cup arborio rice

1 cup Chicken Stock (page 312)

1 pound fresh spinach, stemmed, washed, and sautéed (page 243)

¹/2 pound white mushrooms, cleaned, stems trimmed, and thinly sliced

1¹/2 cups scrubbed and shredded carrots

1 pound ground veal

¹/4 cup grated Parmigiano-Reggiano

1 teaspoon kosher salt

¹/4 teaspoon freshly ground black pepper

1 6-pound veal breast, bone-in, cut with a pocket

2 tablespoons olive oil

1 carrot, scrubbed and coarsely chopped

1 celery rib, washed and coarsely chopped

1 whole head of garlic, quartered

1 small onion, peeled and sliced

Cabernet Sauvignon and Merlot from Italy's Lombardy or Veneto regions go beautifully with the roast.

2 quarts Veal Stock (page 314)
1½ cups white wine

1.   In a 3-quart saucepan, melt 1½ tablespoons of the butter over medium heat. Add the minced onions and cook until translucent, about 10 minutes. Toss in the rice and stir to coat the grains well. Add the chicken stock, bring to a boil, and simmer, covered, until the rice is very tender, about 18 minutes. While the rice is still warm, transfer to a food processor and purée until completely smooth. Set aside to cool.

2.   Drain the cooked spinach well, coarsely chop, and reserve.

3.   Heat the remaining butter in a large skillet over high heat. Sauté the mushrooms and shredded carrots until tender, about 5 minutes. Set aside in a colander to drain and cool.

4.   In a large bowl (or in an electric mixer fitted with a paddle), combine the puréed rice, spinach, mushrooms, carrots, ground veal, and Parmigiano and mix thoroughly. Season with ¾ teaspoon of the salt and ⅛ teaspoon of the pepper.

5.   Fill the pocket in the veal breast with the stuffing. Close off the open end with two trussing needles, one inserted horizontally through the top flap of the opening, the other, parallel, through the bottom flap. Lace the two needles with kitchen thread, and tie the ends together to close the opening.

6.   Preheat the oven to 450 degrees F.

7.   Place half the olive oil with the chopped carrots, celery, garlic, and onions in a large roasting pan. Brush the stuffed veal breast with the remaining oil and season with ¼ teaspoon salt and ⅛ teaspoon pepper. Place the breast of veal, bone side down, atop the vegetables and roast until browned, about 45 minutes.

8.   Bring the veal stock and the wine to a boil in the saucepan. Turn the oven down to 350 degrees and add the wine and stock to the roasting pan. Cover the breast of veal with aluminum foil and continue cooking for 3 hours.

(continued)

9. Uncover the veal and cook an additional 45 minutes, thoroughly basting every 10 minutes.

10. Carefully remove the breast from the pan and allow to rest on a cutting board for 20 to 30 minutes before carving. Strain the braising liquids and reduce by half in the saucepan. Season with additional salt and pepper to taste, if necessary. Reserve and keep warm.

11. To serve, remove the trussing needles and string and turn the breast bone side up. Using your hands, gently pry the rib bones free from the meat and discard. Turn the breast over again and, using a heavy kitchen knife, cut into 1-inch-thick slices. Transfer the slices to a warm serving platter and serve with the reduced cooking juices.

Grilled Veal Lombatina

In Rome, most trattorias offer this simple preparation that uses fruity olive oil, lemon, and balsamic vinegar to highlight the flavor of the veal. A tasty alternative to grilling the chops is to sear them in a red-hot skillet, weighted down with another heavy pan. You'll get a nice brown crust on each side and the chops will stay extra juicy. As a complementary side dish for the veal lombatina, try the Baked Eggplant, Zucchini, and Parmigiano Tortino, Sautéed Spinach, or Fagioli alla Toscana.

SERVES 4

Look for a juicy red wine with lots of fruit to accompany the chops. We'd recommend Rosso di Montalcino, Morellino di Scansano, and Barbera d'Alba.

4 14-ounce veal loin chops, 2 inches thick
4 tablespoons extra-virgin olive oil
$1/2$ teaspoon kosher salt
$1/4$ teaspoon freshly ground black pepper
$2^1/4$ teaspoons balsamic vinegar
2 tablespoons coarsely chopped parsley
2 lemons, halved and seeded

1. Preheat a grill, grill pan, broiler, or outdoor barbecue to very hot.

2. Rub the veal chops with 1 tablespoon of the oil. Season with half the salt and pepper.

3. Place the remaining salt, pepper, olive oil, and balsamic vinegar in a jar. Cover tightly and shake well to combine.

4. Grill the chops 10 minutes a side and transfer to a warm serving platter. Drizzle with the olive oil and balsamic mixture, sprinkle with the parsley, and serve with the lemon halves.

Roast Leg of Veal with Shiitake Mushroom and Goat Cheese Sauce

*T*his is an elegant roast that's also a cinch to prepare. You may want to save this for special occasions since it's an expensive cut—the same one from which veal scaloppine are sliced. Wonderful served with buttered fettuccine, the dish is also complemented by spinach, Hashed Brussels Sprouts, or Mashed Potatoes.

SERVES 6 TO 8

1 3-pound top round veal roast, at room temperature
1 teaspoon kosher salt
$1/2$ teaspoon freshly ground black pepper
2 tablespoons olive oil
4 tablespoons butter
1 pound shiitake mushrooms, stems removed and
   reserved, caps sliced
1 cup sliced shallots
3 tablespoons sliced garlic
$1/2$ cup coarsely chopped parsley
3 fresh thyme sprigs
6 to 8 whole black peppercorns
$1/2$ bay leaf
1 cup white wine
$3^1/2$ cups Veal Stock (page 314)
5 ounces fresh soft goat cheese, at room temperature

Pouilly Fumé and Vouvray are ideal white wine mates for the goat cheese and mushroom sauce, and you'd do equally well with a Loire Valley Cabernet Franc like Chinon or Saumur-Champigny.

1. Preheat the oven to 350 degrees F.

2. Season the roast with $1/2$ teaspoon salt and $1/4$ teaspoon pepper. Heat the olive oil and 1 tablespoon butter in a 3-quart ovenproof

skillet or Dutch oven over medium-high heat. Sear the roast on all sides until golden brown. Transfer to a plate and reserve.

3. Pour the fat from the pan. Add 2 tablespoons butter to the pan and sauté the sliced shiitake mushrooms until softened and light brown, about 4 minutes. Season the mushrooms with $1/4$ teaspoon salt and $1/8$ teaspoon black pepper and remove from the pan. Reserve.

4. Add the remaining tablespoon butter to the pan and stir in the shallots, garlic, parsley, thyme, peppercorns, bay leaf, and shiitake stems. Sauté until wilted, about 3 minutes.

5. Return the roast and its juices to the pan, add the white wine, and bring to a boil. Add the veal stock, return to a boil, and place the pan in the oven.

6. Roast the veal, uncovered, for 1 hour, or until a meat thermometer inserted into the roast reaches 125 degrees. Transfer the roast to a plate and keep warm while you make the sauce.

7. Strain the cooking liquid into a saucepan and boil over high heat to reduce by a third. Whisk in the goat cheese to thicken and add the remaining salt and pepper. Add the reserved shiitake mushrooms to the sauce, return to a boil, and remove from the heat.

8. Slice the veal and arrange on a warm platter. Ladle the hot sauce over the slices and serve.

ORANGE-FENNEL OSSO BUCO

Satisfying for cooler months, osso buco is a succulent dish whose richness is offset by the refreshing combination of orange, fennel, and sherry wine vinegar. Make sure to have tiny spoons on hand to scoop out the marrow from the veal shanks. Serve with mashed turnips and precede with Red Oakleaf and Bibb Salad with Gruyère.

SERVES 4

4 osso buco (approximately 1 pound each)
1 teaspoon kosher salt
$1/2$ teaspoon freshly ground black pepper
Flour for dredging
3 tablespoons olive oil
$1/2$ cup sherry vinegar
3 cups Veal Stock (page 314)
3 medium fennel bulbs, trimmed to stalk
3 cups peeled sliced carrots
1 cup fresh orange juice
1 orange, peeled and cut into segments

A soft, grapey Merlot, whether from California, Bordeaux, or Long Island, would be suitable with the osso buco.

1. Preheat the oven to 375 degrees F.

2. Season the osso buco with $1/2$ teaspoon salt and $1/4$ teaspoon pepper and dredge them in flour.

3. Heat the olive oil in a 12-inch skillet or Dutch oven over medium-high heat. Brown the osso buco on all sides, 15 to 20 minutes. Transfer the osso buco to a platter and reserve.

4. Pour all the fat from the pan. Add the vinegar and, with a wooden spoon, scrape up any browned bits adhering to the pan. Cook over high heat until the vinegar is reduced by half. Add the veal stock to the pan and bring to a simmer. Season with the remaining salt and pepper.

4. Return the osso buco to the pan. Cover and braise in the oven for 1 hour.

5. Split the fennel in half lengthwise, leaving the core intact. Slice each half lengthwise into $1/2$-inch pieces.

6. Uncover the osso buco and add the fennel, carrots, and orange juice. Raise the oven temperature to 400 degrees and cook uncovered an additional 45 to 50 minutes, basting occasionally. The meat should be fork-tender and the vegetables completely cooked.

7. Remove the pan from the oven. Transfer the osso buco to a serving platter and keep warm. Skim the fat from the cooking liquid with a bulb baster or ladle and cook over high heat to thicken slightly, 4 to 5 minutes. Stir in the orange segments, ladle the sauce and vegetables over the meat, and serve.

BRAISED OXTAILS WITH RED WINE AND ONIONS

*O*ne of the most flavorful and underrated cuts of beef, oxtails are a wonderful dinner choice for cool weather entertaining. Serve with Mashed Potatoes or turnips and steamed red Swiss chard—and don't forget the finger bowls!

SERVES 6

6 pounds oxtails, cut 1 1/2 inches thick
6 cups red wine
1/2 cup red wine vinegar
3 cups cipollini onions or pearl onions, peeled
1 1/2 cups sliced celery
2 cups sliced carrots
1 teaspoon juniper berries
1/2 teaspoon black peppercorns
5 parsley sprigs
4 teaspoons kosher salt
Freshly ground black pepper
1/3 cup flour
1/4 cup olive oil
1/3 cup tomato paste
2 tablespoons coarsely chopped parsley

Tannic red wines cut through the richness of the oxtails. Well-structured Châteauneuf-du-Pape, Bordeaux, and Napa Valley Cabernet Sauvignons are particularly good choices.

1. Trim the oxtails of excess fat and place in a large nonreactive bowl. Add the wine, vinegar, cipollini onions, celery, carrots, juniper berries, peppercorns, and parsley. Marinate, covered, in the refrigerator overnight.

2. Preheat the oven to 375 degrees F.

3.   Drain the oxtails, reserving the liquid and vegetables. Dry them on paper towels, season with salt and pepper, and dredge in the flour.

4.   Heat the olive oil in a large Dutch oven over medium heat and brown the oxtails on all sides, 10 to 15 minutes. Do this in several batches if necessary. Remove the oxtails from the pan. Add the vegetables and brown, stirring occasionally, for 10 minutes. Transfer the browned vegetables to a bowl and reserve.

5.   Return the oxtails to the pan with the marinade, juniper berries, peppercorns, and 2 cups water. Stir in the tomato paste until dissolved. Cover and bake for 2 hours.

6.   Add the reserved vegetables to the pot, stir, cover, and return to the oven for 1 additional hour, until tender.

7.   Allow the pot to cool for 10 to 15 minutes. Uncover, tilt the pot slightly, and skim as much fat as possible using a bulb baster or ladle. Return to a simmer over low heat, adjust the seasoning, and serve sprinkled with the chopped parsley.

Roast Peppered Rack of Venison with Dried Cherry and Pearl Onion Sauce

*R*ack of venison provides an unexpected and delicious touch of elegance to a dinner for special friends. The venison is cooked medium rare, as you would rack of lamb, and is crusted with a piquant layer of Dijon mustard and crushed black peppercorns. Pearl onions and sun-dried cherries add a sweet and sour balance to the sauce. For the best result, ask your butcher to remove the rib flap and trim the meat of all sinew and fat so that it is completely exposed. The chopped trimmings will add depth to your sauce. Serve with Parsnip Pancakes, Mashed Yellow Turnips, or Hashed Brussels Sprouts.

SERVES 4

1 tablespoon butter

$^1/_2$ pound pearl onions, peeled (2$^1/_2$ cups)

1 teaspoon plus a pinch of kosher salt

$^1/_2$ cup dried cherries (available at specialty or health food stores)

1$^1/_2$ cups red wine

2 tablespoons olive oil

1 8- or 9-rib rack of venison (about 3 pounds), top flap, sinew, and fat trimmed from the meat, chopped, and reserved for the sauce

$^1/_3$ cup peeled and sliced shallots

1 bay leaf

1 teaspoon juniper berries

3 parsley sprigs

$^1/_2$ cup brandy or Cognac

4 cups Veal Stock (page 314)

The pepper and cherry flavors make Zinfandel, Châteauneuf-du-Pape, and Australian Shiraz excellent matches for the venison.

¹/₈ teaspoon freshly ground black pepper
1 teaspoon Dijon mustard
1 tablespoon coarsely crushed black peppercorns

1. In a small saucepan, melt the butter over medium heat. Add the pearl onions, 1 cup water, and a pinch of salt. Cook until tender, about 10 minutes. Drain and set aside.

2. In the same saucepan, combine the dried cherries and red wine. Bring to a boil over medium-high heat, then immediately set the saucepan aside to cool.

3. In a medium saucepan, heat 1 tablespoon olive oil almost to the smoking point. Sear the reserved meat trimmings over high heat, until well browned, about 5 minutes. Add the shallots, bay leaf, juniper berries, and parsley. Cook 1 minute, stirring with a wooden spoon. Set aside.

4. Reserving the cherries, strain the red wine and add to the pan. Pour in the brandy. Return the saucepan to high heat and reduce the brandy-red wine mixture to a syrup, scraping up any browned bits that may have formed on the bottom of the pan. If the brandy flames, cover to extinguish or simply allow to burn away.

5. Add the veal stock and simmer, uncovered, over medium heat until reduced by half. Strain the sauce, return to the saucepan, and add the plumped cherries and cooked onions. Cook an additional 3 to 5 minutes, season with $3/4$ teaspoon salt and $1/8$ teaspoon freshly ground black pepper. Set aside.

6. Preheat the oven to 500 degrees F. Heat a roasting pan in the oven for 10 minutes and then add the remaining olive oil.

7. Season the venison with $1/4$ teaspoon salt. Place the rack in the pan, meat side down, and roast for 10 minutes. Turn the rack to its other side and roast for an additional 5 minutes, until medium-rare. Remove the venison from the oven and let rest at room temperature for 15 minutes.

(continued)

8. Preheat the broiler. Brush the entire surface of the meat evenly with the mustard and then sprinkle with the crushed peppercorns to cover. Place the rack under the broiler until the mustard-pepper crust is set, 4 to 5 minutes.

9. Return the sauce to a simmer. Cut the rack into individual chops, transfer to a warm platter, and serve with the hot sauce.

GRILLED LAMB CHOPS "SCOTTA DITA"

*T*his is Union Square Cafe's version of lamb chops *alla scotta dita* ("burn the finger")—a classic trattoria specialty in Rome—so named because the lamb bones are picked up from the hot grill with bare fingers and eaten immediately. Ask your butcher for chops with the bones left 3 to 4 inches long. We serve a Sautéed Insalata Tricolore with the chops, and they'd be equally at home with Charred Tomatoes, Onions, and Mint, Basil Mashed Potatoes, or Fagioli alla Toscana.

SERVES 4

Côtes-du-Rhône, Rioja, and Zinfandel are three good red wine choices for the chops.

3 tablespoons Dijon mustard
2 teaspoons minced garlic
2 tablespoons balsamic vinegar
$1/2$ teaspoon kosher salt
$1/8$ teaspoon freshly ground black pepper
$1/2$ cup extra-virgin olive oil
$1/4$ cup julienned basil
12 $1^1/2$-inch-thick rib lamb chops, trimmed of excess fat

1.   In a nonreactive bowl, combine the Dijon mustard, garlic, vinegar, salt, and pepper with 2 teaspoons water. Slowly whisk in the olive oil to form a creamy marinade. Stir in the cut basil.

2.   Add the chops to the marinade and toss to coat evenly. Marinate the chops for 1 to 3 hours, covered and refrigerated.

3.   Preheat a grill, grill pan, or barbecue to very hot. Shake the excess marinade from the chops and grill 4 to 5 minutes a side for medium-rare, or slightly longer for more well done. Transfer to a warm platter and serve.

BRAISED LAMB SHANKS WITH GARLIC AND HERBS

*F*or meat and red wine lovers, these herbed lamb shanks are a superb main course choice. They're also one of the thriftiest cuts of lamb, and not at all difficult to make. The long, slow cooking ensures fork-tender, fall-from-the-bone lamb, delicious with Mashed Yellow Turnips, Baked Eggplant, Zucchini, and Parmigiano Tortino, or Fagioli all'Uccelletto.

SERVES 4

6 garlic cloves
4 lamb shanks
2 teaspoons kosher salt
$1/2$ teaspoon freshly ground black pepper
2 tablespoons flour
2 tablespoons olive oil
$1^1/2$ cups sliced onions
2 tablespoons chopped fresh rosemary
3 tablespoons chopped fresh mint
1 tablespoon fresh thyme leaves
1 tablespoon chopped parsley
1 cup white wine
3 cups Veal Stock (page 314)

1. Preheat the oven to 325 degrees F.

2. Cut one of the garlic cloves in half and rub the lamb shanks with the halves. Cut the remaining cloves into thin slices and set aside. Season the shanks with 1 teaspoon salt and $1/4$ teaspoon freshly ground pepper and dredge in the flour.

Lamb shanks are a wonderfully versatile flavor mate for most big red wines. We love pairing them with Bordeaux and northern Rhone Valley reds like Hermitage, Côte-Rôtie, and St. Joseph.

3. Heat the olive oil over medium heat in a Dutch oven or large ovenproof skillet. Add the lamb shanks and brown on all sides. Remove the shanks from the pan and set aside.

4. Toss in the onions and sliced garlic and cook 3 to 5 minutes, until softened. Add the rosemary, mint, thyme, and parsley and cook an additional 3 to 4 minutes.

5. Add the wine to the pan, raise the heat to high, and reduce by half. Stir in the veal stock, season with the remaining salt and pepper, and bring to a simmer. Place the lamb shanks in the pan, cover, and bake for 2 hours, until the meat is fork-tender.

6. Uncover the pan and turn the oven up to 500 degrees. Let the lamb shanks brown in the oven for 20 minutes, basting the meat thoroughly with the pan gravy every 5 minutes.

7. Remove the shanks from the pan and keep them covered and warm. Strain the pan gravy into a bowl and, using a bulb baster or ladle, skim as much fat as possible from the surface. Return the gravy to the Dutch oven and reduce by half over high heat. Transfer the lamb shanks to a warm serving platter. Spoon part of the gravy over the shanks and serve the rest in a sauceboat on the side.

ROAST STUFFED LEG OF LAMB

*M*ichael's inspiration for this roast is *braciole*—the southern Italian favorite in which beef or pork is stuffed and braised with raisins, pine nuts, and bread crumbs. This is a fun and relatively easy dish to prepare, and one that requires little of your attention once you've stuffed the lamb. Ideal accompaniments are Artichoke and Potato Ragout, Fagioli all'Uccelletto, or Roast Tomato Mashed Potatoes.

SERVES 6 TO 8

1/2 cup golden raisins
2 teaspoons grated lemon zest
1/4 cup mixed chopped fresh herbs (choose at least 3 from
*   parsley, thyme, chives, mint, or oregano)*
1 teaspoon kosher salt
5/8 teaspoon coarsely ground black pepper
1 tablespoon minced garlic
1/4 cup bread crumbs
1 teaspoon balsamic vinegar
2 tablespoons plus 1 teaspoon extra-virgin olive oil
1 5- to 6-pound leg of lamb, butterflied by butcher

1. Place the raisins in a small saucepan with 1/3 cup water. Bring to a boil and remove from the heat. Set aside to plump for 5 minutes. Drain the raisins and chop coarsely.

2. In a bowl, combine the raisins, lemon zest, herbs, 1/4 teaspoon salt, 1/2 teaspoon pepper, garlic, bread crumbs, balsamic vinegar, and 2 tablespoons olive oil. Stir with a wooden spoon to mix thoroughly.

3. Spread open the lamb and distribute the herb mixture evenly over the inside surface. Close the lamb by rolling one end to meet the other. Tie securely with kitchen string in several places. If any of the herb mixture falls out while rolling the lamb, use your fingers to

In Italy's Veneto region, grapes are dried almost to the raisin stage before being turned into wine. A top-flight Valpolicella Classico, Amarone, or Cabernet Franc from that region would be a wonderful complement to the stuffed lamb.

stuff it back into any opening. Refrigerate for at least 4 hours or overnight.

4.   Remove the lamb from the refrigerator and bring to room temperature. Preheat the oven to 450 degrees F.

5.   Rub the lamb with 1 teaspoon olive oil and season with the remaining salt and pepper. Roast the lamb on a rack over a roasting pan. The lamb should cook 12 to 15 minutes per pound for rare to medium rare. Or use a meat thermometer to determine doneness: 125 degrees for very rare, 130 degrees for medium-rare, 140 degrees for medium, and 160 degrees for well done.

6.   Remove the lamb from the oven and let rest for 20 minutes. Remove the strings and slice on a grooved platter to collect the natural juices. Serve.

VEGETABLE AND GOAT CHEESE LASAGNE AL FORNO

*T*his crowd-pleasing vegetarian dish alternates layers of pasta with cooked vegetables, savory vegetable-tomato sauce, and cheese. It takes time and patience to assemble, but the lasagne works well for entertaining since you can bake it a day in advance. If preparing ahead, leave off browning with the Parmigiano until ready to serve. Accompany with Sautéed Broccoli Rabe and crusty whole wheat bread.

SERVES 6

LASAGNE

> 1 medium eggplant (1 1/4 pounds), peeled and sliced
>   into 1/8-inch rounds
> 2 tablespoons kosher salt
> 5/8 cup extra-virgin olive oil
> 3/8 teaspoon freshly ground pepper
> 1 medium zucchini, sliced into 1/8-inch-thick rounds
>   (2 cups)
> 3/8 teaspoon freshly ground black pepper
> 1 medium yellow squash (1/2 pound), sliced into
>   1/8-inch thick rounds
> 1 1/4 pounds fresh, soft goat cheese, at room temperature
> 3 large eggs
> 2 teaspoons minced garlic
> 1/2 cup chopped basil
> 1/4 pound dried lasagne noodles (9 3 × 7-inch sheets)
> 1 1/2 cups drained Oven-Dried Tomatoes (page 318)
> 1/4 cup finely grated Parmigiano-Reggiano

The lasagne is equally good with white and red wines, as long as they have plenty of fruit and acidity. For white, try an assertive Sauvignon Blanc or Pinot Bianco, and for red, pick a young Chianti Classico, Zinfandel or Côtes-du-Rhône.

TOMATO SAUCE

3 tablespoons extra-virgin olive oil

1 cup sliced onion

2 teaspoons minced garlic

1 cup sliced red bell pepper

1 1/2 cups thinly sliced zucchini

Pinch of dried red pepper flakes

1 cup halved canned plum tomatoes

4 medium-size ripe tomatoes (2 pounds),
* cored and coarsely chopped*

1 tablespoon chopped basil

1 1/2 teaspoons kosher salt

1/8 teaspoon freshly ground black pepper

1. Place the slices of eggplant in a colander and sprinkle both sides of each slice with 1 1/2 teaspoons salt. Fit a smooth-bottomed bowl into the colander; its weight will press the eggplant to remove the moisture and bitterness. After a minimum of 30 minutes, rinse the eggplant under cold water to remove the salt and pat dry between two layers of paper towel. Reserve.

2. To make the tomato sauce, heat the olive oil in a 3-quart saucepan over medium heat. Add the onion, garlic, red pepper, zucchini, and red pepper flakes. Cook, stirring occasionally, for 25 minutes, taking care not to let the vegetables brown.

3. Add the canned and fresh tomatoes with their juices, the basil, salt, and pepper to the saucepan. Bring to a boil, lower the heat, and simmer for 1 1/2 hours, stirring occasionally. Allow to cool slightly, then purée the sauce in a blender or food processor. Strain the sauce to remove the tomato seeds and skin and reserve.

4. Preheat the oven to 375 degrees F.

5. Place the eggplant slices on a baking sheet in a single layer, drizzle with 2 tablespoons olive oil, and sprinkle evenly with pepper. Cover with foil and bake 20 minutes until the eggplant is soft. Transfer to a plate and reserve.

(continued)

6. Toss the zucchini with 1 tablespoon olive oil, $^1/_2$ teaspoon salt, and $^1/_8$ teaspoon pepper and spread out on a baking sheet. Bake uncovered for 10 minutes. Transfer to a plate and set aside. Repeat with the yellow squash. (If you have three baking sheets, the eggplant, zucchini, and yellow squash can be cooked simultaneously.)

7. In a large bowl, combine the goat cheese, eggs, garlic, $^1/_4$ cup olive oil, $^1/_2$ teaspoon salt, and $^1/_8$ teaspoon pepper. Mix thoroughly until smooth with an electric mixer or by hand with a wooden spatula. Stir in the basil and set aside.

8. Bring 1 gallon of water to a boil and add 1 tablespoon salt. Cook the pasta until al dente. Drain in a colander and refresh with cold water. Transfer the pasta to a baking sheet, brushing each sheet lightly with olive oil to prevent sticking.

9. To assemble the lasagne, lightly brush a $9 \times 9 \times 2$-inch baking pan with olive oil. Cover the bottom of the pan with a layer of pasta. Spread enough tomato sauce, about $^2/_3$ cup, to cover the pasta. Arrange a layer of the eggplant atop the sauce and repeat with a layer of zucchini. With a rubber spatula, spread half the goat cheese mixture over the vegetables. Place half the oven-dried tomatoes on the cheese. Beginning with a layer of pasta, repeat all the above steps, this time using the yellow squash in place of the zucchini. Finish with a layer of pasta and $^2/_3$ cup tomato sauce. Reserve the remaining sauce.

10. Lower the oven to 350 degrees. Top the lasagne with the grated Parmigiano, cover with foil, and bake 1 hour and 15 minutes. Uncover and continue to bake until the cheese browns, 15 to 20 minutes. Heat the remaining sauce and serve with the lasagne, cut into squares.

ROMAN ROAST PORK LOIN
ARISTA DI MAIALE

*D*anny thought it an endearing gesture when the owner of his favorite Roman trattoria called him "Maiallino." Having followed in his father's footsteps as a regular diner at that trattoria, Danny interpreted the nickname as meaning "little Meyer." It was only after ordering the restaurant's spectacular roast loin of baby pork for the fifth time in as many visits that Danny finally learned what he was really being called: "little pig." Since American pork is far leaner than its Italian counterpart, it is essential to cook this roast slowly and tightly covered so that it ends up moist and fork-tender. Serve the pork with Roast Tomato Mashed Potatoes, Sautéed Spinach, or Fagioli alla Toscana.

SERVES 4

1 8-rib pork loin roast (ask your butcher to notch the
*   chine every 2 bones)*
2 teaspoons kosher salt
1/4 teaspoon freshly ground black pepper
3 tablespoons coarsely chopped fresh rosemary leaves
2 tablespoons sliced garlic
2 tablespoons olive oil
2 cups sliced onions
1 cup white wine
3 cups Veal Stock (page 314)

1. Preheat the oven to 325 degrees F.

2. Season the pork loin with half the salt and pepper. In a small bowl, combine 1 tablespoon of the rosemary and a quarter of the garlic slices. Insert the mixture into the notches between the bones.

This is a hearty, richly flavored roast that will give you a chance to pull a big, tannic red from your cellar. Try it with Barolo, Barbaresco, or Brunello di Montalcino.

3. In a Dutch oven or ovenproof skillet, heat the olive oil over medium-high heat. Sear the pork loin on all sides until golden brown, about 10 minutes. Transfer to a plate.

4. Add the remaining garlic and rosemary to the pan and cook over a medium flame until softened but not browned, about 1 minute. Stir in the onions and cook 3 to 4 minutes. Pour in the white wine and reduce until syrupy. Add the veal stock and remaining salt and pepper and bring to a simmer.

5. Place the pork loin in the pan with the bones facing up. Cover tightly and cook for 1 hour.

6. Remove the cover and turn the roast over. Increase the oven temperature to 500 degrees and cook an additional 25 to 30 minutes, to brown the pork.

7. Remove the roast from the pan and set aside, covered, in a warm spot. Over high heat, reduce the pan juices by half. Transfer the roast to a cutting board and, using the notches as a guide, carve into 4 double chops. Serve with the sauce.

SEARED CALF'S LIVER WITH SPROUTED MUSTARD SEEDS

Sprouting your own mustard seeds adds an element of adventure to this delicious French-inspired calf's liver recipe. Begin sprouting at least 3 days in advance of preparing the liver. Serve with Hashed Brussels Sprouts and Mashed Potatoes.

SERVES 4

$^1/_4$ cup mustard seeds, sprouted 3 days in advance (see below)

2 tablespoons flour

$^3/_4$ teaspoon kosher salt

$^1/_8$ teaspoon freshly ground black pepper

4 4-ounce slices calf's liver

1 tablespoon olive oil

2 tablespoons butter

$^1/_4$ cup minced shallots

$^1/_2$ teaspoon paprika

$^1/_2$ cup white wine

1 cup Veal Stock (page 314)

2 tablespoons Dijon mustard

This versatile dish does equally well with white or red wine. For white, try a Chardonnay from France's Maconnais region or a young Bordeaux blanc. A lightly chilled Beaujolais is a superb choice for a red.

1. To sprout the mustard seeds: Three days before preparing the recipe, moisten a 14-inch piece of cheesecloth with water, wring it out, and spread it over a rack set on a baking sheet. Sprinkle the mustard seeds onto the damp cheesecloth in a single layer. Moisten the seeds evenly with several drops of water and set aside to sprout at room temperature. The seeds should start to sprout within 1 day. Dampen the sprouts with water 1 or 2 times a day so they do not dry out. After 3 days, the sprouts should be about $^3/_4$ inch long. Discard any unsprouted seeds and transfer to a bowl until ready to use. The sprouts will last for about 5 days, covered and refrigerated.

2.   Preheat the oven to 200 degrees F.

3.   Pour the flour onto a dinner plate and season with $^1/_4$ teaspoon salt and half the pepper. Dredge the liver slices in the flour and shake off the excess.

4.   In a large skillet, heat the olive oil and 1 tablespoon butter over medium-high heat. Sauté the liver until golden brown, about 2 minutes on each side for medium-rare. Transfer the cooked liver to a serving platter and keep warm in the oven while you make the sauce.

5.   Discard the browned butter and oil from the pan and add the remaining tablespoon of butter. Add the shallots and cook over moderate heat 1 to 2 minutes, until softened. Stir in the mustard sprouts and paprika and cook an additional 1 to 2 minutes. Add the white wine, raise the heat to high, and reduce until almost dry. Add the veal stock and reduce by one quarter. Stir the Dijon mustard into the sauce until dissolved. Season with the remaining salt and pepper. Spoon over the cooked calf's liver and serve.

Seared Sweetbreads with Mushrooms and Frisée

*T*he key to this recipe is a slow sauté, resulting in sweetbreads crisp on the outside and tender on the inside. The greens create a good balance to the creamy richness of the sweetbreads. Begin with Carrot–Red Lentil Soup or Bruschetta.

SERVES 4

1 1/2 pounds sweetbreads
1 1/2 teaspoons kosher salt
1/4 teaspoon freshly ground black pepper
Flour for dredging
2 tablespoons vegetable or light olive oil
2 tablespoons butter
3/4 pound mushrooms, washed, stems trimmed, and
    quartered
3 tablespoons minced shallots
1 teaspoon minced garlic
1 cup peeled, seeded, and diced tomato (1 large tomato)
1/2 cup white wine
2 cups Veal Stock (page 314)
4 cups washed and trimmed frisée
2 tablespoons chopped parsley

Try Vouvray, sec or demi-sec, or a fruity Pinot Noir with the sweetbreads.

1. Soak the sweetbreads in ice water to cover for 1 hour, changing the water every 15 minutes to remove all traces of blood. Drain and place the sweetbreads in a saucepan with 1 teaspoon salt and cold water to cover. Bring to a boil, skim any foam from the surface, and poach for 3 to 5 minutes, until the sweetbreads are firm but not rubbery. Drain in a colander, return to the pot, and refresh the sweetbreads in cold water. With a paring knife, trim any excess fat and connective membrane. Put the sweetbreads on a plate and cover with

another plate weighted with several cans or 1-pound scale weights (or a 1-gallon can of olive oil). Refrigerate overnight or at least 5 hours, until the sweetbreads have flattened out and lost their moisture.

2. Preheat the oven to 200 degrees F.

3. Season the sweetbreads with $^1/_4$ teaspoon salt and $^1/_8$ teaspoon pepper and dredge in flour.

4. Heat the oil in a 10-inch skillet over moderate heat. Sauté the sweetbreads slowly until golden brown, about 10 minutes. Transfer to an ovenproof serving platter and hold in the oven while you make the sauce.

5. Pour the fat from the pan and return to medium-high heat. Melt half the butter and sauté the mushrooms until soft and lightly browned. Stir in the shallots and garlic. Season with the remaining salt and pepper. Add the tomatoes and white wine and reduce by half. Add the veal stock and cook until the sauce coats the back of a spoon.

6. Toss in the frisée and cook until just wilted. Swirl in the remaining butter and the chopped parsley. Spoon the sauce over the sweetbreads and serve.

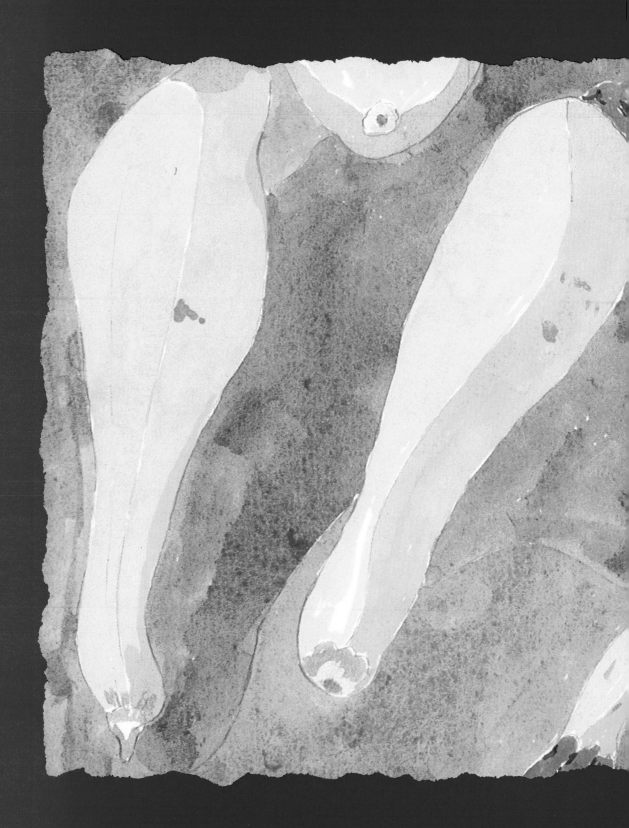

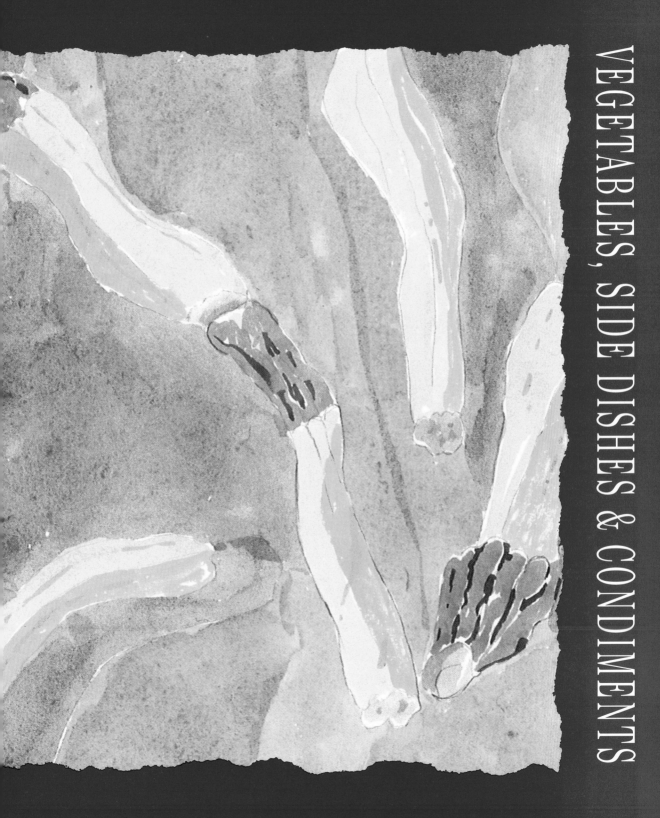

VEGETABLES, SIDE DISHES & CONDIMENTS

Artichoke-Eggplant Hash

Braised Baby Artichokes with Garlic, Basil, and Mint

Mashed French Beans with Garlic and Mint

Sautéed Broccoli Rabe with Garlic

Hashed Brussel Sprouts with Poppy Seeds and Lemon

Spicy Gingered Asian Slaw

Baked Eggplant, Zucchini, and Parmigiano Tortino

Frizzled Leeks

Grilled Sweet Red Onions

Mashed Potatoes

Basil Mashed Potatoes

Roast Tomato Mashed Potatoes

Eggplant Mashed Potatoes

Fennel Mashed Potatoes

Mashed Sweet Potatoes with Balsamic Vinegar

Creamy Potato-Gruyére Gratin

Parsnip Pancakes

Sweet Peas with Escarole, Onions, and Mint

Sautéed Spinach with Garlic

Creamed Spinach

Charred Tomatoes, Onions, and Mint

Mashed Yellow Turnips with Crispy Shallots

Creamy Polenta with Mascarpone

Sauteed Insalata Tricolore

Fagioli alla Toscana

Fagioli all'Uccelletto

Three-Grain Pilaf with Almonds and Shitake Mushrooms

Red Lentil–Basmati Rice Pilaf

Bagna Cauda Sauce

Peach-Fig Chutney

Rhubarb and Dried Cherry Chutney

Herbed Potato Salad with Bacon and Scallions

*B*ack in the spring of 1985 when Union Square Cafe was being built, loyal followers of Brownie's—the vegetarian restaurant that had occupied the space for the previous forty-nine years—stopped by daily, curious as to the whereabouts of their beloved lunch haunt, and wary about what kind of restaurant would dare take its place. We told them Union Square Cafe wouldn't be a vegetarian restaurant, but that vegetables would always play an important role on our menu, and to this day, they always have.

Every dish on our menu is served with its own complementary accompaniment—which often becomes popular in its own right. For example, many Union Square Cafe guests have remarked that they order our Veal Lombatina primarily to enjoy its sidekick, the Baked Eggplant, Zucchini, and Parmigiano Tortino. Additionally, we've always offered a good choice of vegetable side dishes and condiments—so named, because we think they make the rest of our food taste better. See if you don't find your roast leg of lamb more flavorful when you dip it into our creamy mashed turnips.

The recipes in this chapter are the heart and soul of Union Square Cafe's cooking. We encourage you to have fun orchestrating new

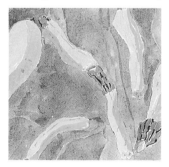

dinner combinations by selecting your own favorites from among our vegetable side dishes. Either match them creatively with our main courses, or do as many of our guests do and make an entire meal out of three or four of them on their own.

ARTICHOKE-EGGPLANT HASH

*H*ere's a succulent variation on the classic American hash, substituting Provençal vegetables for the more standard beef and potatoes. We've had great success serving the hash with whitefish and red snapper, and it would be equally at home with lamb or roast chicken.
SERVES 4 TO 6

> 1 medium eggplant (1 pound)
> 3 tablespoons olive oil
> 1³/4 teaspoons kosher salt
> Freshly ground black pepper
> 1 medium Idaho potato (¹/2 pound)
> 1 tablespoon fresh thyme leaves
> 2 cups drained Braised Baby Artichokes with Garlic,
>   Basil, and Mint (¹/2 recipe, page 220)
> 2 ripe tomatoes, peeled, seeded, and diced
> 1 teaspoon minced garlic
> 1 tablespoon chopped parsley

1. Preheat oven to 400 degrees F.

2. Cut the eggplant in half lengthwise and slice each half lengthwise into thirds. Be sure to keep the slices together, retaining the original shape of the eggplant. This will prevent the eggplant from drying out as it cooks. Slice across the eggplant halves at ¹/2-inch intervals. With a wide spatula, transfer the cut eggplant to a lightly oiled cookie sheet or roasting pan. Drizzle evenly with 1 tablespoon of the olive oil and season with ¹/4 teaspoon of the salt and a sprinkle of freshly ground pepper. Cover with foil and roast in the oven until very tender, about 45 minutes.

3. Peel the potato and cut it in half lengthwise. Cut each half again lengthwise to make four long quarters. Cut across the quarters making ¹/4-inch slices. Place the potato slices in a pot with cold water

to cover and $^1/_2$ teaspoon salt. Bring to a boil over a medium flame and cook until tender. As soon as the water reaches a boil, test the potatoes: they should be just about done. If not, simmer 1 to 2 minutes longer. Drain the potatoes well in a colander.

4.   In a 10-inch skillet, heat the remaining 2 tablespoons olive oil over medium-high heat. Add the potatoes and brown evenly, stirring occasionally, about 10 minutes. Sprinkle the browned potatoes with the thyme leaves and stir to release the flavor of the herb.

5.   Combine the garlic-simmered artichokes and roasted eggplant with the potatoes. Toss together over high heat until heated through. Add the tomatoes and garlic and cook 2 minutes longer. Season with the remaining salt and pepper to taste. Sprinkle with chopped parsley and serve.

BRAISED BABY ARTICHOKES WITH GARLIC, BASIL, AND MINT

*T*his makes a satisfying antipasto, served with toasted peasant bread, or a fine accompaniment for a grilled main course.

SERVES 4 TO 6

Juice of 1 lemon
12 baby artichokes
$^1/_2$ cup white wine
$^1/_2$ cup extra-virgin olive oil
$^1/_2$ cup water
4 garlic cloves, peeled and cut in half
2 tablespoons chopped basil
2 tablespoons chopped mint
1 teaspoon coriander seeds, cracked
$^1/_8$ teaspoon black peppercorns, cracked
1 bay leaf
$^1/_2$ teaspoon kosher salt

Artichokes have a difficult time with wine, but if you can find a crisp rosé with lots of fruit— Cassis rosé, Tavel, and Sancerre rosé are good choices— you'll be pleased with the results.

1.   In a large bowl, combine the lemon juice and enough cold water to cover the artichokes. Cut off only the very tip of the artichoke stem. Peel the outer layer of the remaining stem with a paring knife or vegetable peeler. Slice off the tops of the artichokes, about $^1/_4$ inch down, and peel away 2 to 3 layers of tough outer leaves until the tender yellow inner leaves are exposed. Cut the artichokes in half lengthwise.With a paring knife, remove the small choke. To prevent discoloration, place each artichoke in the lemon water as soon as it is cleaned.

2.   Drain the artichokes and place them in a 2-quart nonreactive saucepan with the remaining ingredients. Gently simmer, covered, until tender, about 20 minutes. Serve warm or chilled with the cooking liquid spooned over.

MASHED FRENCH BEANS WITH GARLIC AND MINT

*T*he French consume their *flageolet* beans with as much passion as Italians devour *fagioli*. Flageolets simmered with tomato and garlic are a classic accompaniment to roast leg of lamb. In this recipe, the beans are puréed with fresh mint and roasted garlic, which we've found to be a great match with dishes as diverse as Braised Lamb Shanks and steamed fillet of halibut.

SERVES 4

> *1 cup flageolet beans*
> *1 head garlic*
> *1 celery rib*
> *1 carrot, scrubbed and cut in half lengthwise*
> *1 medium onion, peeled, and halved*
> *$1/2$ teaspoon kosher salt, more to taste*
> *4 tablespoons extra-virgin olive oil*
> *2 tablespoons chopped fresh mint*
> *Freshly ground black pepper*

1.   Soak the beans, covered with cold water, overnight. Discard any beans or loose skins that float to the surface.

2.   Preheat the oven to 375 degrees F.

3.   Place the head of garlic in an ovenproof dish and roast in the oven until completely tender, about 30 to 40 minutes. Cool, slice off the top $1/4$ inch from the pointed end and squeeze the softened garlic cloves from their papery skins. They will now have the consistency of a purée. Set aside.

4.   Place the beans in a medium saucepan and cover generously with water. Add the celery, carrot, and onion. Bring to a boil, reduce the

heat, cover, and simmer 1 hour. Add salt and continue cooking for an additional 30 minutes, or until tender.

5. Drain the beans, reserving the liquid and discarding the vegetables. Purée the beans, adding $1/2$ cup and perhaps a few tablespoons more of their cooking liquid. The beans will resemble mashed potatoes but will not be completely smooth.

6. Heat a skillet with 3 tablespoons of olive oil over a medium flame. Sauté the roast garlic purée for 1 minute. Add the puréed beans and stir to heat through and incorporate the garlic. Finish with the chopped mint, salt, and freshly ground pepper. Drizzle the remaining olive oil on top and serve.

Sautéed Broccoli Rabe with Garlic

*T*he natural bitterness of this nutritious green tames as you cook it. Be sure to choose young broccoli rabe that has a vibrant green color, no yellowing in the florets, and tender, not woody, stalks. Traditionally served with grilled pork sausage, this recipe is also a great match for seared sea scallops, chicken, and steak. On its own, try it with a light sprinkling of Pecorino Romano cheese.

SERVES 4

2 pounds broccoli rabe, washed, largest stems discarded
1/4 cup extra-virgin olive oil, plus more for drizzling
2 teaspoons finely minced garlic
1/3 teaspoon dried red pepper flakes
1/2 teaspoon kosher salt
1/8 teaspoon freshly ground black pepper
3/4 cup water
4 lemon wedges

1.   Separate the leaves from the florets of the broccoli rabe. Chop the leaves and their stems into 2- to 3-inch pieces.

2.   In a 3-quart saucepan or skillet large enough to hold all the broccoli rabe, combine the olive oil, garlic, and red pepper flakes. Cook over moderately high heat for about 45 seconds to flavor the oil, but do not allow the garlic to brown. Add the broccoli rabe. The pan will be overflowing, but the broccoli rabe will lose considerable volume during cooking. Continuously toss with tongs or a kitchen fork to avoid any browning of the greens. It will take 1 to 2 minutes to wilt the broccoli rabe.

3. Add the salt and pepper, toss, and cook approximately 1 minute longer. Add the water and cook until tender, 3 to 5 minutes. Any water that does not evaporate will blend with the olive oil to create a flavorful juice for the broccoli rabe, and should definitely be served. Garnish with the lemon wedges and a light drizzle of olive oil.

HASHED BRUSSELS SPROUTS WITH POPPY SEEDS AND LEMON

*T*his simple recipe has converted lots of sworn brussels-sprouts haters into devoted connoisseurs. We've turned the sprouts into comfort food by "hashing" and stir-frying them with poppy seeds. Serve with poultry, veal, and beef.

SERVES 4 TO 6

1 pound large brussels sprouts
Juice of $1/2$ lemon
2 tablespoons olive oil
2 garlic cloves, peeled and minced
1 tablespoon poppy seeds
$1/4$ cup white wine
$1/4$ teaspoon kosher salt
$1/8$ teaspoon freshly ground black pepper

1.   Cut the stems from the brussels sprouts and halve each one lengthwise. Slice each half into thin slices, about $1/8$ inch thick, and toss with the lemon juice in a large bowl.

2.   Heat the olive oil in a sauté pan over high heat almost to the smoking point. Stir in the hashed sprouts with the garlic and poppy seeds. Add the white wine and continue stirring for about 3 minutes, until the sprouts are bright green and barely crunchy. Reduce the heat to low, season with salt and pepper, and cook for 1 additional minute. Transfer to a warm bowl and serve.

Spicy Gingered Asian Slaw

*T*his zesty slaw is packed with flavor. Try it alongside our Fillet Mignon of Tuna. Alone it makes a light yet satisfying lunch.
SERVES 4 TO 6

1/4 cup lime juice
1/4 cup minced shallots
1 tablespoon soy sauce
1 1/2 tablespoons peeled and minced ginger
1 tablespoon minced jalapeño, seeded
2 teaspoons peeled and minced garlic
1 tablespoon honey
2 teaspoons Thai red curry paste
1 tablespoon dark sesame oil
1/2 cup peanut, soy, or canola oil
5 cups finely sliced napa cabbage
1 1/2 cups julienned carrots
1 large red pepper, cored, seeded, and thinly sliced
1 large yellow pepper, cored, seeded, and thinly sliced
1/2 cup sliced scallions, green and white parts
1/4 cup chopped cilantro leaves
2 tablespoons unsalted, roasted, skinless peanuts,
*   coarsely chopped*
1 tablespoon toasted sesame seeds
2 teaspoons kosher salt
1/8 teaspoon freshly ground black pepper

1. In a glass jar, combine the lime juice, shallots, soy sauce, ginger, jalapeño, garlic, honey, curry paste, sesame oil, and peanut oil. Cover tightly and shake vigorously until well blended.

2. In a large bowl, toss together the cabbage, carrots, peppers, scallions, cilantro, peanuts, and sesame seeds. Season with the salt and pepper. Pour the sauce over the slaw and toss to combine. Allow the slaw to marinate for 10 minutes before serving.

Baked Eggplant, Zucchini, and Parmigiano Tortino

Crusty and chock-full of delicious vegetables, this easy-to-prepare dish is versatile enough to be enjoyed as an appetizer, side dish, or even as a main course—accompanied by a green salad and some good bread. At the restaurant, we serve the tortino alongside our grilled loin veal chop, but it would taste equally good with almost any other grilled or roast meat. Once you get the knack of making this tortino, you can vary its flavor by substituting other vegetables like asparagus, artichokes, leeks, or fennel for the eggplant and zucchini. The tortino can be prepared as far as two days in advance of serving. In that case, hold off topping with the Parmigiano and browning until just before you are ready to serve.

SERVES 4 AS A MAIN COURSE, 6 AS A SIDE DISH

$^{1}/_{2}$ cup olive oil

1 Spanish onion, peeled, cut in half, and each half cut
  into $^{1}/_{4}$-inch slices (1$^{1}/_{2}$ cups)

1 medium eggplant (1 pound), peeled, quartered, and
  cut into $^{1}/_{4}$-inch slices

1 zucchini ($^{1}/_{2}$ pound), washed and sliced into
  $^{1}/_{4}$-inch rounds

1 yellow squash ($^{1}/_{2}$ pound), washed and cut into
  $^{1}/_{4}$-inch rounds

1 teaspoon kosher salt

$^{1}/_{4}$ teaspoon freshly ground black pepper

5 eggs

4 tablespoons balsamic vinegar

1 cup heavy cream

1 cup grated Parmigiano-Reggiano (3 ounces)

1. Preheat the oven to 325 degrees F.

2. Heat 2 tablespoons of the olive oil over low heat in a medium sauté pan and cook the onion, stirring occasionally, until very tender and golden colored, 15 to 20 minutes. Set aside.

3. In the same sauté pan, heat 4 tablespoons olive oil and add the eggplant. Cook over medium heat for 3 to 4 minutes, then add the zucchini and the yellow squash. Continue to sauté on medium heat until all the vegetables are tender, about 5 minutes. Combine the cooked vegetables with the reserved onions, season with half the salt and pepper, and allow to cool.

4. In a large mixing bowl, beat the eggs. Combine with 1 tablespoon olive oil, the balsamic vinegar, cream, $2/3$ cup of the cheese, and remaining salt and pepper. Mix well to form a somewhat thick batter and stir in the sautéed vegetables.

5. Oil a 2-quart, 9-inch round or square baking dish or casserole with the remaining tablespoon of olive oil and pour in the tortino mixture. Be sure the mixture is level on all sides. Cover the dish with foil and bake for 35 to 40 minutes.

6. Preheat the broiler. Remove the foil from the dish and sprinkle on the remaining Parmigiano. Bake until the eggs are set, about 15 minutes longer. Just before serving, place the tortino under the broiler until the cheese forms a golden crust. Let rest for 5 minutes and serve in squares.

FRIZZLED LEEKS

*A*n addictive garnish for many of our dishes, frizzled leeks are great over carrot soup, corn pudding, seared fish, and any of our mashed potato recipes. Three secrets to successful frizzled leeks: Cut the leeks as fine as you can, cook them just to light golden brown, and always serve piping hot.

SERVES 4 TO 6 AS A GARNISH

> 3 cups julienned leeks (about $^1/_{16}$ inch thick
>   and 2 inches long), white part only,
>   washed and dried thoroughly
> 2 tablespoons flour
> 2 cups vegetable oil
> Salt

1.   In a 2-quart heavy-bottomed saucepan, heat the oil to 320 degrees F on a deep-fat thermometer. (To check the temperature without a thermometer, drop a small piece of bread the size of a crouton into the oil. It should float to the surface and lightly brown in about 2 minutes.) Toss the cut leeks in the flour and place them in a strainer to shake off the excess.

2.   Cook the leeks in three separate batches. Place each batch of leeks in the oil and cook for 3 to 4 minutes, until light blond. Remove with a skimmer or slotted spoon and drain on paper towels. Repeat with the remaining leeks. Sprinkle the cooked leeks lightly with salt and serve hot.

GRILLED SWEET RED ONIONS

*W*hile the onions cook mostly in the oven, it's the final minutes on the grill that add the appealing smoky, caramelized flavors. One of our favorite customers makes an entire meal of 4 to 6 orders of these onions every time she lunches at Union Square Cafe! We love them with our Tuna Burgers, and they're great with almost anything barbecued.

SERVES 4 TO 6

4 medium red onions (2 pounds)
$^1/_4$ cup olive oil
$^1/_2$ teaspoon kosher salt
$^1/_8$ teaspoon freshly ground black pepper
2 to 3 tablespoons extra-virgin olive oil
1 tablespoon chopped parsley

1. Preheat the oven to 400 degrees F.

2. Peel the onions and cut them into slices $^3/_4$ inch thick. On a lightly oiled cookie sheet or roasting pan, neatly arrange the onion slices in rows. Be sure to keep the rings of each slice intact and don't crowd the slices. Evenly drizzle the remaining olive oil onto each of the onion slices and season with the salt and pepper.

3. Roast in the oven for 35 to 40 minutes, until the onions are softened and very lightly browned. (The recipe can be done ahead up to this point. Allow the onions to cool, then store them, tightly covered in the refrigerator, until ready to use. They will keep up to 3 days.)

4. Just before serving, heat a grill or grill pan until very hot. Use a spatula to place the onion slices on the grill, taking care that the rings stay intact. Cook 3 to 5 minutes a side to give the onions attractive grill marks and a delicious smoky flavor. Arrange the grilled onions on a platter, drizzle on the extra-virgin olive oil, sprinkle with the chopped parsley, and serve.

MASHED POTATOES

*W*ho of us can resist the creamy comfort of perfect mashed potatoes? We've found that even the most persnickety diner can be convinced to try almost any new or unusual dish on our menu—so long as it's accompanied by mashed potatoes. These creamy spuds make everything they come in contact with taste better. A few tips for making perfect, smooth mashed potatoes: Use a food mill or ricer. A hand-held masher will give you lumpy potatoes and a food processor makes them gummy and tough. Also, mashed potatoes are never as good as when freshly made. While this recipe explains how to hold mashed potatoes for up to an hour, they'll change dramatically if you reheat them the next day. Once you've learned this basic recipe, have fun with some of the flavored mashed potato variations we offer on the following pages. Frizzled Leeks provide a sweet-crunchy garnish when sprinkled over these or any of our mashed potato variations.

YIELDS 4 CUPS, SERVES 4

2 pounds Idaho potatoes, peeled and quartered
2 teaspoons kosher salt
8 tablespoons (1 stick) unsalted butter
1/2 cup heavy cream
1/2 cup milk
1/4 teaspoon freshly ground white pepper

1.   Place the potatoes in a 2-quart saucepan with 1 teaspoon of the salt and cold water to cover. Bring to a boil, lower the heat, and simmer, covered, until completely tender, about 30 minutes. Test the potatoes by piercing them with a paring knife—there should be no resistance. Place in a colander and allow to drain well for several minutes.

2.   Combine the butter, heavy cream, and milk in another saucepan and heat gently until the butter has melted. Keep warm.

3.   Working over the saucepan used to cook the potatoes, pass the potatoes through a food mill or a potato ricer. If you have any difficulty, add a little of the hot milk and butter to the potatoes.

4.   To serve, place the potatoes over a low flame and begin adding the warm milk mixture. Whip the potatoes with a wooden spoon or spatula while heating. When all the liquid is absorbed, season with the remaining salt and white pepper. Serve piping hot. Mashed potatoes are best served immediately, but if you are unable to do so, or need them for another recipe, keep the potatoes hot for up to 1 hour by placing them in the top of a double boiler, covered, and held over barely simmering water.

BASIL MASHED POTATOES

*I*f you're lucky enough to have an abundant source of basil in the summer, this recipe is a great way to use it. The bright green basil purée—sort of a cheeseless pesto—is also wonderful stirred into soups, mixed into salad vinaigrettes, or spooned over pizza. Prepared and stored properly, the purée will keep for weeks. Just make sure to start with very dry basil and transfer to a clean, dry jar. Top with a $1/8$-inch layer of olive oil, cover tightly, and refrigerate.

SERVES 4

> 2 tablespoons pine nuts
> $1/4$ cup extra-virgin olive oil
> 3 medium garlic cloves, peeled and sliced
> $1/2$ teaspoon kosher salt
> $1/4$ teaspoon freshly ground black pepper
> 2 cups basil leaves, washed and dried (2 ounces)
> 4 cups Mashed Potatoes (page 232)

1.   In a blender, combine the pine nuts, extra-virgin olive oil, garlic, salt, and pepper; purée. With the motor running, add the basil leaves and continue to purée until smooth.

2.   Add the basil purée to the warm mashed potatoes and, over low heat, stir with a wooden spoon until the purée is completely incorporated and the mixture is piping hot. Serve.

Roast Tomato Mashed Potatoes

*H*ere's another spin on the basic mashed potato recipe, this time using slow-baked, oven-dried plum tomatoes to add a potent tomato flavor. Try these with lamb, chicken, veal scaloppine, broccoli rabe, and garlic-simmered artichokes.

SERVES 4

1/2 pound Oven-Dried Tomatoes, drained (page 318)
4 cups Mashed Potatoes (page 232)

1. In a food processor, purée the oven-dried tomatoes to a nearly smooth consistency.

2. Add the tomato purée to the warm mashed potatoes and, over low heat, stir with a wooden spoon until the tomatoes are completely incorporated and the mixture is piping hot. Serve.

Eggplant Mashed Potatoes

*T*his unusual mashed potato variation accompanies our grilled marinated Fillet Mignon of Tuna. It's also great with lamb, pork, chicken, or fish dishes accented with Asian spices.

SERVES 4

> 2 medium eggplants (about 2 pounds total), peeled
> 1/4 cup olive oil
> 1 teaspoon salt
> Freshly ground black pepper
> 1 tablespoon sesame oil
> 1 teaspoon minced garlic
> 1 tablespoon peeled and grated ginger
> 1 tablespoon tahini
> 2 tablespoons soy sauce (preferably tamari)
> 2 cups Mashed Potatoes (page 232)
> 1 recipe Frizzled Leeks (optional; page 230)

1. Preheat the oven to 400 degrees F.

2. Cut the eggplants in half lengthwise, then slice each half lengthwise into thirds. Keep the slices together. Slice across the halves at 1/2-inch intervals. With a wide spatula, transfer the cut eggplant to a lightly oiled roasting pan. Drizzle evenly with 3 tablespoons of the olive oil and season with salt and pepper. Cover with foil and roast in the oven for 45 minutes. The cooked eggplant should be very tender and soft to the touch. Purée in a food processor until smooth.

3. In a medium sauté pan, heat the remaining olive oil and the sesame oil over a low flame. Add the garlic and ginger and cook for 3 to 4 minutes. Add the eggplant purée, tahini, and soy sauce; cook for 10 minutes longer. Stir in the warm mashed potatoes and heat thoroughly. Add pepper and serve piping hot.

FENNEL MASHED POTATOES

*W*e love the fennel mashed potatoes served with firmly textured seafood such as lobster, scallops, monkfish, tuna, and swordfish. Or, served with lamb, try shaving some fresh Parmigiano-Reggiano over the top and finish with a few drops of good olive oil. SERVES 4

2 pounds Idaho potatoes, peeled and quartered
2 teaspoons kosher salt
2 cups sliced fennel, bulb and top
$1/2$ cup milk
$1/2$ cup heavy cream
8 tablespoons (1 stick) unsalted butter
1 teaspoon Pernod
$1/4$ teaspoon freshly ground white pepper

1. Place the potatoes in a 2-quart saucepan with 1 teaspoon of the salt and cold water to cover. Bring to a boil, lower the heat, and simmer, covered, until completely tender, about 30 minutes. Drain.

2. In a saucepan, combine the fennel milk, cream, and butter. Simmer covered, until tender, about 30 minutes.

3. Pour the fennel and its cooking liquid into a blender or processor, cover, and purée, adding 1 teaspoon Pernod.

4. Working over the saucepan you used for the potatoes, pass the potatoes through a food mill or a potato ricer. If you have any difficulty, add a little of the hot fennel purée to the potatoes.

5. To serve, place the potatoes over a low flame and begin adding the warm fennel purée. Whip the potatoes with a wooden spoon or spatula while heating. When all the purée is incorporated, season with the remaining salt and white pepper. Serve piping hot.

MASHED SWEET POTATOES WITH BALSAMIC VINEGAR

*G*ently spiced and sweetly tart, these mashed sweet potatoes can be served with roast pork, duck, and even lamb chops. Use more or less of the balsamic vinegar to vary the tartness of the potatoes according to your taste.

SERVES 4

4 to 5 large sweet potatoes (4 pounds), scrubbed
2 tablespoons butter
^{1}/$_8$ teaspoon ground cinnamon
^{1}/$_8$ teaspoon freshly grated nutmeg
1 cup milk
1 teaspoon salt
Freshly ground black pepper
1 to 2 teaspoons balsamic vinegar

1. Preheat the oven to 400 degrees F.

2. Place the sweet potatoes in the oven and bake for 50 minutes, or until easily pierced with a paring knife. Allow the potatoes to cool just enough to handle. Peel and pass through a food mill or ricer. Reserve.

3. In a medium saucepan, heat the butter over a low flame until it browns. Stir in the cinnamon and nutmeg. Off the heat, stir in the milk, then return to the stove and bring the milk to a boil. Add the sweet potato purée and stir with a wooden spoon to combine thoroughly. Season with salt and pepper and stir in the balsamic vinegar. Serve.

CREAMY POTATO-GRUYÈRE GRATIN

*T*his wonderfully rich and delicious potato gratin recipe is adapted from the Chez Max restaurant in Zurich, where Michael was chef in the early eighties. Michael remembers it as one of proprietor Max Kehl's favorite. Serve it with roast beef, venison, or leg of lamb.
SERVES 4 TO 6

1 teaspoon butter
1 garlic clove, peeled and split in half
3 cups heavy cream
1/8 teaspoon freshly grated nutmeg
1 1/2 teaspoons kosher salt
1/8 teaspoon white pepper
1/8 teaspoon cayenne
4 medium Idaho potatoes (2 pounds)
2 1/2 cups finely grated Gruyère cheese (1/2 pound)

1. Preheat the oven to 350 degrees F.

2. Lightly butter a 10-cup gratin dish. Rub the dish with both halves of the cut garlic clove.

3. Combine the cream, nutmeg, salt, pepper, and cayenne in a bowl. Peel the potatoes and slice them paper-thin on a mandoline. As you work, place the potato slices in the bowl with the cream and seasonings. Add the Gruyère and combine thoroughly.

4. Pour the potato-cheese mix into the prepared gratin dish, making sure the potato slices are flat and level. Place the gratin dish inside a roasting pan and fill the pan to three quarters full with hot water, creating a *bain-marie*. Carefully place the *bain-marie* in the center of the oven and bake for 2 hours, or until completely set and golden on top. Serve.

PARSNIP PANCAKES

*H*ere's a variation on classic potato latkes, made sweet by substituting parsnips for spuds. They're great for brunch, served on their own, topped with a heaping spoonful of apple sauce and a dollop of sour cream or crème fraîche. We enjoy them with venison and they also make a winning match for roast turkey.

SERVES 4

1 1/2 pounds parsnips, peeled
1 small white onion
1 large egg, beaten
1/4 cup all-purpose flour
1/8 teaspoon cayenne
Pinch of freshly grated nutmeg
1/2 teaspoon kosher salt
1/8 teaspoon freshly ground black pepper
1/4 cup olive oil (or enough to fill pan to 1/8 inch)
1 tablespoon unsalted butter

1. Bring 2 quarts lightly salted water to a boil and add the parsnips. Return to a boil and cook 3 minutes, to soften. Remove the parsnips from the water and let cool.

2. Shred the onion in a food processor or through the largest holes of a hand grater. Shred the parsnips in the same manner.

3. Using a wooden spatula, combine the parsnips, onion, and egg in a mixing bowl. When well blended, lightly stir in the flour without overworking the mixture. Season with the cayenne, nutmeg, salt, and pepper. Form into 8 equal-sized pancakes, about 3 inches in diameter and 1/2 inch thick, placing each pancake on a cookie sheet lined with wax paper.

4. Heat the olive oil and butter in a heavy skillet. Over a medium flame, cook the parsnip pancakes until golden brown on both sides, 5 to 7 minutes a side. (You may need to do this in two batches, depending on the size of your pan.) Place the cooked pancakes on paper towels and keep them warm in a 200-degree-F oven until ready to serve.

NOTE: As with potato latkes, making parsnip pancakes can be a smoky and somewhat splattery endeavor. The natural sugar in parsnips will caramelize and then blacken if you cook them too quickly. If you cook them slowly and carefully, you will end up with beautifully browned pancakes and a minimal mess.

SWEET PEAS WITH ESCAROLE, ONIONS, AND MINT

A delicious medley of spring vegetables to accompany lamb, baked ham, or salmon. You can save time by first soaking the onions in warm water to loosen their skins.

SERVES 4 TO 6

2 cups pearl onions, peeled ($^1/_2$ pound)
1$^3/_4$ cups Vegetable Stock (page 316) or Chicken Stock (page 312)
2 tablespoons butter
2 tablespoons flour
3 cups cleaned and quartered white mushrooms ($^1/_2$ pound)
4 cups cleaned and roughly chopped escarole (4 ounces)
2 cups shelled peas (10 ounces)
$^1/_4$ cup chopped fresh mint
$^3/_4$ teaspoon kosher salt
$^1/_8$ teaspoon freshly ground black pepper

1.   Place the onions in a small saucepan with the vegetable stock. Bring to a boil, turn the flame down to low, cover, and simmer until tender but not mushy, 10 to 12 minutes. Set aside.

2.   Make a *beurre manié:* In a small dish, with your fingers, make a paste of 1 tablespoon of the butter and the flour. Reserve.

3.   In a 10-inch lidded skillet or saucepan, melt the remaining butter over medium-high heat. Add the mushrooms and cook until browned, 3 to 5 minutes. Add the escarole and toss until wilted.

4.   Add the peas, mint, onions, and onion broth to the skillet. Season with salt and pepper and whisk the *beurre manié* into the cooking liquid. Cover and cook until the peas are tender and the sauce has thickened, 4 to 5 minutes. Serve.

Sautéed Spinach with Garlic

*T*his quick-stir method of cooking spinach allows the spinach to keep its bright green color and flavor. You'll find our trick of stirring with a fork and garlic clove to be a simple and quick way to give potent garlic flavor to spinach and other greens. Enjoy the spinach with veal chops, steak, chicken, or lamb. It also goes well with legumes and grains. If you have leftovers, you can chop them and make a sandwich on good bread with olive oil and fresh mozzarella. SERVES 4

2 pounds fresh spinach
1 garlic clove, peeled
3 tablespoons extra-virgin olive oil
$^1/_8$ teaspoon kosher salt
Freshly ground black pepper
1 lemon, quartered (optional)

1.   Remove the stems from the spinach leaves. Discard any leaves that are discolored or tough. Soak the spinach in a large bowl of cold water, stirring to dislodge sand and grit. Change the water at least three times to ensure that the spinach is absolutely clean. (With each change of water, lift the spinach out of the bowl with your hands rather than draining the water into a colander. That way you won't pour the sandy water back onto the spinach.) Thoroughly dry the spinach in a salad spinner or on paper towels.

2.   Spear the clove of garlic with the prongs of a dinner fork. Over a high flame, heat the olive oil in a skillet or saucepan large enough to accommodate all the spinach. Add the spinach and stir quickly and constantly with the garlic-stuck fork. Continue to cook until the spinach is wilted, 3 to 4 minutes. Season with salt and pepper just as the spinach begins to wilt. Cook, stirring, 1 or 2 minutes longer, until the spinach is tender. Serve either hot or at room temperature, in the Italian style. Serve with a generous squeeze of lemon at the last moment.

CREAMED SPINACH

Creamed spinach has got to be one of America's great comfort foods. It's also versatile, and works well with everything from fried chicken to roast rack of venison. From his years in French kitchens, Michael learned that using béchamel—milk thickened with a flour and butter roux—allows you to make great creamed spinach that is light, economical, and hardly uses any cream.

SERVES 4

> 3 pounds spinach
> 4 tablespoons butter
> 2 tablespoons flour
> 1 cup milk
> 2 tablespoons heavy cream
> $1/4$ teaspoon freshly grated nutmeg
> 1 teaspoon kosher salt
> $1/8$ teaspoon freshly ground black pepper

1. Remove the stems from the spinach leaves. Discard any leaves that are discolored or tough. Soak the spinach in a large bowl of cold water, stirring to dislodge sand and grit. Change the water at least two or three times to ensure that the spinach is absolutely clean. (With each change of water, lift the spinach out of the bowl with your hands rather than draining the water into a colander. That way you won't pour the sandy water back onto the spinach.) Thoroughly dry the spinach in a salad spinner or on paper towels.

2. To make the béchamel, melt 2 tablespoons of the butter in a non-reactive saucepan over low heat. Sift in the flour and stir with a wooden spoon until the flour is completely incorporated into the butter. Cook gently, stirring, for 5 minutes. Don't let the flour brown. Remove the roux from the heat and whisk in the milk. Return to a boil, whisking constantly, and cook 2 to 3 minutes longer. Cover and set aside while you cook the spinach.

3. In a large skillet, melt 1 tablespoon butter. Cook the spinach, stirring until wilted, and simmer 1 minute longer if necessary to remove any excess water from the spinach.

4. Pulse the cooked spinach in a food processor to make a coarse purée.

5. Add the puréed spinach to the saucepan with the béchamel. Bring to a simmer and stir in the heavy cream, nutmeg, salt, pepper, and remaining butter. Serve.

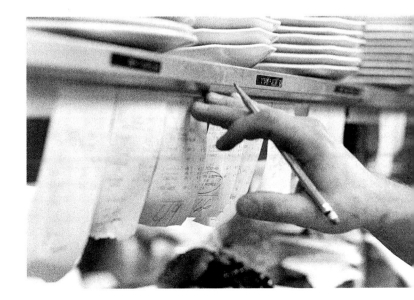

CHARRED TOMATOES, ONIONS, AND MINT

*M*int is a refreshing alternative to basil for adding flavor to tomatoes. You'll find plenty of uses for this delicious condiment, including enjoying it on its own as a salad. The charred flavor in the tomatoes makes it a savory accompaniment to grilled mint-friendly foods like chicken, lamb, tuna, and swordfish. Letting the mint oil sit for two days before using it mellows the flavor dramatically and allows the fragrant aroma to develop.

SERVES 4

MINT OIL

¹/₂ cup chopped fresh mint leaves
¹/₂ cup olive oil

TOMATO SALAD

5 medium-size ripe tomatoes (3 pounds)
1 tablespoon olive oil
1 cup thinly sliced red onion
2 tablespoons red wine vinegar
¹/₄ cup thinly sliced mint
¹/₂ cup mint oil
1 teaspoon kosher salt, plus to taste
¹/₄ teaspoon freshly ground black pepper

1. Combine the mint and oil in a small saucepan over low heat. Simmer very gently for 5 minutes; remove from the heat and pour into a nonmetal bowl to cool. Cover and allow to sit at room temperature for 2 days. Strain into a tightly lidded jar and refrigerate for up to 1 month.

2. Slice the tomatoes in half crosswise. Use your fingers to scoop out the seeds from the tomato halves, leaving the juice and meat intact.

Discard the seeds. Dry the cut surface of the tomatoes with a paper towel. This will facilitate the charring process.

3.   Heat a heavy cast iron skillet over a high flame for about 5 minutes. Lightly brush both sides of the tomatoes with the olive oil. Char the tomatoes by placing them in the skillet, cut side down, until the flesh blackens, 4 to 5 minutes. Turn the tomatoes over with a spatula and char the other side for 1 minute. Remove from the pan and let cool.

4.   Chop the tomatoes into 1-inch chunks and combine with the remaining ingredients. Toss together well and serve at room temperature.

MASHED YELLOW TURNIPS WITH CRISPY SHALLOTS

One of Danny's fondest food memories is eating his grandmother's mashed potatoes topped with fried onion crisps. She served them with barbecued St. Louis baby back ribs, and even after all the meat was cleaned from the bones, he would dip the ribs into a second or third helping of mashed potatoes, enjoying the trace flavor of the barbecue sauce with the spuds.

The idea of substituting turnips for the potatoes and shallots for the onions came to Danny while strolling through the Greenmarket one fall day just before the restaurant opened. Mashed turnips have become one of Union Square Cafe's most beloved dishes, and the only person who has never been persuaded to try them is Danny's grandmother.

SERVES 4 TO 6

1 1/2 cups light olive or vegetable oil
3 tablespoons butter
5 to 6 shallots, peeled and sliced into thin rings
2 large yellow turnips (rutabaga), about 4 pounds
2 teaspoons kosher salt
1 cup milk
6 tablespoons butter
1/2 teaspoon freshly ground black pepper

1.   In a saucepan, heat the oil with 3 tablespoons butter over medium-low heat until it begins to bubble. Reduce the heat to low, add the shallots, and cook until they are a rich golden brown, 30 to 40 minutes. Stir the shallots occasionally while they are cooking to make sure they brown evenly.

2. Remove the shallots from the oil with a slotted spoon and drain on paper towels. Once the shallots have dried and crisped, in about 15 minutes, they can be stored in a cool place, covered, for several days. Serve the shallots at room temperature.

3. Peel the turnips to remove their waxy skins and cut them into generous 1-inch chunks. Place them in a saucepan with water to cover and 1 teaspoon of salt. Bring to a boil and simmer, covered, until easily pierced by a paring knife, about 35 minutes.

4. In a separate saucepan, heat the milk and remaining 6 tablespoons butter over low heat until the butter has melted and the milk just begins to simmer.

5. Drain the turnips and purée (in several batches, if necessary) in a food processor. With the motor running, add the melted butter and milk in a steady stream. The turnips should be very smooth.

6. Return the turnip purée to the saucepan, season with 1 teaspoon salt and the pepper and reheat, stirring, over a medium flame. Serve piping hot, sprinkled generously with crispy shallots.

CREAMY POLENTA WITH MASCARPONE

*P*olenta—sometimes translated as "cornmeal mush"—is often characterized as "bland," "insipid," and "tasteless." Follow this recipe and you'll create a polenta that is rich in flavor, yet fluffy and light in texture. The secret is in the long, slow cooking process, which transforms the raw cornmeal taste and gritty texture into a subtle, nutty, and smooth delight. When serving the polenta as an appetizer or on its own as a main course, we love the addition of melted Gorgonzola cheese and toasted walnuts. The polenta also makes a wonderful accompaniment to poultry and rabbit—in which case we omit the strongly flavored cheese and nuts.

SERVES 4

> 5 cups milk
> 1 cup polenta (medium-grain yellow cornmeal,
>   not instant)
> 5 tablespoons mascarpone cheese (2$^{1}/_{2}$ ounces)
> 1 teaspoon kosher salt
> $^{1}/_{8}$ teaspoon freshly ground white pepper
> 3 tablespoons crumbled Gorgonzola (2 ounces)
>   (optional)
> $^{1}/_{4}$ cup shelled walnuts, lightly toasted (optional)

1.   In a 2-quart, nonreactive saucepan, slowly bring the milk to a boil, stirring every few minutes with a wooden spoon to prevent scorching. To avoid lumpy polenta, follow this method carefully: Hold the cup of polenta in one hand and a firm whisk in the other. Slowly pour the polenta into the milk with a sprinkling motion and whisk constantly until all the polenta is absorbed.

2. Turn the heat down *very* low. Switch back to the wooden spoon and thoroughly stir the polenta every 10 minutes for 1 hour. The polenta should have the consistency of firm mashed potatoes. It will have completely lost its raw corn taste and gritty texture. Stir in the mascarpone and season with salt and white pepper.

3. Preheat the broiler. Spoon the polenta into a heat-resistant dish, dot evenly with the crumbled Gorgonzola, and melt the cheese under the broiler. Sprinkle with the toasted walnuts and serve.

Sautéed Insalata Tricolore

*A*mericans enjoy their salad before the meal, the French prefer it afterward. We wonder, why can't salad be served on the same plate—with the meat. Michael loves doing just that—using the same ingredients we keep on hand for our endive, radicchio, and arugula salad. Lightly sautéed just to the point of wilting, this warm, slightly bitter salad makes a wonderful accompaniment for lamb, beef, and veal.

SERVES 4

> 1 medium head radicchio, cleaned and cut into
> $^3/_4$-inch slices
> 2 heads Belgian endive, trimmed of any discolored leaves
>   and cut crosswise into $^3/_4$-inch slices
> 5 cups cleaned and coarsely chopped arugula (5 ounces)
> $^1/_4$ cup extra-virgin olive oil
> 1 teaspoon minced garlic
> Pinch of dried red pepper flakes
> $^1/_4$ teaspoon kosher salt
> Freshly ground black pepper

1. Combine the radicchio, endive, and arugula.

2. In a sauté pan large enough to hold all the greens, combine the olive oil, garlic, and red pepper flakes. Cook together over moderately high heat for about 45 seconds to flavor the oil, but do not allow the garlic to brown. Add the greens, tossing continuously until they wilt, about 2 minutes. Season with salt and pepper. Serve immediately, or at room temperature.

FAGIOLI ALLA TOSCANA

*W*ith tongue in cheek, Tuscans often refer to themselves as *mangiafagioli* (bean eaters)—so addicted are they to eating beans. Classically served with their beloved *bistecca alla fiorentina*—a hefty grilled T-bone steak slathered with olive oil and lemon—white beans are a satisfying accompaniment to roast meats and, we've found, even to grilled seafood and fish. Many Union Square Cafe guests enjoy the fagioli on their own as a hearty appetizer. Make sure to have plenty of good olive oil on hand to drizzle over the beans at the table.

It is important not to undercook fagioli. Unlike pasta, beans cooked al dente are both unpleasant to eat and difficult to digest.
SERVES 4

1 cup dried cannellini or Great Northern beans
1 celery rib
1 carrot, scrubbed and cut in half lengthwise
1 medium onion, peeled, halved, and stuck with 2 cloves
1 bay leaf
1 teaspoon kosher salt, plus more to taste
¹/₃ cup extra-virgin olive oil
1 tablespoon minced garlic
1 teaspoon each minced rosemary, sage, and thyme
¹/₂ cup grated Pecorino Romano
Freshly ground black pepper

1. Cover the beans with cold water and soak overnight.

2. Drain the beans and place them in a saucepan with cold water to cover by at least 3 inches. Add the celery, carrot, onion halves, and the bay leaf. Bring to a boil and immediately turn down to a simmer. With a slotted spoon or ladle, carefully skim off any foam that rises to the surface of the water. Continue simmering, covered, for 1 hour. Add the salt and continue cooking an additional 30 minutes, or until

(continued)

the beans are completely cooked and tender. Test for doneness by gently squeezing a bean between your fingers—it should give without any resistance. Discard the vegetables and, if not serving right away, let the beans cool in their cooking liquid.

3.   To serve, heat the olive oil and garlic in a skillet over medium heat; be careful not to brown the garlic. Add the beans to the skillet with $1^{1}/_{2}$ cups of their cooking liquid. Bring to a boil, add the herbs, and three quarters of the cheese. Continue to boil briskly until the liquid reduces to form a sauce, about 10 minutes. Don't be concerned if some of the beans disintegrate. Along with the olive oil and cheese, they will thicken and enrich the sauce. Add additional salt and pepper to taste. Transfer the beans to a serving dish, sprinkle with the remaining cheese and some additional extra-virgin olive oil, if you like.

Fagioli all'Uccelletto

*T*his is a richer version of Fagioli alla Toscana. Danny first had this savory white bean and tomato dish in a Roman trattoria and could never get a straight answer as to what the beans had to do with *uccelletti*, or "little birds." The most sensible answer he ever got was that the dish called for the same herbs—rosemary, sage, and thyme—as most recipes suggest for roasting little birds. Whatever the case, these beans pack a lot of flavor and are well worth the lengthy simmering time. Try them with any well-seasoned meat or fowl dish (they're great with roast quail) or have a plateful of them on their own for lunch on a chilly autumn day. All you'll need is some crusty bread and a glass of red wine to complete the meal.

SERVES 4 TO 6

Try Dolcetto d' Alba, Barbaresco, or Valpolicella with these rich-tasting beans.

1 recipe Fagioli alla Toscana, through step 2 (page 253)
1 cup Veal Stock (page 314)
¹/₃ cup extra-virgin olive oil
2 large tomatoes, peeled, seeded, and diced
1 teaspoon each minced rosemary, sage, and thyme
¹/₃ cup grated Pecorino Romano
Kosher salt
Freshly ground black pepper

1. In a large skillet, heat the fagioli with 1 cup of their cooking liquid, the veal stock, and the olive oil. Bring to a boil and cook over high heat until the starch in the beans, combined with the rapidly boiling stock, has formed a rich sauce.

2. Add the tomatoes and herbs and continue cooking 2 to 3 minutes. Finish with the Pecorino, salt, and freshly ground black pepper to taste.

Three-Grain Pilaf with Almonds and Shiitake Mushrooms

*T*ogether, these grains have a wonderfully nutty flavor that improves and completes the overall flavor of many dishes. Serve with Pan-Roasted Salmon with Citrus-Balsamic Vinaigrette, poultry, or lamb. Be sure to select hulled wheat berries—available at health food stores—to assure a synchronized cooking time for the pilaf.

SERVES 4

1/4 cup wheat berries
1 tablespoon butter
1/4 cup wild rice
1 1/2 cups water
1/4 cup white wine
1 bay leaf
1/8 teaspoon kosher salt
Freshly ground black pepper
1/4 cup basmati rice
1 cup quartered shiitake mushrooms,
   stems removed (4 ounces)
2 ounces whole almonds, with skin,
   coarsely chopped (1/3 cup)
4 scallions, beards removed, outer layer peeled,
   and thinly sliced (1/3 cup)

1. Soak the wheat berries in water to cover for 2 hours. Drain.

2. Melt half the butter in a 2-quart saucepan over medium heat. Add the wild rice and wheat berries; stir well to coat the grains. Add the water, white wine, bay leaf, salt, and pepper and bring to a boil. Cover, lower the heat, and gently simmer for 30 minutes.

3. Stir in the basmati rice and return to a simmer. Continue cooking, covered, without further stirring, for 20 more minutes. Remove from the heat and allow to finish steaming, covered, while you prepare the mushrooms and almonds.

4. Heat the remaining butter in a large skillet over high heat and sauté the shiitake mushrooms until softened, 3 to 4 minutes. Toss in the almonds and cook an additional 3 to 4 minutes. Stir in the scallions and cooked grains. When heated through, spoon the pilaf into a warm bowl and serve.

Red Lentil–Basmati Rice Pilaf

The rice and lentils are cooked separately to retain their individual characters. Serve the pilaf with Seared Curried Whitefish or Grilled Marinated Chicken Breast with Asian Spices.

SERVES 4

4 teaspoons vegetable oil
$^1/_2$ cup peeled and diced onion
$^3/_4$ cup imported basmati rice, rinsed
   (if using domestic, do not rinse)
$^1/_2$ bay leaf
1 teaspoon kosher salt
$^1/_4$ teaspoon freshly ground black pepper
3 cups water
1 tablespoon peeled, minced ginger
$^3/_4$ teaspoon ground cumin
$^3/_4$ teaspoon ground coriander
$^1/_2$ teaspoon dried red pepper flakes
$^3/_4$ cup split red lentils
1 scallion, white and green parts, trimmed and sliced

1.   In a $1^1/_2$-quart saucepan, heat 2 teaspoons of the oil over medium heat. Add the onion and cook for 3 minutes, stirring, until translucent. Stir in the rice, bay leaf, $^1/_2$ teaspoon salt, and $^1/_8$ teaspoon pepper. Add $1^1/_2$ cups water and bring to a boil. Lower the heat and simmer, covered, for 15 minutes. Remove from the heat and set aside to rest, covered, for 5 minutes.

2.   In a separate $1^1/_2$-quart saucepan, heat the remaining oil over medium heat. Stir in the ginger, cumin, coriander, and red pepper flakes and cook 1 minute. Add the red lentils and stir to coat evenly

with the spices. Add the remaining $1^1/_2$ cups water, season with the remaining salt and pepper, and bring to a boil. Lower the heat and simmer, covered, for 15 minutes.

3. In a large, warm serving bowl, combine the cooked rice and lentils, mixing thoroughly, and serve topped with the sliced scallion.

NOTE: If you can find them, split red lentils imported from India are preferable to their domestic counterparts for this recipe. They're slightly smaller and firmer, and will do a better job of retaining their shape and color after you've cooked them.

BAGNA CAUDA SAUCE

*T*his is Union Square Cafe's variation on the classic Piemontese *bagna cauda*—a culinary and social ritual in which crispy raw winter vegetables are dipped into a "hot bath" of olive oil flavored with garlic and anchovies. Though a Piedmont native might blanch at the thought, we serve our bagna cauda sauce at room temperature, drizzled over grilled or lightly steamed vegetables. We'd suggest sliced zucchini, quartered radicchio, young fennel, bell peppers, portobello mushrooms, cauliflower or broccoli florets. Additionally, this makes a nice eggless version of Caesar dressing, and a tangy condiment for grilled fish or steak.

SERVES 4 TO 6

> 2 tablespoons minced shallots
> 16 anchovy fillets
> 1 $^1/_3$ teaspoons minced garlic
> 4 tablespoons Italian red wine vinegar
> 1 teaspoon lemon juice
> 2 tablespoons finely grated Parmigiano-Reggiano
> $^1/_2$ teaspoon kosher salt
> $^1/_8$ teaspoon freshly ground black pepper
> 1 cup extra-virgin olive oil

1. In a food processor, combine all the ingredients except the olive oil. Purée until the anchovies are completely smooth. With the motor running, slowly add the olive oil and mix until creamy. If the sauce emulsifies to a mayonnaise consistency, add 1 to 2 tablespoons water so that it is pourable.

2. Serve at room temperature, drizzled over grilled or blanched vegetables, or as a dip for crudités.

PEACH-FIG CHUTNEY

A spicy, refreshing, and low-fat condiment for grilled chicken, roast duck, grilled vegetables, or roast pork. Tamarind paste and dried pomegranate seeds add subtle flavoring and acidity to the chutney, and are worth seeking out in specialty Indian and Middle Eastern markets. The chutney will keep up to a week, tightly covered and refrigerated.
YIELDS 2 1/2 CUPS

> 1 pound ripe peaches, unpeeled
> 1 tablespoon fresh lime juice
> 1/2 pound fresh ripe figs, such as Black Mission
> 3/4 cup cider vinegar, premium quality, unfiltered if possible
> 4 tablespoons honey
> 1 1/4 teaspoons mustard seeds
> 1 1/2 tablespoons minced pickled ginger
> Pinch of kosher salt
> 1/4 teaspoon tamarind paste (optional)
> 1 teaspoon ground dried pomegranate seeds, ground in a
>   spice mill (optional)
> 1 tablespoon seeded and minced jalapeño

1. Cut the peaches in half, remove the pits, and cut each half into 1 1/2-inch chunks. Toss the peaches with the lime juice and set aside. Remove the fig stems and quarter the figs lengthwise. Set aside.

2. In an 8-inch skillet, combine the cider, honey, mustard seeds, pickled ginger, salt, tamarind, and ground pomegranate seeds. Place over moderate heat and reduce to a syrup, 6 to 7 minutes. Stir in the peaches and cook over low heat, covered, until softened but not mushy. This will take 5 to 15 minutes, depending on the ripeness of the fruit. Add the figs and jalapeño and cook, covered, an additional 5 minutes.

3. Remove from the heat, transfer to a bowl, and cool. Serve at room temperature or chilled.

Rhubarb and Dried Cherry Chutney

*R*hubarb is a harbinger of spring, and here it stars with "cherry raisins" to make a fabulous sweet-spicy chutney. We serve it with Roast Lemon-Pepper Duck; it's also a great balance for other rich-tasting foods like pork and venison. Very young and tender rhubarb doesn't need to be peeled. But as the season progresses, larger stalks can become tough and stringy. Use a vegetable peeler to remove only the outermost layer.

4 CUPS

*2 pounds fresh rhubarb, both ends trimmed, peeled and
   cut into 1/2-inch pieces*
3 tablespoons sugar
1/2 cup honey
1/2 cup dried cherries
5 tablespoons red wine vinegar
3 tablespoons red wine
2 teaspoons mustard seeds
1/2 teaspoon kosher salt
Pinch each of cinnamon, allspice, and cayenne
1/2 cup minced red onion
3/4 cup 1/2-inch slices of celery
2 teaspoons grated orange zest
1 tablespoon minced jalapeño pepper (no seeds)
2 teaspoons lime juice

1.   Place the rhubarb in a colander over a bowl and sprinkle with the sugar. Let the rhubarb macerate and drain for 30 minutes.

2.   In a 10-inch skillet, cook the honey, cherries, vinegar, wine, mustard seeds, salt, and spices over medium heat until syrupy.

3. Stir in the onion and celery and cook for 2 minutes to soften. Add the rhubarb and cook over medium heat for 10 minutes, stirring occasionally to cook evenly. Avoid overcooking the rhubarb. When done, it should be tender but still have some texture to it.

4. Add the orange zest and jalapeño pepper and cook for 1 minute longer. Stir in the lime juice, remove from the pan, and let cool. Serve at room temperature or chilled.

NOTE: Sun-dried cherries from Washington State and Michigan are a relatively recent and worthy addition to the shelves of specialty food shops around the country. Some stores also carry sun-dried cranberries and strawberries—either of which would stand in nicely for the cherries in this recipe. The fruits are great for snacks in their dried state, but should always be reconstituted before using them in a recipe that does not include sauce or a liquid (e.g., pancakes or muffins).

HERBED POTATO SALAD WITH BACON AND SCALLIONS

*H*ere's a lively oil- and vinegar-based potato salad flavored with fresh herbs, smoky slab bacon, and crisp raw scallions. Serve with your favorite sandwich.

SERVES 4 TO 6

2 pounds red new potatoes, scrubbed and cut into
   eighths
3 medium garlic cloves, peeled and halved
1 fresh rosemary sprig
3 parsley sprigs
2 fresh thyme sprigs
1 teaspoon black peppercorns
1 tablespoon plus $1^1/_4$ teaspoons kosher salt
Pinch of dried red pepper flakes
6 ounces slab bacon, sliced $^1/_4$ inch thick
6 scallions, beards removed, outer layer peeled,
   and thinly sliced ($^1/_2$ cup)
$^1/_4$ cup extra-virgin olive oil
$1^1/_2$ tablespoons Italian red wine vinegar
1 tablespoon coarsely chopped parsley
$^1/_4$ teaspoon freshly ground black pepper

1. Preheat the oven to 375 degrees F.

2. Place the potatoes in a medium saucepan and cover with 6 cups water. Add the garlic, rosemary, parsley sprigs, thyme, peppercorns, 1 tablespoon salt, and red pepper flakes. Bring to a simmer and cook until the potatoes are tender but not mushy, 10 to 12 minutes. Set the saucepan aside to cool, leaving the potatoes in the cooking liquid.

3. Lay the bacon on a rack over a baking sheet (or directly on a baking sheet if you don't have a rack) and roast until crisp, 20 to 25 minutes. When cool enough to handle, cut each slice into $1/4$-inch pieces.

4. Reserve $1/4$ cup of the potato cooking liquid, then drain the potatoes in a colander. In a large bowl, combine the potatoes, bacon, and scallions.

5. Combine the reserved cooking liquid, olive oil, vinegar, parsley, the remaining salt, and $1/4$ teaspoon pepper in a glass jar. Cover tightly and shake vigorously. Pour the sauce over the potatoes and toss thoroughly to combine. Serve at room temperature.

Baked Banana Tart with Caramel and Macadamia Nuts

Individual Baked Apple Tarts with Apple Butter

Biscotti

Chocolate Sorbet

Blueberry and Peach Cobbler

Rosemary-Raisin Sponge Cake with Honeyed Goat Cheese

Marble Fudge Brownies

Panna Cotta

Frozen Goat's Milk Yogurt

Pear-Almond Crisp

Chilled Pineapple-Moscato Zabaglione

Rhubarb Crisp

Chilled Spiced Red Wine–Fig Soup

Pumpkin Flan

"Reverse" Chocolate Chunk Cookies

Pumpkin Bread Pudding

Mocha Semifreddo Layered with Toasted Hazelnut Dacquoise

Sardinian Lemon and Sheep's Milk Cheese Fritters with Honey

Ginger-Walnut Tart

*A*merican and Italian in inspiration, Union Square Cafe's desserts are straightforward, homey, and about comfort. The roster of recipes provides seasonal options as well as the opportunity to please lovers of chocolate, devotees of fruit desserts, and even those who prefer something slightly less sweet to nibble on while enjoying their last sips of wine.

A note on dessert wines: We love sweet wines and always have at least eight on hand, offered by the glass as an accompaniment to dessert, or as the dessert itself. It's very tricky to match sweet wines with dessert, since frequently the sugar content of one is far greater than that of the other. A sparkling flute of Italy's Muscato d'Asti, no matter how delicious and refreshing, may not be sweet enough to stand up to a sugary slice of pecan pie. And even a deliciously concentrated glass of Sauternes will leave disappointed chocolate lovers wondering why they ever let the two meet. Our advice: Experiment, have fun, but decide ahead of time which will be the star—the wine or the dessert—and make your pairing on that basis. If you can't decide, serve the sweet wine after the dessert as a course unto itself. Most of your happy guests will end up washing down their last bite with the dessert wine anyway, and if it works, you'll have found a combination you can serve together the next time.

Delicious dessert wines are made throughout the world, and once you find a style and level of sweetness you enjoy, there are literally dozens of flavor nuances you can experience. If you are fond of Sauternes—the sweet wine made from botrytised ("nobly rotted") sémillon and sauvignon blanc grapes in Bordeaux—it's worth seeking out Barsac, Loupiac, and Jurançon, or any good California or Australian Late Harvest Sauvignon Blanc or Sémillon. If you like the peachy-grapefruit flavor of the muscat grape, try Italy's sparkling Moscato d'Asti, France's Muscat de Beaumes de Venise, or a late harvest California wine made from Muscat Canelli. Riesling makes unctuously delicious dessert wines, and beyond Germany and Alsace, we've found great examples from Australia, New York State, and California. Often overlooked by dessert wine drinkers is Vouvray Moelleux—the luscious wine made from botrytised chenin blanc grapes in France's Loire Valley. The wine is a great value, it is long-lived, and with maturity, it's often indistinguishable from an outstanding Sauternes.

BAKED BANANA TART WITH CARAMEL AND MACADAMIA NUTS

*T*his is far and away the most popular dessert we've ever served at Union Square Cafe. We've adapted our individual tart recipe to make one 9-inch tart at home. When glazing the tart, make sure to time things so the hot caramel is ready just as the tart comes out of the oven.

SERVES 6 TO 8

TART DOUGH

8 tablespoons (1 stick) unsalted butter

1/4 cup sugar

1 egg yolk

2 teaspoons water

1 teaspoon vanilla extract

1 cup all-purpose flour

BANANA TOPPING

4 large ripe bananas

1 tablespoon very soft butter

1 tablespoon superfine sugar

TART GLAZE

1/2 cup sugar

1 tablespoon corn syrup

1 tablespoon butter

*1 cup lightly toasted and coarsely chopped macadamia
    nuts*

2 pints vanilla, honey-vanilla, or chocolate ice cream

1.   In the bowl of an electric mixer fitted with the paddle attachment, cream the butter and sugar until light. Add the yolk, water, and vanilla and blend well. Add the flour and mix until just blended.

(continued)

Place on a sheet of plastic wrap and, with lightly floured hands, form the dough into a flat patty. Wrap in the plastic and refrigerate at least 3 hours, or overnight.

2. Preheat the oven to 450 degrees F.

3. Remove the dough from the refrigerator and let sit for 10 to 15 minutes. Remove the bottom from an 8 ½-inch or 9-inch springform pan and dust lightly with flour. Set aside the ring of the springform pan, which will not be used. Unwrap the dough and place on the floured pan bottom. With a floured rolling pin, roll the dough to fill the pan bottom. Press firmly on the dough while rolling toward and over the edge of the circle. Some of the dough will be pushed over the edge as the bottom is covered. The dough should be ¼ inch thick, filling the bottom to its edge. Run a paper towel around the raised edge of the circle to wipe off any smeared dough. Cover a baking sheet with aluminum foil and place the pan bottom on it. Bake 12 to 14 minutes, until the crust is lightly golden. Remove from the oven and let cool. Lower the oven temperature to 375 degrees.

4. Peel the bananas, keeping them whole. Place 1 banana on a cutting surface with the back of the curve toward you. Using a sharp paring knife, slice off the end of the banana on a sharp diagonal and reserve the cut end. Thinly slice the entire banana on the diagonal, keeping the slices together. Repeat with the remaining bananas, reserving the cut ends. Carefully transfer 1 of the sliced bananas, intact, onto the baked tart shell. Position the banana 1 inch from the edge of the circle with the curve of the banana following the curve of the circle. Press your hand gently on the inside curve of the banana, causing the slices to lay flat and spread toward the outer edge of the circle. With the tips of your fingers, continue spreading until the banana is fanned over half the circle's edge. Repeat with the second banana over the other half of the circle's edge, connecting the ends to form an unbroken circle of fanned banana slices. Continue in the same manner to fill the inner part of the tart shell. Use the reserved

end banana pieces to fill the center of the tart. Brush the banana lightly with the soft butter and sprinkle with the tablespoon of sugar. Place the tart in the oven to bake the bananas for approximately 10 minutes while you prepare the caramel.

5. In a 1-quart saucepan, combine the sugar, corn syrup and butter. Place the saucepan over medium-high heat and stir to combine. Bring the caramel mixture to a boil, stirring occasionally, to melt the butter. When the mixture reaches a boil, stop stirring and allow it to caramelize to a medium amber. (If one area begins to brown faster than the rest, swirl the pan to blend the caramelization.) Remove from the heat and immediately dip the pan into very cold water to halt the cooking. Set aside while still hot.

6. Remove the tart from the oven. Dip a spoon into the hot caramel and drizzle it back and forth, vertically and horizontally, to create a grid pattern over the surface of the bananas. Allow the tart to sit until the caramel hardens, 1 to 2 minutes. With a sharp knife, cut away any excess caramel from the outside edge of the tart. Leaving it on the pan bottom, transfer the tart to a serving platter. Cut into wedges, sprinkle with the macadamia nuts, and serve while warm with a scoop of ice cream.

INDIVIDUAL BAKED APPLE TARTS WITH APPLE BUTTER

*T*his has been a favorite Union Square Cafe dessert from the day we opened. Choose crisp tart apples and cut them as thin as possible for best results. The apple butter is outstanding on its own, spread on cinnamon-raisin toast or served over vanilla ice cream.

MAKES FOUR 5-INCH TARTS

APPLE BUTTER

> *5 Granny Smith or McIntosh apples, unpeeled, cored,*
>   *and coarsely chopped*
> *1 quart fresh apple cider*
> *1 cinnamon stick*

TARTS

> *1/2 pound puff pastry, available frozen in supermarkets*
> *1/4 cup apple butter*
> *2 to 3 Granny Smith or McIntosh apples*
> *2 tablespoons butter, melted*
> *1 to 2 tablespoons superfine sugar*
> *1/3 cup crème fraîche or whipped cream, or 1 pint*
>   *vanilla ice cream as garnish*

1. Prepare the apple butter: Combine all the ingredients in a large pot and bring to a boil. Lower to a simmer and reduce by half, stirring occasionally, for approximately 1 hour. Remove the cinnamon stick and pass through a food mill. (If you don't have a food mill, peel the apples prior to chopping and purée the cooked mixture in a food processor.) Cool.

2. Prepare the tarts: On a lightly floured surface, roll the puff pastry to an 11-inch square. Cut out four 5-inch circles with a sharp paring knife, using a 5-inch plate, the top of a bowl, or similar object as your

guide. Transfer the circles to a baking sheet lined with parchment paper. Place a tablespoon of apple butter on each circle and spread out evenly with the back of a spoon, stopping $1/4$ inch short of the edges. Refrigerate.

3. Preheat the oven to 375 degrees F.

4. Peel, halve, and core the apples. Place the halves on a cutting board, cut side down, with the stem end point to the left. With a sharp paring knife, thinly slice the apples horizontally, across the core.

5. Remove the pastry circles from the refrigerator. Arrange the apple slices in a tight concentric circle, edges overlapping, over each pastry circle. Carefully brush the slices with half the melted butter. Bake 25 minutes, brush with the remaining butter, and continue baking an additional 10 to 12 minutes, until the apples are lightly golden and the pastry well browned. Remove from the oven and immediately sprinkle each tart with 1 to 2 teaspoons of superfine sugar. Transfer to individual plates and serve warm with a dollop of crème fraîche, whipped cream, or ice cream.

BISCOTTI

*H*ere's Union Square Cafe's version of Italy's famous "twice-baked" cookies. When the cafe first opened, we served them only in their classic role, as an accompaniment to the Tuscan dessert wine, Vin Santo. The biscotti have become so popular that guests now dip them into every sweet wine we serve, and often request them on their own.

YIELDS 5 DOZEN

2 3/4 cups all-purpose flour
1 1/3 cups plus 1 tablespoon sugar
1/2 cup whole almonds
1/3 cup sliced almonds
2 tablespoons cornmeal
1 1/2 tablespoons whole aniseed
1 1/2 teaspoons baking powder
1/8 teaspoon salt
8 tablespoons unsalted butter, at room temperature
2 eggs
1 tablespoon vanilla extract
1 tablespoon Pernod
1 egg white, lightly beaten

1. Preheat the oven to 350 degrees F.

2. Combine the flour, sugar, almonds, cornmeal, aniseed, baking powder, and salt in the bowl of a standing mixer fitted with the paddle attachment. Using low speed, mix thoroughly. Alternatively, mix by hand with a wooden spoon until thoroughly combined.

3. Add the butter and continue mixing on low speed until the dough has the consistency of wet sand.

4. Mix in the eggs, vanilla, and Pernod until a soft dough is formed.

5. Divide the dough in half and form into 2 logs, each 4 × 15 inches. Place the logs on a cookie sheet lined with parchment paper. Lightly beat the egg white. Brush evenly on the logs and sprinkle with 1 tablespoon sugar. Bake for 30 minutes, until golden brown. The logs should be firm but still pliable. Cool to room temperature.

6. When the logs are cool enough to handle, cut them into $1/4$-inch-thick slices with a serrated knife. Lay the sliced cookies out on the cookie sheet. Lower the oven to 325 degrees and bake until lightly golden and crisp, about 15 minutes. Cool and store, well covered.

CHOCOLATE SORBET

This amazing sorbet combines an intense chocolate punch with a light, refreshing texture. For maximum flavor, allow to soften 10 to 15 minutes in your refrigerator before serving.

YIELDS 2 ½ TO 3 PINTS

> *2 cups sugar*
> *1 cup premium quality cocoa (alkalized or dutch-*
>   *processed)*
> *1 teaspoon ground cinnamon*
> *Pinch of salt*
> *4 cups water*
> *1 cup strong brewed coffee*
> *1 tablespoon coffee liqueur*
> *Fresh mint sprigs for garnish (optional)*

1.   Mix all dry ingredients in a large saucepan. Stir in the water and coffee. Bring to a simmer over moderate heat and cook for a few minutes until the ingredients are dissolved. Remove from the heat and stir in the liqueur. Allow to cool and then refrigerate until chilled thoroughly.

2.   Freeze in an ice cream machine according to manufacturer's directions. If the sorbet is still soft when removed from the machine, place in the freezer overnight to harden. Garnish with mint sprigs and serve.

BLUEBERRY AND PEACH COBBLER

A wonderful deep-dish pie to celebrate two of summer's favorite fruits. Serve warm, with whipped cream, or a scoop of vanilla or strawberry ice cream.

SERVES 4 TO 6

> 2 cups blueberries
> 2 pounds fresh peaches, peeled and sliced (7 cups)
> $1/2$ teaspoon ground cardamom
> $1/2$ teaspoon grated lemon zest
> 5 tablespoons sugar
> 2 cups plus 1 tablespoon cake flour
> 1 tablespoon baking powder
> Pinch of salt
> 5 tablespoons unsalted butter, cut into bits
> $3/4$ cup plus 1 tablespoon heavy cream

1. Preheat the oven to 400 degrees F.

2. Combine the blueberries and sliced peaches in a bowl. Toss with the cardamom, lemon zest, 2 tablespoons sugar, and 1 tablespoon flour. Transfer the fruit to a deep, 10-inch ovenproof serving dish.

3. To make the pastry, sift together the 2 cups cake flour, remaining sugar, baking powder, and salt in a large bowl. Using two butter knives, combine the butter with the flour until the mixture resembles coarse meal. Using a light touch, stir in $3/4$ cup cream to make a soft and tender dough.

4. Turn the dough out onto a table and roll $3/4$ inch thick. With a cookie cutter, cut out 3-inch rounds. Arrange the rounds atop the blueberries and peaches and brush with 1 tablespoon heavy cream. Bake for 30 to 35 minutes, until bubbly and lightly browned. Serve warm.

Rosemary-Raisin Sponge Cake with Honeyed Goat Cheese

*A*n unusual, not-too-sweet dessert for cheese lovers, this is delicious served with dessert wine, or with the last few drops of the dinner's red wine.

SERVES 6 TO 8

HONEY SAUCE

>*1/2 cup honey*
>*1/3 cup white wine*
>*1 1/2 tablespoons fresh rosemary*
>*2 teaspoons lemon juice*

HONEYED GOAT CHEESE

>*5 ounces fresh soft goat cheese*
>*4 ounces cream cheese*
>*1 1/2 ounces sour cream*
>*3/4 teaspoon chopped rosemary*
>*3 tablespoons finely chopped hazelnuts*
>*2 1/2 teaspoons applejack or Calvados*
>*1 1/2 tablespoons honey*
>*1 teaspoon salt*
>*Freshly ground black pepper*
>*1/2 cup heavy cream*

ROSEMARY-RAISIN CAKE

>*2 tablespoons extra-virgin olive oil, plus more for the
>   cake pan*
>*1 cup all-purpose flour, plus more for the cake pan*
>*1/2 cup cake flour*
>*1 1/2 teaspoons baking powder*
>*Pinch of salt*
>*1 1/2 tablespoons chopped fresh rosemary*

3 eggs
³/₄ cup light brown sugar
³/₄ teaspoon vanilla extract
1¹/₂ cups golden raisins

1. Combine the honey and white wine in a small nonreactive saucepan and bring to a boil. Lower the heat and simmer for 3 to 5 minutes. Remove from the heat, add the fresh rosemary, and allow to infuse for 10 minutes. Strain, add the lemon juice, and set aside.

2. In the bowl of a kitchen mixer, combine the goat cheese, cream cheese, and sour cream. Cream until smooth and light, 3 to 4 minutes. Stir in the rosemary, hazelnuts, applejack, honey, salt, and pepper.

3. Whip the cream to soft peaks and fold into the goat cheese base with a rubber spatula. Line a colander with a square of cheesecloth. Transfer the cheese mixture to the colander, twist the cheesecloth closed around it, and flatten slightly to form a disk. Place the colander over a bowl to drain, and refrigerate for at least 2 hours, or overnight.

4. Preheat the oven to 350 degrees F. Lightly oil and flour a 9-inch square cake pan.

5. Sift together the flours, baking powder, and salt. Add the chopped rosemary.

6. Beat the eggs and brown sugar until well blended but not increased in volume. Stir in the vanilla and 2 tablespoons olive oil. Add the egg mixture to the dry ingredients, stirring until just combined. Fold in the raisins, but don't overmix or the cake will be dry.

7. Spread the batter evenly into the cake pan and bake for 20 minutes, until golden brown and slightly firm to the touch. Cool on a rack.

8. Slice the rosemary cake and serve each portion topped a with a spoonful of the chilled honeyed-goat cheese and a drizzle of the honey sauce.

MARBLE FUDGE BROWNIES

*T*hese cream cheese-swirled brownies baked in individual molds raise an old comfort dessert to new heights of elegance. The brownies are a guaranteed hit for entertaining. For best results, serve with hot chocolate sauce and a scoop of vanilla, pistachio, or chocolate-mint ice cream.

SERVES 4

FOR THE MOLDS

1 tablespoon butter, at room temperature

2 tablespoons cocoa powder

4 round 6-ounce molds, fluted if possible, 1 1/8 inches
   deep by 4 inches in diameter

FUDGE MIX

4 1/2 ounces semisweet chocolate

9 tablespoons unsalted butter

2 large eggs

3/4 cup plus 1 tablespoon sugar

1/2 cup all-purpose flour

Pinch of salt

CREAM CHEESE SWIRL

1/4 cup sugar

8 ounces cream cheese

1/2 teaspoon vanilla extract

1 large egg

1. Preheat the oven to 300 degrees F. Butter the molds and dust with the cocoa powder.

2. To make the fudge mix, place the chocolate and butter in the top of a double boiler set over simmering water and melt, stirring to combine thoroughly.

3. In a large bowl, whisk together the eggs with the sugar until well combined but not increased in volume.

4. Add the chocolate to the egg mixture and stir well to incorporate. Stir in the flour and salt until just blended, not overmixed.

5. To make the cream cheese topping, cream the sugar and the cream cheese in the bowl of a standing mixer, scraping down the sides as you work. Continue until completely smooth. Add the vanilla and the egg and mix until incorporated.

6. Fill the molds to three-quarters full with the chocolate mixture, then top with the cream cheese mixture. Using a folding motion with a fork, swirl the cream cheese mixture into the chocolate two or three times.

7. Bake in the oven for 35 minutes. The top of the brownie will be light golden brown and slightly puffed, and the center will be tender.

8. Cool on a rack for 15 minutes before unmolding. Best served while still warm.

PANNA COTTA

Since this satin-textured custard contains no eggs, it gets its consistency from gelatin. It is worth the trouble to seek out a source for sheet gelatin, since the results are so good.

SERVES 6

1/2 cup sugar
3 tablespoons water
1 teaspoon fresh lemon juice
3 sheets gelatin (1/4 ounce, total)
2 3/4 cups heavy cream (preferably 40 percent milk fat)
1/2 cup sweetened condensed milk
4 cups fresh fruit to garnish (choose from strawberries, rasp-
berries, blueberries, tangerine, or orange sections)

1. In a small, heavy-bottomed saucepan, combine the sugar, water, and lemon juice. Cook over medium heat, without stirring, until the sugar turns a golden caramel color. Pour equal amounts of the caramel into six 5-ounce soufflé molds. Set aside.

2. Place the sheets of gelatin in a bowl with ice water to cover. Stir the gelatin with your fingers until it has softened. Set aside.

3. In a nonreactive saucepan over medium heat, bring the cream and condensed milk barely to a simmer. Do not allow to boil. Lift the gelatin sheets from the water, squeeze them dry, and stir into the heated cream to dissolve. Strain the mixture and pour into the caramel-lined molds. Cover with plastic wrap and place in the refrigerator to set for at least 4 hours.

4. To serve, run a knife around the inside edge of the mold and invert each panna cotta on a plate. Garnish with fruit.

FROZEN GOAT'S MILK YOGURT

*A*n unusual and refreshing frozen dessert using tangy goat's milk yogurt as its base. Serve with Chilled Spiced Red Wine–Fig Soup, fresh berries, poached fruit, or cinnamon cookies.

YIELDS 2 ½ PINTS

> 5 cups goat's milk yogurt, such as Coach Dairy Farm's
>   "Yo-Goat"
> 1 cup sugar
> ⅓ cup corn syrup

1. Combine 1 cup of the yogurt with the sugar and corn syrup in a medium saucepan. Heat over medium-high heat, stirring frequently, until the mixture begins to simmer. Remove from the heat and chill thoroughly.

2. Whisk in the remaining 4 cups yogurt and freeze in an ice cream machine according to manufacturer's directions. If the frozen yogurt remains soft, place in the freezer overnight to harden.

PEAR-ALMOND CRISP

A wonderful autumn dessert that substitutes almondy amaretti cookies for some of the sugar normally found in fruit crisps. Chilled heavy cream provides a refreshing contrast to the piping hot crisp.
SERVES 10

> 4 pounds ripe Bosc pears, peeled and cored
> $^1/_2$ cup Poire Williams brandy
> 2 tablespoons sugar
> $^1/_2$ cup whole blanched almonds
> $1^3/_4$ cups all-purpose flour
> 1 cup brown sugar
> 1 teaspoon ground cinnamon
> 11 tablespoons unsalted butter, softened
> $^1/_2$ cup crushed amaretti cookies
> 1 pint chilled heavy cream

1. Preheat the oven to 375 degrees F.

2. Halve the pears lengthwise and cut into $^1/_4$-inch slices. Place the pear slices in a bowl, drizzle with pear brandy, sprinkle with sugar, and stir with a wooden spoon to coat evenly. Set aside to macerate for 30 minutes.

3. Toast the almonds on a baking sheet for 7 to 10 minutes, or until evenly toasted. Remove and cool. Finely chop the almonds and set aside.

4. In a mixing bowl, combine the flour, brown sugar, and cinnamon. Mix in the butter, working with your fingers until the mixture holds together and is crumbly. Stir in the chopped almonds and the crushed amaretti cookies. Set aside.

5. Place the pears and their juice in a 12-inch round porcelain tart pan. Spread the almond mixture evenly over them. Bake for 1 hour, or until the pears are bubbling and the topping is golden brown.

6. To serve, scoop the hot crisp into individual dessert bowls and drizzle the chilled heavy cream evenly over each portion.

CHILLED PINEAPPLE-MOSCATO ZABAGLIONE

*O*ur chilled variation on the classic zabaglione substitutes the light and citrusy Italian dessert wine, Moscato d'Asti, for rich Marsala. Pineapple lends a distinctive sweet-tart note. Serve as an accompaniment to Ginger-Walnut Tart or dolloped over fresh berries or sliced tropical fruits. Enjoy a well-chilled glass of the remaining Moscato d'Asti with your dessert.

SERVES 4 TO 6

4 egg yolks
$1/2$ cup sugar
$1/2$ cup frozen, pure, unsweetened pineapple juice
  concentrate, thawed
$1/4$ cup Moscato d'Asti wine
1 cup heavy cream

1. In the bowl of an electric mixer, combine all ingredients except the cream. Place over simmering water and whisk constantly until mixture is well aerated, hot, and thickened.

2. Return the bowl to the mixer and whip on medium-high speed until the zabaglione is cooled and as thick as softly whipped cream. Refrigerate until chilled, up to 1 hour.

3. Just before serving, whip the cream until soft peaks form and fold gently into the chilled zabaglione.

RHUBARB CRISP

*R*hubarb is plentiful in early spring and this simple dessert puts it to good use. If you are unable to find young, tender rhubarb stalks, make sure to peel the outermost stringy layer.

SERVES 6

3/4 cup plus 3 tablespoons all-purpose flour
1/3 cup brown sugar
1/8 teaspoon ground cinnamon
1 1/4 tablespoons plus 3/4 cup sugar
5 1/3 tablespoons unsalted butter, softened
1/2 cup toasted walnuts
2 pounds rhubarb, cut into 1/2-inch pieces
1 pint strawberry or vanilla ice cream

1. Preheat the oven to 400 degrees F.

2. In a bowl, combine the 3/4 cup flour, brown sugar, cinnamon, and 1 1/4 tablespoons white sugar. Work in the butter with your fingers until the mixture is crumbly. Add the walnut pieces.

3. In a 10-inch pie plate or ovenproof serving dish, toss the rhubarb with the sugar and 3 tablespoons flour, to coat evenly. Scatter the crisp topping evenly over the surface of the rhubarb. Bake for 35 minutes, until the rhubarb bubbles at the sides and the topping is crisp and brown. Serve warm topped with ice cream.

Chilled Spiced
Red Wine–Fig Soup

*H*ere's a captivating and refreshing late summer dessert that's sure to win over red wine lovers. We love it served with a scoop of Frozen Goat's Milk Yogurt, but it's equally good with cinnamon cookies or as a postscript to a platter of after-dinner cheeses.

SERVES 4

1 cinnamon stick
2 to 3 star anise, broken up
$^1/_8$ teaspoon dried red pepper flakes
2 strips orange zest
2 dozen small figs, stemmed, such as Black Mission
1 750-ml bottle of dry red wine, such as Beaujolais,
    Dolcetto d'Alba, or Zinfandel
$^1/_4$ cup sugar
Juice of $^1/_2$ lemon

1.   In a small piece of cheesecloth, bundle the cinnamon stick, star anise, red pepper flakes, and orange zest; tie securely.

2.   Set aside half the figs. Place the remaining figs in a large saucepan with the cheesecloth bundle and the remaining ingredients. Bring to a boil, lower the heat, and simmer for 1 minute. Remove from the heat, steep for 5 minutes, and discard the cheesecloth bundle.

3.   Purée the cooked soup in a food processor, then strain back into the saucepan through a sieve lined with several layers of cheesecloth. (The remaining fig paste may be cooled and reserved for baking cookies.)

4.   Add the reserved figs to the saucepan with the soup. Bring to a boil, lower the heat, and simmer, covered, 5 to 7 minutes, until the figs are tender. Transfer the poached figs and soup to a bowl and chill thoroughly.

5.   Just before serving, remove the figs with a slotted spoon, split lengthwise, and transfer 6 halves to each of four chilled soup bowls. Ladle the soup into each bowl and serve.

PUMPKIN FLAN

*T*his variation on crème caramel is delicately flavored with spiced pumpkin purée. We bake our flans in individual ramekins, but as the recipe indicates, you may also make the recipe in a single 9-inch cake or pie pan. If you do, the flan will resemble a crustless pumpkin pie. Cinnamon-flavored whipped cream, spooned over the chilled flan just before serving, is a wonderful accompaniment.

SERVES 8

CARAMEL

$1^1/_2$ cups sugar
$^1/_2$ cup water

FLAN

1 cup sugar
1 teaspoon ground cinnamon
$^1/_2$ teaspoon salt
$^1/_4$ teaspoon ground nutmeg
$^1/_4$ teaspoon powdered ginger
6 eggs
1 cup canned pumpkin purée
1 12-ounce can evaporated milk
1 teaspoon vanilla extract
$^1/_2$ cup water

1.   To prepare the caramel, combine the sugar and water in a heavy-bottomed saucepan and cook over medium heat without stirring until it caramelizes into a rich amber color, 8 to 10 minutes. Remove from the heat immediately to stop the cooking. If the sugar begins to color unevenly, you may swirl the pan, if necessary, to assure thorough caramelization.

2.   Pour equal amounts of the liquid caramel into eight 1-cup crème caramel ramekins, or into a 9-inch cake or pie pan. Set aside.

3.   Preheat the oven to 350 degrees F.

4.   In the bowl of a standing electric mixer, using the whisk attachment, combine the sugar, cinnamon, salt, nutmeg, and ginger. Begin mixing at moderate speed and add the eggs. When the eggs are well mixed, about 1 minute, add the pumpkin purée. Continue mixing for 30 seconds until the eggs and purée are incorporated. With the mixer still running, add the evaporated milk, vanilla, and water; continue blending for an additional 1 minute until you have a smooth, homogeneous mass.

5.   Divide the pumpkin flan mixture evenly among the ramekins, or pour it all into the cake pan.

6.   Place the filled ramekins or cake pan in a deep-sided roasting pan and pour in hot tap water to reach halfway up the sides of the ramekins to make a *bain-marie.* Cover the roasting pan with foil and carefully transfer to the middle shelf of the oven. Bake the filled ramekins for 30 to 40 minutes until the flan is *just* firm and set. (If you use a cake pan, increase the baking time to 60 to 75 minutes.) The cooked flan should jiggle slightly when shaken, and a paring knife will come out clean when inserted in the center. Remove the ramekins or pan from the *bain-marie* and set aside to cool. Once cooled, refrigerate the flan until well chilled to allow it to set.

7.   To serve, unmold the flan by running the point of a small paring knife along the inside of the ramekins or pan. Cover each ramekin or the pan with a chilled plate and invert. The caramel should spill out to form a sauce for the flan. Serve garnished with cinnamon-flavored whipped cream if desired.

"Reverse" Chocolate Chunk Cookies

*T*hese rich brown cookies studded with chunks of white chocolate are a delicious, inside-out version of chocolate chip cookies. Since the cookie batter is brown to begin with, you won't be able to use its toasty color as a visual indication of doneness. To avoid overcooking, remove the cookies from the oven as soon as they puff up and are still slightly soft to the touch. The cookies will set as they cool, but should remain pliable rather than hard or crunchy.

MAKES 60 COOKIES

> $1^3/_4$ *cups all-purpose flour*
> $1^1/_4$ *cups cocoa powder*
> *2 teaspoons baking soda*
> *20 tablespoons ($2^1/_2$ sticks) unsalted butter, at room tem-*
> *perature*
> $1^1/_4$ *cups sugar*
> $^3/_4$ *cup brown sugar*
> *2 eggs*
> *10 ounces solid white chocolate, broken into $^1/_4$-inch*
> *chunks (or 8 ounces white chocolate chips)*

1. Preheat the oven to 350 degrees F.

2. Lightly butter a cookie sheet, or alternatively, line the sheet with a strip of parchment paper. Set aside.

3. In a mixing bowl, combine the flour, cocoa powder, and baking soda. Set aside.

4. Using an electric mixer or a hand-held beater, cream the butter and sugars until the mixture is light and fluffy. Add the eggs and con-

tinue to beat until they are well combined, about 1 minute. Mix in the flour mixture until well incorporated. Fold in the white chocolate chunks with a rubber spatula.

5. Form the cookies, using a tablespoon of batter for each one, and place in even rows on the cookie sheet. Leave 2 inches between each cookie.

6. Transfer the cookie sheet to the middle shelf of the oven and bake for 8 to 10 minutes, until the cookies are puffed and still soft to the touch. Remove the cookie sheet from the oven and allow the cookies to cool and set for 5 to 7 minutes before carefully removing them with a spatula. If you have used a sheet of parchment paper, slide the entire sheet off the tray and allow the cookies to cool for 5 to 7 minutes. Meanwhile, you may reuse the cookie sheet immediately for baking the next batch.

Pumpkin Bread Pudding

*H*ere's a versatile recipe that's actually two desserts in one. The pumpkin bread stands on its own as a terrific accompaniment to a steaming cup of tea, coffee, apple cider, or hot chocolate. The addition of an easy-to-prepare custard turns it into a comforting bread pudding with plenty of flavor. For convenience, bake the pumpkin bread 1 to 3 days ahead, wrap, and refrigerate. The bread can be successfully frozen for up to 2 months.

SERVES 6 TO 8

PUMPKIN BREAD

1 cup currants

3 tablespoons dark rum

1³/4 cups all-purpose flour

2 teaspoons baking powder

¹/2 teaspoon baking soda

¹/4 teaspoon salt

1 tablespoon ground cinnamon

1 teaspoon grated nutmeg

¹/8 teaspoon ground cloves

1 cup canned pumpkin purée

¹/2 pound (2 sticks) unsalted butter

1¹/4 cups sugar

3 eggs, lightly beaten

CUSTARD

2¹/2 cups half-and-half

²/3 cup sugar

2 tablespoons peeled and grated fresh ginger

3 eggs

1 teaspoon vanilla extract

1 teaspoon cinnamon

Confectioners' sugar for dusting

1. Preheat the oven to 350 degrees F.

2. In a small saucepan, combine the currants and dark rum and place over medium heat. Bring to a boil, remove from the heat, and set aside to plump the currants, 5 to 10 minutes.

3. Butter and flour a 9 × 5-inch loaf pan. In a bowl, whisk together the flour, baking powder, baking soda, salt, cinnamon, nutmeg, and cloves.

4. Place the pumpkin purée in a bowl. Strain the currants into a colander held over the bowl and incorporate the rum into the pumpkin purée. Set aside the currants.

5. In the bowl of a standing mixer fitted with the paddle attachment, cream the butter and sugar on medium-high speed until light and airy. Reduce the speed to low and gradually add the eggs until well incorporated. Add the dry ingredients to the butter mixture alternately with the pumpkin purée, beginning and ending with the dry ingredients. Stir in the currants.

6. Pour the batter into the loaf pan and bake 1 hour and 40 minutes, until firm to the touch. Cool 10 minutes in the pan, then invert onto a wire rack and allow the cake to cool completely.

7. In a medium saucepan, mix the half-and-half, sugar, and ginger. Bring to a boil over medium heat, stirring frequently. Remove from the heat and steep the ginger for 20 minutes. Strain and reserve.

8. Whisk together the eggs and the vanilla until foamy. Whisk in the half-and-half mixture until thoroughly blended.

9. To assemble the pudding, cut the loaf of pumpkin bread in half lengthwise. Wrap one half and refrigerate or freeze for another use. Cut the other half into 16 square slices, then cut each square diagonally to make 32 triangles.

10. In a shallow, 12 × 7-inch oval gratin dish, arrange the triangles cut side down in overlapping rows to fill the dish completely. Pour the

(continued)

custard mixture into the dish, pouring around the pumpkin bread to keep the top edges dry. Sprinkle the cinnamon over the pumpkin bread and set aside for 10 minutes to allow the bread to soak up the custard.

11. Place the gratin dish in a large roasting pan and fill the pan with enough water to come halfway up the sides of the dish. Bake in the center of the oven for 45 to 50 minutes, until the custard is set around the edges yet still slightly soft toward the center. Remove the gratin dish from the water as soon as it is taken from the oven. Dust with confectioners' sugar, scoop out portions, and serve warm.

Mocha Semifreddo Layered with Toasted Hazelnut Dacquoise

Semifreddo, the Italian "half-frozen" dessert, stays light and fluffy thanks to folded-in egg whites and whipped cream. Here's an eye-opening rendition, flavored with a punch of espresso and layered with crispy hazelnut dacquoise.

SERVES 6 TO 8

DACQUOISE

1 cup toasted hazelnuts (4 ounces)
^{1}/2 cup sugar
2 teaspoons flour
3 egg whites, at room temperature
Pinch of salt

SEMIFREDDO

4 egg yolks
6 tablespoons sugar
1 teaspoon vanilla extract
6 tablespoons brewed espresso, or 1 heaping tablespoon instant espresso powder mixed into 6 tablespoons boiling water.
^{1}/2 cup heavy cream
2 egg whites, at room temperature
Pinch of salt
3 tablespoons sugar

GARNISH

1 cup heavy cream, whipped
2 tablespoons shaved semisweet chocolate

(continued)

1.   Preheat the oven to 325 degrees F.

2.   Line the bottom of a baking sheet with parchment paper. Using the bottom of a 9 × 5-inch loaf pan as a guide, trace 3 rectangular outlines onto the paper with the point of a dinner knife.

3.   In a food processor fitted with the metal blade, grind the hazelnuts with $1/4$ cup of the sugar until fine. Transfer to a bowl, stir in the flour, and set aside.

4.   In the bowl of a standing mixer, heat the egg whites, salt and remaining $1/4$ cup sugar over simmering water until warm to the touch. Return the bowl to the mixer and whip on medium-high speed until firm peaks are formed. Fold in the nut mixture.

5.   Fill a large pastry bag fitted with a $1/4$-inch plain round tip with the meringue. Pipe the meringue to fill the three outlined rectangles. Bake 30 to 40 minutes, until lightly browned and firm to the touch. Allow to cool on the sheet pan. (If the meringues have browned before becoming adequately firm, turn off the heat and allow them to dry in the oven.)

6.   Carefully turn over the parchment paper and peel off the meringues. Trim the meringue rectangles, if necessary, to fit the inside of the loaf pan and set aside. Line the inside of the loaf pan with plastic wrap, allowing for a 2-inch overlap over the top edges and set aside.

7.   For the semifreddo, combine the egg yolks, sugar, vanilla, and espresso in the bowl of an electric mixer. Place over simmering water and whisk constantly until thick, foamy, and hot. Return the bowl to the mixer and whip on medium-high speed until cooled and well aerated. Transfer to a large, nonreactive bowl and refrigerate.

8.   Whip the heavy cream until soft peaks form. Transfer the whipped cream to the bowl with the egg yolk-espresso mixture without combining and return to the refrigerator.

9. Whip the egg whites with a pinch of salt until foamy and beginning to hold a peak. Continue to whip, gradually adding the 3 tablespoons sugar, until firm peaks form.

10. Remove the large bowl from the refrigerator and add the firmly whipped egg whites. Fold together the egg yolk mixture, the whipped cream, and the whipped whites until blended.

11. To assemble, place 1 meringue layer in the bottom of the lined pan. Pour in half of the whipped mixture. Top with a second meringue. Pour in the remaining mixture and top with the third meringue. Fold the ends of the plastic wrap neatly over the top, cover tightly with an additional sheet of plastic wrap, and freeze overnight.

12. To serve, take the semifreddo from the freezer and remove the covering plastic wrap. Unfold the ends of the plastic wrap lining the pan to expose the top layer of meringue. Carefully turn the loaf over onto a cutting surface and lift the pan from the semifreddo. Peel off all the plastic wrap. With a sharp serrated knife, slice the semifreddo into 1-inch slices. Place one slice on each dessert plate, and garnish, if desired, with a generous dollop of lightly sweetened whipped cream and chocolate shavings.

Sardinian Lemon and Sheep's Milk Cheese Fritters with Honey

*T*he beautiful and wild island of Sardinia has captivated us with its exotic and tangled culinary heritage—Moorish, North African, Spanish, Greek, and Italian. We've always found it amazing that on one small island—no bigger than Rhode Island—a traditional dessert like this *seadas al miele* is prepared slightly differently in scores of tiny villages, each one entirely sure that its version is the best. While all *seadas* recipes contain sheep's milk cheese and honey (for an exquisite salty-sweet contrast), our favorite version—from Sardinia's south—is made with a touch of vanilla and tangy lemon zest. For the most authentic results, try to find a bitter, herbaceous Italian honey, available in specialty stores.

SERVES 6

DOUGH

> 1 1/4 cups all-purpose flour
> 1/4 cup cake flour
> 3 tablespoons sugar
> 1 teaspoon baking powder
> 1 1/4 tablespoons cold butter, cubed
> 1 1/4 tablespoons vegetable shortening

CHEESE AND LEMON FILLING

> 1/2 pound young, semihard sheep's milk cheese, such as Dolce Pecorino or Mufflone d'Oro, finely grated (1 1/2 cups)
> 1 vanilla bean, split
> Grated zest of 1 lemon
> 1 egg, beaten

This warm dessert works very well with ripe, raisiny dessert wines, such as the Sardinian Vernaccia di Oristano or Tuscany's fabled Vin Santo.

1 quart vegetable oil
6 tablespoons premium honey
2 tablespoons confectioners' sugar

1. For the dough, sift the flours into the bowl of a standing mixer fitted with the paddle attachment. Add the sugar and baking powder and mix on low speed. With the mixer running, add the butter cubes and shortening and mix until the dough resembles coarse meal. Continue mixing and begin pouring in 6 tablespoons cold water, stopping as soon as the dough begins to hold together. Remove the dough from the bowl, fold over once or twice, and divide in half. Wrap each half in plastic and refrigerate at least 3 hours. The dough may be prepared up to 2 days in advance.

2. For the filling, place the grated cheese in a medium bowl. Scrape the seeds from the inside of the vanilla bean into the bowl. Add the grated lemon zest and toss well. Form the mixture into 6 round patties, each one 2 inches in diameter and $1/2$ inch thick. Refrigerate until ready to use.

3. Take one piece of dough from the refrigerator and, on a lightly floured surface, roll into an extended rectangle, about 5 inches wide and 26 inches long. (If you have a pasta machine, roll the dough to No. 3.) Refrigerate the strip and repeat with the second piece of dough. After the second piece has been rolled out, brush the entire surface with the beaten egg and cut the strip across its width into 6 equal pieces, each approximately 5 inches by 5 inches. Place a cheese patty in the center of each square.

4. Remove the refrigerated strip of dough and cut into 6 equal pieces, also 5 inches square. Working with one piece at a time, cover each cheese patty and press to bond both layers of the dough. With the tips of your fingers, carefully push out any air bubbles trapped between the pieces of dough and close any remaining openings along the seam. Repeat with the remaining squares. Using a round, fluted cutter, $3 1/2$ inches in diameter, cut out a circle from each of the closed squares, making sure that the cheese remains in the center. Refrigerate until ready to use.

(continued)

5. In a 3-quart saucepan, heat the oil to 365 degrees F. (If you don't have a deep-fat thermometer, a piece of bread dropped into the oil will float up almost immediately and brown lightly in about 45 seconds at this temperature.) Carefully slide 3 of the fritters into the oil and fry 2 minutes. Turn over with a slotted spoon and cook until golden brown, an additional 1 to 2 minutes. Drain on paper towels and repeat with remaining fritters. Immediately transfer the hot fritters to a serving platter, drizzle with the honey, sprinkle with the confectioners' sugar, and serve.

GINGER-WALNUT TART

*F*resh ginger adds an exotic spicy note to this sweet nut tart. Select the youngest ginger you can find to avoid a stringy filling. The tart is delicious enough on its own, but the flavor truly soars if you serve it with a dollop of Pineapple-Moscato Zabaglione.

SERVES 8

DOUGH

2 cups all-purpose flour
1 tablespoon sugar
$^1/_8$ teaspoon salt
12 tablespoons ($1^1/_2$ sticks) cold butter, cut into
    $^1/_2$-inch pieces
1 egg, lightly beaten

FILLING

4 eggs
1 pound light brown sugar
$^1/_2$ cup very finely minced fresh young ginger
    (may be done in a food processor)
2 tablespoons heavy cream
1 teaspoon vanilla extract
Pinch of salt
1 teaspoon ground ginger
8 tablespoons (1 stick) butter, melted
2 cups coarsely chopped walnuts

1. In a medium bowl, combine the flour, sugar, and salt. With the tips of your fingers or two butter knives, work the cold butter into the dry ingredients until it resembles coarse meal. Add the egg and continue blending until the dough comes together. Form the dough into a disk and wrap in plastic wrap. Refrigerate until thoroughly chilled, about 1 hour.

2.   On a lightly floured surface, roll the dough into a circle $1/4$ inch thick. Rotate often while rolling to assure that the dough is not sticking to the surface. Flour the surface and rolling pin as needed. Drape the dough over the lightly floured rolling pin, unroll it over a 12-inch tart pan, and press it into the pan. Place the tart shell in the freezer and chill thoroughly, about 30 minutes.

3.   Preheat the oven to 425 degrees F.

4.   Line the tart shell with aluminum foil and fill with dried beans or pastry weights. Bake for 12 to 15 minutes, until the dough is set. Remove the foil and weights and continue to cook for 5 to 7 minutes, until the dough is light brown. Set aside. Lower the oven temperature to 325 degrees.

5.   For the filling: in a medium bowl whisk together the eggs, sugar, both gingers, heavy cream, vanilla extract, and salt; thoroughly combine. Mix in the melted butter.

6.   Sprinkle the walnuts into the prebaked tart shell. Pour the ginger mixture over the walnuts, spread to level, and bake in the center of the oven for 1 hour, or until completely set. Transfer to a wire rack to cool before serving.

Chicken Stock

Fish Stock

Veal Stock

Vegetable Stock

Basic Tomato Sauce

Oven-Dried Tomatoes

Tomato Coulis

Mayonnaise

We use the following recipes as the basis for many of Union Square Cafe's dishes. You *can* prepare our recipes using store-bought replacements for these pantry items, but the added quality and satisfaction that comes from using homemade products makes it worth taking a stab at cooking them from scratch. Though foundation stocks are used far more frequently in restaurants than in home kitchens, they are simple enough to make at home, and the added depth and richness they provide make them well deserving of a place in your pantry.

With the exception of mayonnaise, you can make these pantry items well in advance. When you next have roast chicken, save the carcass and make chicken stock. It will freeze well for several months and you'll be ahead of the game the next time you want to make risotto—or any other dish that calls for chicken stock. The same holds true for veal,

fish, and vegetable stock; make them when it's convenient, freeze, and use as needed.

A handy trick is to freeze the stock in ice cube trays, then store the frozen cubes in an airtight plastic bag for accessibility.

CHICKEN STOCK

A clear, flavorful chicken stock is indispensable for sauces, soups, and most risotto recipes. The key to a clear, brilliant stock is to skim as much fat and foam as possible from the surface, and to cook the stock at a barely perceptible simmer. For a darker, more richly flavored chicken stock that can be substituted for veal stock, roast the chicken bones with the vegetables and 1 tablespoon tomato paste in a 350-degree oven for 30 minutes, or until browned. Add the water, herbs, and spices and proceed with the recipe below. In addition to chicken bones from your butcher, use leftover carcasses from roast chicken.

YIELDS APPROXIMATELY 3 QUARTS

> 5 pounds chicken bones, rinsed well in cold water
> 4 quarts water
> 1 large onion, peeled and coarsely chopped (2^1/$_2$ cups)
> 3 medium carrots, scrubbed and quartered (2^1/$_2$ cups)
> 3 celery ribs, quartered
> 1 medium parsnip, peeled and coarsely chopped (1^1/$_2$ cups)
> 1 bay leaf
> 1 teaspoon fresh thyme
> 10 whole black peppercorns
> ^{1}/$_4$ cup parsley sprigs

1. Combine all the ingredients in an 8-quart stockpot. Over medium heat, bring slowly to a boil. Skim the foam that rises to the surface with a ladle.

2. Reduce the heat and simmer very slowly, uncovered, 4 to 5 hours. Skim the surface with a ladle every half hour to remove any accumulated fat or impurities.

3. Strain the stock into a clean pot or metal bowl and chill over ice. Refrigerate 1 or 2 days, or freeze for several months. Remove any hardened fat from refrigerated stock before reheating.

FISH STOCK

*F*or a brilliant and flavorful fish stock, rinse the bones and heads well to remove any blood or impurities. If you are using fish heads, be sure to have the gills removed. Also, never cook the stock beyond a barely perceptible simmer to prevent it from becoming murky and unappealing.
YIELDS 3½ CUPS

1 tablespoon olive oil
1 cup peeled and sliced onions
1 cup sliced leeks, cleaned white and light green
*   parts only*
½ cup chopped celery
1 fresh thyme sprig
3 parsley sprigs
1 small bay leaf
1 teaspoon whole black peppercorns
1 pound fish bones, cleaned and chopped (from white-
*   fleshed fish such as flounder, sole, bass, or snapper)*
½ cup white wine
4 cups cold water

1. Heat the olive oil over medium heat in a 3-quart stockpot or saucepan. Add the vegetables, herbs, and peppercorns and cook over medium heat, stirring frequently, until softened, about 10 minutes.

2. Raise the heat to high, add the fish bones, and stir well for 3 to 4 minutes. Add the white wine and reduce, an additional 3 to 4 minutes.

3. Add the cold water, lower the heat to medium, and slowly bring the stock to a boil. Skim the surface with a ladle to remove any foam that rises. Lower the heat and simmer very slowly for 45 minutes.

4. Strain the stock through a fine-mesh strainer or cheesecloth and chill over ice. Refrigerate up to 4 days, or freeze for future use.

VEAL STOCK

*O*ften considered the backbone of classic French cuisine, well-made veal stock is essential to the success of slow-cooked dishes like Braised Oxtail, Osso Buco, and Roast Breast of Veal. As with any stock, freeze what you don't need for future use.

YIELDS 12 CUPS

7 pounds veal bones, preferably knuckle and shank
5 quarts water
2 cups scrubbed and coarsely chopped carrots
3 cups quartered medium onions with skins
2 cups coarsely chopped celery
2 cups sliced leeks
1 head garlic, halved
2 tablespoons olive oil
3 tablespoons tomato paste
1/2 teaspoon whole black peppercorns
1 teaspoon thyme
1 bay leaf
6 parsley sprigs

1. Preheat the oven to 450 degrees F.

2. Rinse the veal bones well in cold water. Place the bones in an 8-quart stockpot and cover with the water. Bring to a boil over medium heat. With a small ladle, skim the surface to remove the foam and impurities. Reduce the heat to low and simmer very slowly.

3. Place the vegetables in a roasting pan and toss with the oil and the tomato paste to coat. Roast 45 minutes to 1 hour, until the vegetables are well browned.

4. Transfer the roasted vegetables to the stockpot and add the peppercorns, thyme, bay leaf, and parsley. Pour 1 cup of water into the

roasting pan and place it on the stove over high heat. Deglaze the pan by stirring to dissolve and incorporate any browned bits into the water. Transfer the water to the stock. Cook over low heat at a barely perceptible simmer, uncovered, for 12 to 16 hours. Skim occasionally to remove any fat or foam that rises to the surface.

5. Strain the stock into a clean pot or metal bowl and chill over ice. Remove any fat that rises to the top. Refrigerate 1 to 2 days, or freeze for later use.

VEGETABLE STOCK

*H*ere's an all-purpose, all-season vegetable stock, to be enjoyed on its own as a broth or as a soup base. It is also a superb stand-in for chicken stock when cooking risotto, legumes, or braised vegetables.
YIELDS 12 CUPS

1 tablespoon extra-virgin olive oil
3 cups scrubbed and sliced carrots
3 cups peeled and sliced onions
1 medium head Bibb lettuce, washed and chopped
2 cups chopped savoy cabbage
2 cups sliced leeks, washed
1 1/2 cups sliced celery
1 cup peeled and sliced parsnips
1/2 cup parsley sprigs
3 garlic cloves, sliced
2 fresh thyme sprigs
2 tablespoons chopped basil
1 bay leaf
1 teaspoon whole black peppercorns
2 teaspoons kosher salt
1 Idaho potato, sliced
2 tomatoes cored and chopped
3 quarts water

1. Heat the olive oil in a 5-quart stockpot over high heat. Add all the ingredients except the potato, tomatoes, and water and cook, stirring occasionally, to soften and wilt, about 7 minutes.

2. Add the potato, tomatoes, and the water. Bring to a boil, lower the heat, and simmer, covered, for 40 minutes. Strain in a colander over a bowl, pressing the vegetables to extract the maximum amount of stock. Refrigerate, tightly covered, up to 1 week, or freeze.

BASIC TOMATO SAUCE

This sauce is perfectly good on its own with pasta or as an enriching base for vegetable dishes. We combine the lively acidity of fresh tomatoes with the meatiness of canned plum tomatoes for a well-balanced sauce. If seasoning with cheese, we recommend Pecorino Romano as a complement to the sauce.

YIELDS 5 CUPS

1 1/2 pounds fresh ripe tomatoes, cored and chopped
1 35-ounce can of Italian plum tomatoes (4 cups)
2 tablespoons olive oil
1/2 cup peeled and diced onion
1 teaspoon minced garlic
1 tablespoon rinsed and chopped basil
1/2 teaspoon kosher salt
1/4 teaspoon freshly ground black pepper

1. In a 3-quart saucepan, combine the fresh and canned tomatoes with their juices. Cook over medium heat for 15 minutes, or until the tomatoes are quite soft. Pass the tomatoes through a food mill to remove all seeds and skin.

2. In the same saucepan, rinsed and wiped dry, heat the olive oil over medium heat. Sauté the onion and garlic until softened, but not browned. Add the puréed tomatoes and the basil. Continue cooking at a simmer until the sauce thickens, about 1/2 hour. Season with salt and pepper. The sauce can be kept for up to one week, tightly covered and refrigerated, or frozen for several months.

OVEN-DRIED TOMATOES

*P*lum tomatoes have won acceptance primarily as an ingredient for making cooked tomato sauce. Their sturdiness also makes them superb candidates for enduring a long, slow day in the oven. These roast plum tomatoes can be enjoyed any way you've ever used sun-dried tomatoes, but they're even more versatile since they're a lot less salty. We use them to intensify the flavor of pasta sauces and for our popular Roast Tomato Mashed Potatoes.

YIELDS 1½ CUPS

> *2 pounds ripe plum tomatoes, washed, cored,*
>   *and split lengthwise*
> *1 teaspoon kosher salt*
> *2 cups extra-virgin olive oil*
> *2 large fresh thyme sprigs*
> *1 fresh rosemary, sprig cut in half*
> *2 to 3 sage leaves*
> *3 medium garlic cloves, split*

1.   Place the tomatoes cut side up on a baking sheet. Sprinkle with the salt and let sit for 1 hour.

2.   Preheat the oven to 200 degrees F.

3.   Roast the tomatoes for 5 to 6 hours. The tomatoes are done when they are dried but still slightly plump; they should definitely not be leathery, nor as dry as commercial sun-dried tomatoes.

4.   Allow the tomatoes to cool to room temperature, then transfer them to a jar or bowl. Stir in the olive oil, herbs, and garlic, cover tightly, and refrigerate. The tomatoes will improve if marinated 2 to 3 days before using. They will keep for up to 2 weeks stored in the refrigerator.

TOMATO COULIS

A coulis is a simple vegetable or fruit purée that relies more on the ripeness of its primary ingredient than on added seasonings. This sauce blends the sweetness of ripe tomatoes with the warmth of cayenne and the mellow fruitiness of extra-virgin olive oil. Use the coulis to accompany grilled or roasted vegetables and fish.

YIELDS 2 CUPS

2 pounds ripe fresh tomatoes, cored and chopped
1 tablespoon cold butter
$1/3$ cup extra-virgin olive oil
$1/2$ teaspoon kosher salt
$1/8$ teaspoon freshly ground black pepper
$1/8$ teaspoon cayenne

1.   Place the tomatoes in a saucepan and cook over medium heat, covered, until very juicy, about 20 minutes. Strain into a bowl through a fine-mesh strainer.

2.   Return the strained tomatoes to the pan and slowly reduce over medium heat until thickened to a sauce consistency. Reduce the heat to very low and whisk in the butter. Slowly whisk in the olive oil to enrich and thicken the sauce. Season with the salt, pepper, and cayenne. Serve warm.

MAYONNAISE

*W*hile the food processor has taken the elbow grease out of preparing homemade mayonnaise, here's a helpful tip if you choose to whisk it up the old-fashioned way: Dampen a kitchen towel and roll it lengthwise into a cylinder. Form the towel into a tight ring on your kitchen counter and center the bowl on the ring. Your bowl will stay put while you vigorously whisk in the oil. Use the mayonnaise for sandwiches, salads, seafood, and vegetables.

YIELDS 2 CUPS

> *2 egg yolks*
> *1 tablespoon fresh lemon juice*
> *2 tablespoons Dijon mustard*
> *1 1/2 tablespoons red wine vinegar*
> *3/4 teaspoon kosher salt*
> *1/4 teaspoon fresh black pepper*
> *2 cups olive, canola, or other quality oil*

1. In a nonreactive bowl or in a food processor, combine the egg yolks, lemon juice, mustard, vinegar, salt, and pepper. Whisk vigorously or pulse with the machine to combine.

2. If making by hand, slowly drizzle in the oil, whisking constantly as you pour, to form a thick emulsion. If using a food processor, add the oil in a slow and constant stream with the machine running until all the oil has been incorporated and the mayonnaise has thickened. Will keep 4 to 5 days refrigerated and tightly covered.

MAIL-ORDER SOURCES FOR SPECIAL PRODUCTS

WHITE TRUFFLE OIL

Terra Mare
22 E. 65th Street
New York, NY 10021
(212) 717-5020

Todaro Brothers
555 Second Avenue
New York, NY 10016
(212) 679-7766

BALSAMICO TRADIZIONALE

Dean & Deluca
560 Broadway
New York, NY 10012
(800) 221-7714

Todaro Brothers
(See above)

Balducci's
11-02 Bridge Plaza South
Long Island City, NY 11101
(800) 225-3822

PICKLED GINGER

Katagiri & Company, Inc.
224 E. 59th Street
New York, NY 10022
(212) 755-3566

SHEET GELATIN

Dean & Deluca
(See above)

GOAT CHEESE AND GOAT'S MILK YOGURT

Todaro Brothers
(See above)

Balducci's
(See above)

Dean & Deluca
(See above)

VENISON

D'Artagnan, Inc.
399 St. Paul Avenue
Jersey City, NJ 07306
(800) 327-8246

POLENTA

Dean & Deluca
(See above)

Todaro Brothers
(See above)

Balducci's
(See above)

SWEET FENNEL SAUSAGE

Dean & Deluca
(See above)

Todaro Brothers
(See above)

Balducci's
(See above)

ROASTED RED CHILI PASTE

Thai Kitchen
P.O. Box 13242
Berkeley, CA 94701
(800) 967-THAI

Dean & Deluca
(See above)

WHEAT BERRIES

Oak Grove Mills
266 Oak Grove Road
Pittstown, NJ 08867
(908) 782-9618

Dean & Deluca
(See above)

MALLOREDDUS SARDINIAN PASTA

Dean & Deluca
(See above)

Balducci's
(See above)

SOUFFLÉ CUPS, RAMEKINS, COOKWARE, ETC.

Bridge Kitchenware
214 East 52nd Street
New York, NY 10022
(212) 688-4220

METRIC CONVERSION TABLES

CONVERSIONS OF OUNCES TO GRAMS	
Ounces (oz)	Grams (g)
1 oz	30 g[1]
2 oz	60 g
3 oz	85 g
4 oz	115 g
5 oz	140 g
6 oz	180 g
7 oz	200 g
8 oz	225 g
9 oz	250 g
10 oz	285 g
11 oz	300 g
12 oz	340 g
13 oz	370 g
14 oz	400 g
15 oz	425 g
16 oz	450 g
20 oz	565 g
24 oz	675 g
28 oz	800 g
32 oz	900 g

CONVERSIONS OF POUNDS TO GRAMS AND KILOGRAMS	
Pounds (lb)	Grams (g) Kilograms (kg)
1 lb	450 g[2]
1$\frac{1}{4}$ lb	565 g
1$\frac{1}{2}$ lb	675 g
1$\frac{3}{4}$ lb	800 g
2 lb	900 g
2$\frac{1}{2}$ lb	1,125 g; 1$\frac{1}{4}$ kg
3 lb	1,350 g
3$\frac{1}{2}$ lb	1,500 g; 1$\frac{1}{2}$ kg
4 lb	1,800 g
4$\frac{1}{2}$ lb	2 kg
5 lb	2$\frac{1}{4}$ kg
5$\frac{1}{2}$ lb	2$\frac{1}{2}$ kg
6 lb	2$\frac{3}{4}$ kg
6$\frac{1}{2}$ lb	3 kg
7 lb	3$\frac{1}{4}$ kg
7$\frac{1}{2}$ lb	3$\frac{1}{2}$ kg
8 lb	3$\frac{3}{4}$ kg
9 lb	4 kg
10 lb	4$\frac{1}{2}$ kg

1. Approximate. To convert ounces to grams, multiply number of ounces by 28.35.

2. Approximate. To convert pounds into grams, multiply number of pounds by 453.6.

CONVERSIONS OF FAHRENHEIT TO CELSIUS	
Fahrenheit (F)	Celsius (C)
170°F	77°C[3]
180°F	82°C
190°F	88°C
200°F	95°C
225°F	110°C
250°F	120°C
275°F	135°C
300°F	150°C
325°F	165°C
350°F	180°C
375°F	190°C
400°F	205°C
425°F	220°C
450°F	230°C
475°F	245°C
500°F	260°C
525°F	275°C
550°F	290°C

CONVERSIONS OF QUARTS TO LITERS	
Quarts (qt)	Liters (L)
1 qt	1 L[4]
1$\frac{1}{2}$ qt	1$\frac{1}{2}$ L
2 qt	2 L
2$\frac{1}{2}$ qt	2$\frac{1}{2}$ L
3 qt	2$\frac{3}{4}$ L
4 qt	3$\frac{3}{4}$ L
5 qt	4$\frac{3}{4}$ L
6 qt	5$\frac{1}{2}$ L
7 qt	6$\frac{1}{2}$ L
8 qt	7$\frac{1}{2}$ L
9 qt	8$\frac{1}{2}$ L
10 qt	9$\frac{1}{2}$ L

4. Approximate. To convert quarts to liters, multiply number of quarts by .95.

3. Approximate. To convert Fahrenheit into Celsius, subtract 32, multiply by 5, then divide by 9.

Almond(s):
  -pear crisp, 286–287
  three-grain pilaf with shiitake
    mushrooms and, 256–257
Anchovy:
  mayonnaise, spicy, fried cala-
    mari with, 16–17
  -tomato sauce, seared filet
    mignon with, 182
Apple tarts, individual baked,
  with apple butter, 274–275
Artichoke(s):
  braised baby, with garlic,
    basil and mint, 220
  -eggplant hash, 218–219
  and potato frittata, 118–119
  and potato ragout, 10–11
Arugula:
  endive, and radicchio salad,
    with oregano vinaigrette,
    76–77
  seared rib steak with rose-
    mary and, 184–185
Asparagus:
  penne with red peppers and,
    48
  steamed, with Sauternes
    vinaigrette, 6

Bagna cauda sauce, 260
Balsamic vinegar:
  butter sauce, seared salmon
    with sweet corn, shiitake
    mushrooms and, 140–141
  mashed sweet potatoes with,
    238
  pan-roasted salmon with
    citrus-balsamic vinaigrette,
    146–147
  sweet onion frittata with,
    120–121
Banana tart, baked, with
  caramel and macadamia
  nuts, 271–273
Bass, sea:
  black, "carpaccio" of, al
    Forno, 134–135
  polenta-crusted, with corn
    and tomatillo salsa,
    136–137
Bean(s):
  black, soup with lemon and

sherry, 92–93
  crunchy fava, salad with
    frisée, peppers, and
    pecorino, 78–79
  fagioli alla Toscana, 253–254
  fagioli all'uccelletti, 255
  French, mashed, with garlic
    and mint, 222–223
Bean(s), white:
  braised escarole and, with
    tomatoes, mushrooms and
    pecorino, 20–21
  and broccoli soup with
    Parmigiano and
    prosciutto, 106–107
  cod with radicchio, lemon
    vinaigrette and, 138–139
  salad, warm seafood and,
    26–27
Beef:
  braised oxtails with red wine
    and onions, 194–195
  seared filet mignon with
    tomato-anchovy sauce, 182
  seared rib steak with rose-
    mary and arugula, 184–185
Beets:
  haricots verts, mâche, and
    goat cheese salad, 84–85
  penne with Gorgonzola,
    toasted walnuts, and, 50–51
Biscotti, 276–277
B.L.T. sandwich, 112
Blueberry and peach cobbler,
  279
Bombolotti al modo mio, 38–39
Bread pudding, pumpkin,
  296–298
Broccoli and white bean soup
  with Parmigiano and prosciutto, 106–107
Broccoli rabe:
  orecchiette with tomatoes
    and, 44–45
  sautéed, with garlic, 224–225
  seared sea scallops with
    lemon vinaigrette, roast
    tomatoes and, 158–159
Brownies, marble fudge, 282–283
Bruschetta:
  bianca, 14–15
  rossa, 12–13

Brussels sprouts, hashed, with
  poppy seeds and lemon,
  226
Bucatini all'Amatriciana, 46–47
Burgers, yellowfin tuna, with
  ginger-mustard glaze,
  124–125

Cacciucco di pesce, 168–169
Cake, sponge, rosemary-raisin,
  with honeyed goat cheese,
  280–281
Calamari, fried, with spicy
  anchovy mayonnaise,
  16–17
Calf's liver, seared, with sprouted
  mustard seeds, 210–211
Caramel, baked banana tart
  with macadamia nuts and,
  271–273
"Carpaccio" of black sea bass al
  Forno, 134–135
Carrot:
  -red lentil soup with Asian
    spices, 94–95
  sauce, spicy, sizzled soft-shell
    crabs with, 160–161
Cheese:
  Gorgonzola, penne with,
    beets, toasted walnuts and,
    50–51
  Pecorino, crunchy fava bean
    salad with frisée, peppers
    and, 78–79
  ricotta, and spinach tart,
    baked, 24–25
  sheep's milk, and lemon frit-
    ters with honey, Sardinian,
    302–304
  see also Goat cheese; Gruyère;
    Parmigiano
Cherry(ies), dried:
  and pearl onion sauce, roast
    peppered rack of venison
    with, 196–198
  and rhubarb chutney,
    262–263
Chicken, 170–176
  herb-roasted, 170–171
  Mama Romano's baked
    lemon, 172–173
  stock, 312

Chicken breast:
  with herbed goat cheese, stuffed, 176
  with yogurt and Asian spices, grilled marinated, 174–175
Chicken livers, risotto with Moscato d'Asti, mushrooms and, 58–59
Chicken salad "deluxe," 114–115
Chocolate:
  chunk cookies, "reverse," 294–295
  sorbet, 278
Chutney, 261–263
  peach-fig, 261
  rhubarb and dried cherry, 262–263
Cobbler, peach and blueberry, 279
Cod:
  with radicchio, white beans, and lemon vinaigrette, 138–139
  salt cod, onion, and squash gratin, 154–155
Compote:
  tomato and roast pepper, grilled swordfish with, 144–145
  tomato-onion, red snapper with, 150–151
Condiments, 260–263
  bagna cauda sauce, 260
  peach-fig chutney, 261
  rhubarb and dried cherry chutney, 262–263
Cookies, "reverse" chocolate chunk, 294–295
Corn:
  pudding with red peppers and okra, 18–19
  and tomatillo salsa, polenta-crusted sea bass with, 136–137
Corn, sweet:
  -lobster chowder, 165–167
  and potato vichyssoise, 96–97
  seared salmon with shiitake mushrooms, balsamic vinegar butter sauce and, 140–141
Cotechino with wine-soaked crostini, 32–33

Coulis, tomato, 319
Crabmeat frittata with tomatoes and herbs, 116–117
Crabs, soft-shell, sizzled, with spicy carrot sauce, 160–161
Crisps:
  pear-almond, 286–287
  rhubarb, 289
Crostini, wine soaked, cotechino with, 32–33
Custard:
  chilled pineapple–Moscato zabaglione, 288
  panna cotta, 284
  pumpkin flan, 292–293

Dacquoise, toasted hazelnut, mocha semifreddo layered with, 299–301
Desserts, 266–307
  baked banana tart with caramel and macadamia nuts, 271–273
  biscotti, 276–277
  chilled pineapple–Moscato zabaglione, 288
  chilled spiced red wine–fig soup, 290–291
  chocolate sorbet, 278
  frozen goat's milk yogurt, 285
  ginger-walnut tart, 306–307
  individual baked apple tarts with apple butter, 274–275
  marble fudge brownies, 282–283
  mocha semifreddo layered with toasted hazelnut dacquoise, 299–301
  panna cotta, 284
  peach and blueberry cobbler, 279
  pear-almond crisp, 286–287
  pumpkin bread pudding, 296–298
  pumpkin flan, 292–293
  "reverse" chocolate chunk cookies, 294–295
  rhubarb crisp, 289
  rosemary-raisin sponge cake with honeyed goat cheese, 280–281
  Sardinian lemon and sheep's

milk cheese fritters with honey, 302–304
Duck, 178–188
  roast lemon-pepper, with red wine vinegar sauce, 178–179
  stew, rustic, with rigatoni, 180–181

Eggplant:
  -artichoke hash, 218–219
  mashed potatoes, 236
  penne with roasted pepper and, 52–53
  roast stuffed, with spicy tomato sauce, 28–29
  zucchini and Parmigiano tortino, baked, 228–229
Eggs, 116–121
  artichoke and potato frittata, 118–119
  crabmeat frittata with tomatoes and herbs, 116–117
  sweet onion frittata with balsamic vinegar, 120–121
  uove al forno, 128–129
Escarole:
  braised, and white beans with tomatoes, mushrooms and pecorino, 20–21
  sweet peas with onions, mint and, 242

Fagioli,
  see Bean(s)
Fig(s):
  -peach chutney, 261
  –red wine soup, chilled spiced, 290–291
Filet mignon, seared, with tomato-anchovy sauce, 182
Fillet mignon of tuna, grilled marinated, 148–149
Fish, 134–135
  "carpaccio" of black sea bass al Forno, 134–135
  cod with radicchio, white beans, and lemon vinai-grette, 138–139
  grilled marinated fillet mignon of tuna, 148–149

grilled swordfish with tomato and roast pepper compote, 144–145

grilled trout with warm rosemary vinaigrette, 142–143

pan-roasted salmon with citrus-balsamic vinaigrette, 146–147

polenta-crusted sea bass with corn tomatillo salsa, 136–137

red snapper with tomato-onion compote, 150–151

salt cod, onion, and squash gratin, 154–155

seared curried whitefish with raïta, 152–153

seared salmon with sweet corn, shiitake mushrooms, and balsamic vinegar butter sauce, 140–141

stock, 313

tuna club sandwich, 126–127

yellowfin tuna burgers with ginger-mustard glaze, 124–125

Flan, pumpkin, 292–293

Frisée:
crunchy fava bean salad with peppers, pecorino and, 78–79

salad with shrimp, fennel, and clementines, 86–87

seared sweetbreads with mushrooms and, 212–213

Frittatas, 116–121
artichoke and potato, 118–119

crabmeat, with tomatoes and herbs, 116–117

sweet onion, with balsamic vinegar, 120–121

Fritters, lemon and sheep's milk cheese, with honey, Sardinian, 302–304

Fudge brownies, marble, 282–283

Garlic:
braised baby artichokes with basil, mint and, 220

braised lamb shanks with herbs and, 200–201

broccoli rabe sautéed with, 224–225

croutons, red oakleaf and Bibb salad with Gruyère, dijon vinaigrette and, 80–81

linguine with spinach, olive oil and, 40–41

mashed French beans with mint and, 222–223

potato chips, hot, 30–31

spinach with, sautéed, 243

"Gazpacho" sauce, shrimp with, 156–157

Ginger(ed):
-mustard glaze, yellowfin tuna burger with, 124–125

spicy Asian slaw, 227

-walnut tart, 306–307

Gnocchi, porcini, with prosciutto and Parmigiano cream, 54–57

Goat cheese:
haricots verts, mâche and beet salad, 84–85

herbed, stuffed chicken breasts with, 176

honeyed, rosemary-raisin sponge cake with, 280–281

and shiitake mushroom sauce, roast leg of veal with, 190–191

and summer tomato, salad, 82

and vegetable lasagne al forno, 204–206

Goat's milk, yogurt, frozen, 285

Gorgonzola, penne with beets, toasted walnuts and, 50–51

Gruyère:
-potato gratin, creamy, 239

red oakleaf and Bibb salad with garlic croutons, dijon vinaigrette and, 80–81

Haricots verts, mâche, beet, and goat cheese salad, 84–85

Hash(ed):
artichoke-eggplant, 218–219

brussels sprouts with poppy seeds and lemon, 226

Hazelnut, toasted dacquoise,

mocha semifreddo layered with, 299–301

Lamb:
chops, grilled, "scotta dita," 199

roast stuffed leg of, 202–203

shanks, braised, with garlic and herbs, 200–201

Lasagne al forno, vegetable and goat cheese, 204–206

Leeks, frizzled, 230

Lemon:
black bean soup with sherry and, 92–93

chicken, Mama Romano's baked, 172–173

hashed brussels sprouts with poppy seeds and, 226

-pepper duck, roast, with red wine vinegar sauce, 178–179

and sheep's milk cheese fritters with honey, Sardinian, 302–304

see also Vinaigrette, lemon

Lentil, red:
–basmati rice pilaf, 258–259

–carrot soup with Asian spices, 94–95

Liver, calf's, seared, with sprouted mustard seeds, 210–211

Lobster:
salad, Sardinian, 122–123

shepherd's pie, 162–164

–sweet corn chowder, 165–167

Mâche, haricots verts, beet and goat cheese salad, 84–85

Malloreddus alla Campidanese, 42–43

Mama Romano's baked lemon chicken, 172–173

Mascarpone, creamy polenta with, 250–251

Matzo polenta with sauteed mushrooms, 22–23

Mayonnaise, 320
spicy anchovy, with fried calamari, 16–17

Mint:
braised baby artichokes with

Mint *(cont.)*
    garlic, basil and, 220
    mashed French beans with
        garlic and, 222–223
    sweet peas with escarole,
        onions and, 242
    tomatoes, onions and,
        charred, 246–247
Moscato d'Asti:
    -pineapple zabaglione,
        chilled, 288
    risotto with chicken livers,
        mushrooms and, 58–59
Mushroom(s):
    braised escarole and white
        beans with tomatoes,
        pecorino and, 20–21
    porcini gnocchi with pro-
        sciutto and Parmigiano
        cream, 54–57
    risotto with chicken livers,
        Moscato d'Asti and, 58–59
    roast breast of veal with
        spinach, rice stuffing and,
        186–188
    sautéed, matzo polenta with,
        22–23
    seared sweetbreads with
        frisée and, 212–213
Mushrooms, shiitake:
    and goat cheese sauce, roast
        leg of veal with, 190–191
    seared salmon with sweet
        corn, balsamic vinegar
        butter sauce and, 140–141
    three-grain pilaf with
        almonds and, 256–257
Mushroom soup, 98–100
    with barley and wild rice,
        98–99
    creamless, 100

Okra, corn pudding with red
        peppers and, 18–19
Olives, marinated,
        Roman-style, 5
Onion(s):
    braised oxtails with red wine
        and, 194–195
    charred tomatoes, mint and,
        246–247
    pearl, and dried cherry
        sauce, roast peppered rack

of venison with, 196–198
    red, sweet, grilled, 231
    salt cod, and squash gratin,
        154–155
    sweet, frittata with balsamic
        vinegar, 120–121
    sweet peas with escarole, and
        mint, 242
    -tomato compote, red
        snapper with, 150–151
Orecchiette with broccoli rabe
        and tomatoes, 44–45
Osso buco, orange-fennel,
        192–193
Oxtails, braised, with red wine
        and onions, 194–195

Pancakes, parsnip, 240–241
Pancetta, risotto with snails,
        red wine and, 66–67
Panna cotta, 284
Pantry staples, 308–320
    basic tomato sauce, 317
    chicken stock, 312
    fish stock, 313
    mayonnaise, 320
    oven-dried tomatoes, 318
    tomato coulis, 319
    veal stock, 314–315
    vegetable stock, 316
"Panzanella," cracked wheat,
        72–73
Panzanella, sourdough, 74–75
Pappardelle of zucchini, 36
Parmigiano:
    cream, porcini gnocchi with
        prosciutto and, 54–57
    eggplant and zucchini
        tortino, baked, 228–229
    white bean and broccoli
        soup with prosciutto and,
        106–107
Parsnip pancakes, 240–241
Pasta, 38–53
    bombolotti al modo mio,
        38–39
    bucatini all'Amatriciana,
        46–47
    linguine with spinach, garlic,
        and olive oil, 40–41
    malloreddus alla Campi-
        danese, 42–43
    orecchiette with broccoli

rabe and tomatoes, 44–45
    penne with asparagus and
        red peppers, 48
    penne with eggplant and
        roasted pepper, 52–53
    penne with Gorgonzola,
        beets, and toasted walnuts,
        50–51
    rustic duck stew with riga-
        toni, 180–181
Peach:
    and blueberry cobbler,
        279
    -fig chutney, 261
Pear-almond crisp, 286–287
Pearl onion and dried cherry
        sauce, roast peppered rack
        of venison with, 196–198
Peas, sweet, with escarole,
        onions and mint, 242
Pecorino:
    braised escarole and white
        beans with tomatoes,
        mushrooms and, 20–21
    crunchy fava bean salad with
        frisée, peppers and, 78–79
Penne:
    with asparagus and red
        peppers, 48
    with eggplant and roasted
        pepper, 52–53
    with Gorgonzola, beets, and
        toasted walnuts, 50–51
Pepper, roast(ed):
    compote, grilled swordfish
        with tomato and, 144–145
    penne with eggplant and,
        52–53
Peppers, crunchy fava bean
        salad with frisée, pecorino
        and, 78–79
Peppers, red:
    corn pudding with okra and,
        18–19
    penne with asparagus and,
        48
Pie, lobster shepherd's, 162–164
Pilaf:
    red lentil–basmati rice,
        258–259
    three-grain, with almonds
        and shiitake mushrooms,
        256–257

Pineapple-Moscato zabaglione, chilled, 288

Polenta:
-crusted sea bass with corn and tomatillo salsa, 136–137
with mascarpone, creamy, 250–251
matzo, with sautéed mushrooms, 22–23

Porcini gnocchi with prosciutto and Parmigiano cream, 54–57

Pork loin, Roman roast, arista di Maiale, 208–209

Potato(es):
and artichoke frittata, 118–119
and artichoke ragout, 10–11
chips, hot garlic, 30–31
-Gruyère gratin, creamy, 239
salad, herbed, with bacon and scallions, 264–265
and sweet corn vichyssoise, 96–97

Potatoes, mashed, 232–233
basil, 234
eggplant, 236
fennel, 237
roast tomato, 235
sweet, mashed, with balsamic vinegar, 238

Prosciutto:
porcini gnocchi with, and Parmigiano cream, 54–57
white bean and broccoli soup with Parmigiano and, 106–107

Pumpkin:
bread pudding, 296–298
flan, 292–293
risotto, 60–61

Radicchio:
cod with white beans, lemon vinaigrette and, 138–139
endive, arugula and, with oregano vinaigrette, 76–77

Raisin-rosemary sponge cake with honeyed goat cheese, 280–281

Raïta, seared curried whitefish with, 152–153

Ratatouille:
soup, 102–103
-stuffed zucchini blossoms, 34–35

Red snapper with tomato-onion compote, 150–151

"Reverse" chocolate chunk cookies, 294–295

Rhubarb:
crisp, 289
and dried cherry chutney, 262–263

Ribollita, 104–105

Rice, 58–67
pumpkin risotto, 60–61
risotto d'Oro, 62–63
risotto with chicken livers, Moscato d'Asti, and mushrooms, 58–59
risotto with snails, pancetta, and red wine, 66–67
shrimp risotto with cucumber and jalapeño, 64–65
stuffing, spinach, mushroom and, roast breast of veal with, 186–188
wild, mushroom soup with barley and, 98–99

Rice, basmati:
–red lentil pilaf, 258–259
three-grain pilaf with almonds and shiitake mushrooms, 256–257

Ricotta and spinach tart, baked, 24–25

Risotto,
see Rice

Rosemary:
-raisin sponge cake with honeyed goat cheese, 280–281
seared rib steak with arugula and, 184–185

Salad(s), 68–87
chicken, "deluxe," 114–115
cracked wheat "panzanella," 72–73
crunchy fava bean, with frisée, peppers, and pecorino, 78–79
endive, radicchio, and arugula, with oregano vinaigrette, 76–77
frisée, with shrimp, fennel, and clementines, 86–87
haricots verts, mâche, beet, and goat cheese, 84–85
potato, herbed, with bacon and scallions, 264–265
red oakleaf and Bibb, with Gruyère, garlic croutons, and dijon vinaigrette, 80–81
Sardinian lobster, 122–123
sautéed insalata tricolore, 252
sourdough panzanella, 74–75
summer tomato and goat cheese, 82
warm seafood and white bean, 26–27

Salmon:
pan roasted, with citrus-balsamic vinaigrette, 146–147
seared, with sweet corn, shiitake mushrooms, and balsamic vinegar butter sauce, 140–141

Salsa, corn and tomatillo, polenta-crusted sea bass with, 136–137

Sandwiches:
B.L.T., 112
tuna club, 126–127

Sauces:
bagna cauda, 260
balsamic vinegar butter, seared salmon with sweet corn, shiitake mushrooms and, 140–141
basic tomato, 317
dried cherry and pearl onion, roast peppered rack of venison with, 196–198
"gazpacho," shrimp with, 156–157
red wine vinegar, roast lemon-pepper duck with, 178–179
shiitake mushroom and goat cheese, roast leg of veal with, 190–191

Sauces (cont.)
spicy carrot, sizzled soft-shell
crabs with, 160–161
spicy tomato, roast stuffed
eggplant with, 28–29
tomato-anchovy, seared filet
mignon with, 182
Scallops, sea, seared, with lemon
vinaigrette, broccoli rabe,
and roast tomatoes,
158–159
Seafood:
cacciucco di pesce, 168–169
fried calamari with spicy
anchovy mayonnaise, 16–17
warm, and white bean salad,
26–27
see also Fish; Lobster; Shellfish; Shrimp
Semifreddo, mocha, layered
with toasted hazelnut
dacquoise, 299–301
Sheep's milk cheese and lemon
fritters with honey,
Sardinian, 302–304
Shellfish:
seared sea scallops with
lemon vinaigrette,
broccoli rabe, and roast
tomatoes, 158–159
sizzled soft-shell crabs with
spicy carrot sauce, 160–161
see also Lobster; Shrimp
Shepherd's pie, lobster, 162–164
Shrimp:
frisée salad with, fennel,
clementines and, 86–87
with "gazpacho" sauce,
156–157
risotto with cucumber and
jalapeño, 64–65
Snails, risotto with pancetta,
red wine and, 66–67
Soft-shell crabs, sizzled, with
spicy carrot sauce, 160–161
Sorbet, chocolate, 278
Soup(s), 88–107
black bean, with lemon and
sherry, 92–93
carrot–red lentil, with Asian
spices, 94–95
chilled spiced red wine–fig,
290–291

creamless mushroom, 100
lobster–sweet corn chowder,
165–167
mushroom, with barley and
wild rice, 98–99
ratatouille, 102–103
ribollita, 104–105
sweet corn and potato vichyssoise, 96–97
white bean and broccoli,
with Parmigiano and
proscuitto, 106–107
Spinach:
creamed, 244–245
with garlic, sautéed, 243
linguine with garlic, olive oil
and, 40–41
and ricotta tart, baked, 24–25
roast breast of veal with
mushroom, rice stuffing
and, 186–188
Squash, salt cod and onion
gratin, 154–155
Stocks, 312–316
chicken, 312
fish, 313
veal, 314–315
vegetable, 316
Stuffing, spinach, mushroom
and rice, roast breast of
veal with, 186–188
Sweetbreads, seared, with
mushrooms and frisée,
212–213
Swordfish, grilled, with tomato
and roast pepper com-
pote, 144–145

Tarts:
baked banana, with caramel
and macadamia nuts,
271–273
baked individual apple, with
apple butter, 274–275
baked ricotta and spinach,
24–25
ginger-walnut, 306–307
Tomato(es):
-anchovy sauce, seared filet
mignon with, 182
braised escarole and white
beans with mushrooms
pecorino and, 20–21

coulis, 319
crabmeat frittata with, herbs
and, 116–117
-onion compote, red snapper
with, 150–151
onions, mint and, charred,
246–247
orecchiette with brocolli
rabe and, 44–45
oven-dried, 318
and roast pepper compote,
grilled swordfish with,
144–145
summer, and goat cheese
salad, 82
Tomato(es), roast(ed):
mashed potatoes, 235
seared sea scallops with
lemon vinaigrette, broccoli
rabe and, 158–159
Tomato sauce:
basic, 317
spicy, roast stuffed eggplant
with, 28–29
Tortinos, eggplant, zucchini,
and Parmigiano, baked,
228–229
Trout, grilled, with warm
rosemary vinaigrette,
142–143
Tuna:
burger, yellowfin, with ginger-mustard glaze,
124–125
club sandwich, 126–127
fillet mignon of, grilled
marinated, 148–149
Turnips, yellow, mashed, with
crispy shallots, 248–249

Uove al forno, 128–129

Veal, 186–193
lombatina, grilled, 189
orange-fennel osso buco,
192–193
roast breast of, with spinach,
mushroom and rice
stuffing, 186–188
roast leg of, with shiitake
mushroom and goat
cheese sauce, 190–191
stock, 314–315

Vegetable and goat cheese lasagne al forno, 204–206

Vegetable stock, 316

Venison, roast peppered rack of, with dried cherry and pearl onion sauce, 196–198

Vichyssoise, sweet corn and potato, 96–97

Vinaigrette(s):
citrus-balsamic, pan-roasted salmon with, 146–147
dijon, red oakleaf and Bibb salad with Gruyère, garlic croutons and, 80–81
oregano, endive, radicchio, and arugula salad with, 76–77
Sauternes, steamed asparagus with, 6–7
warm rosemary, grilled trout with, 142–143

Vinaigrette, lemon:
cod with radicchio, white beans and, 138–139
seared sea scallops with broccoli rabe, roast tomatoes and, 158–159

Walnut(s):
-ginger tart, 306–307
toasted, penne with Gorgonzola, beets and, 50–51

Whitefish, seared curried, with raïta, 152–153

Wild rice, mushroom soup with barley and, 98–99

Wine, red:
braised oxtails with onions and, 194–195
-fig soup, chilled spiced, 290–291
risotto with snails, pancetta and, 66–67

vinegar sauce, roast lemon-pepper duck with, 178–179

Yellowfin tuna burgers with ginger-mustard glaze, 124–125

Yogurt:
goat's milk, frozen, 285
grilled marinated chicken breast with Asian spices and, 174–175

Zabaglione, pineapple-Moscato, chilled, 288

Zucchini:
eggplant and Parmigiano tortino, baked, 228–229
pappardelle of, 36

Zucchini blossoms, ratatouille-stuffed, 34–35